THE RECALL

THE RECALL

Tribunal of the People

Joseph F. Zimmerman

PRAEGER

Westport, Connecticut
London

Library of Congress Cataloging-in-Publication Data

Zimmerman, Joseph Francis, 1928–
    The recall : tribunal of the people / Joseph F. Zimmerman.
      p.   cm.
    Includes bibliographical references and index.
    ISBN 0–275–96008–0 (alk. paper)
    1. Recall—United States. I. Title.
KF4884.Z56   1997
324.6'8'0973—dc21   97–9179

British Library Cataloguing in Publication Data is available.

Library of Congress Catalog Card Number: 97–9179
ISBN: 0–275–96008–0

First published in 1997

Praeger Publishers, 88 Post Road West, Westport, CT 06881
An imprint of Greenwood Publishing Group, Inc.

Printed in the United States of America

The paper used in this book complies with the
Permanent Paper Standard issued by the National
Information Standards Organization (Z39.48–1984).

10 9 8 7 6 5 4 3 2 1

Every reasonable effort has been made to trace the owners of copyright
materials in this book, but in some instances this has proven impossible.
The author and publisher will be glad to receive information leading to
more complete acknowledgments in subsequent printings of the book and in
the meantime extend their apologies for any omissions.

Contents

Preface

The recall allows voters by means of petitions to place on the ballot the question of removing an elected public officer prior to the expiration of the term of office, thereby recognizing the electorate as the fountainhead of sovereign power. This corrective device was unconventional when first adopted in 1903 as a democratic process modifying the representative principle and immediately generated intense public controversy about the nature of representative government. The strongest opposition came from elective officers, who charged that representative government would be undermined if the recall was adopted.

Surprisingly, relatively little has been published on the recall during the past seven decades. This book is the first one since 1912 devoted to a national examination and evaluation of the recall since its first employment in 1903 in Los Angeles to remove a member of the city council.

The recall reflects a long history of distrust of public officers dating to Jacksonian democracy with its emphasis upon electing all public officers for short terms and voter ratification of constitutional restraints on actions by state legislatures in the nineteenth century in reaction to scandals associated with canal and railroad building.

There can be no doubt that the plebiscite trinity — the recall and its often associated protest referendum and initiative — encourage voters to shadow government officers and play a more informed and important role in the governance process. Progressive leader Robert M. La Follette referred in 1920 to the admonitory effect of the plebiscitary devices by noting they "will prove so effective a check against unworthy representatives that it will rarely be found necessary to invoke them."[1] His prediction was an accurate one and suggests that the public good is the principle guiding most elected public officers.

Where authorized, the recall is viewed either as a process to be employed only for legal cause with judicial safeguards for the targeted public officer or as a political question with voters acting as a tribunal that determines the fate of the officer, with no judicial appeal if the voters decide to remove the officer.

Collecting data and information on the recall of state public officers is not difficult, because there have been relatively few such recall elections and there is a central repository of data in each state. In contrast, collecting data and information on the recall of local government officers is a difficult task because of the lack of central repository on recall elections in states where the device is authorized. There is no count of the total number of local governments where the recall can be employed. Its use is authorized by voters in certain types of local governments in several states by a constitutional provision, by a general statute, by special statutes for individual local governments, or by home rule charters.

NOTE

1.   Ellen Torelle, compiler, *The Political Philosophy of Robert M. La Follette* (Madison, Wisc.: Robert M. La Follette, 1920), p. 174.

Acknowledgments

Although it is not possible to acknowledge every individual and organization that supplied information in response to my requests, a special debt of gratitude must be expressed to colleague Ronald M. Stout, who examined the manuscript chapters very carefully and offered suggestions for their improvement. A debt of gratitude also is owed to Reshma Prakash and Nicole C. Carey for research assistance and to Addie Napolitano for excellence in preparing the manuscript.

1

The Sovereign Citizen

The process of recalling a public officer from office prior to expiration of the stipulated term of office is commenced by proponents filing petitions that contain the required number of signatures with a designated officer responsible for conducting a special election to determine whether the officer should be removed from office for specified reasons. Recall elections may be limited to the question of removing the targeted officer or also may involve the selection of a replacement in the event the officer is removed.

The recall is authorized today by a constitutional or statutory provision in 26 states. In addition, the state legislature in several states (Connecticut, for example) has enacted special acts authorizing specific local governments to use the recall. Home rule constitutional provisions in several other states, including Massachusetts and New York, allow general purpose local governments to draft and adopt charters authorizing the electorate to employ the recall, and other local governments in these states have employed home rule powers and amended their existing charters to provide for the recall.[1]

The number of public officers subject to the recall in the United States is unknown, but the total is large, because there are 18,828 elected state government officers and 491,669 elected local government officers, a total larger than the number of elected officers in any other nation.[2]

Voters employing the recall in effect act *de facto* as a petit jury trying a public officer on charges contained on petitions initiated by a recall group, which acted as a grand jury. In contrast to criminal charges, the regular grand jury process is bypassed, although the officer subject to a recall petition and election also may be subject to criminal prosecution if such a wrong has been committed. The officer, of course, can seek judicial review of alleged procedural errors in the petition process and alleged invalid signatures on petitions.

Proposals for voters to employ recall elections to keep public officers continuously responsible to the voters have generated controversies in states and municipalities since the recall first was proposed in Los Angeles in 1903. The recall proposal immediately raised the question of whether the fundamental nature of representative government would be transformed if the recall was authorized and utilized by voters on a regular basis.

The proposition that citizens should play an informed and active role in the governance process is enshrined deeply in the political culture of the United States and is epitomized by the open town meeting in many New England towns today. Nevertheless, there is wide disagreement as to the forms and the extent of citizen participation that are desirable.

At one extreme, the view prevails that voters directly should make all laws and those holding an office should do so on a part-time basis. The early New England town meeting accepted this concept of citizen participation and made voting and office holding by freemen compulsory.[3] At the other extreme, the leadership-feedback theory limits the role of citizens primarily to electing periodically for fixed terms government officers who provide leadership in public affairs by proposing policies. This model is reflected in the due process requirement for public hearings on many types of proposed or requested governmental actions.[4] Citizen feedback on proposals may induce the elected officers to modify the proposals prior to their adoption and implementation. Decision-making responsibility, however, remains with the officers.

If the principle guiding all government officers was for the public good, the leadership-feedback concept would be an adequate guide for and check upon decision making by public officers. Opponents of this type of decision making are convinced that periodic election of officers for fixed terms is an inadequate safeguard of the public weal and that more immediate mechanisms must be available to the voters to ensure that elected officers act as agents of their constituents when making decisions on important matters. Thus, opponents argue that a popular mechanism must be available to voters to remove elected officers accused of malfeasance (bad or corrupt conduct), misfeasance (incompetent performance of duties), and nonfeasance (nonperformance of duties).

The possibility of corrupt behavior by officeholders in the United States long has been recognized. Thomas Jefferson in 1782 stressed the importance of informed citizens in the following terms: "In every government on earth is some trace of human weakness, some germ of corruption and degeneracy, which cunning will discover, wickedness insensibly open, cultivate, and improve. Every government degenerates when trusted to the rulers of the people alone. The people themselves therefore are its only safe depositories. And to render even them safe, their minds must be improved to a certain extent."[5] Although his proposal was described as one establishing a spoils system, President Andrew Jackson in an 1829 message to Congress emphasized:

There are perhaps few men who can for any great length of time enjoy office and power, without being more or less under the influence of feelings unfavorable to the faithful discharge of their public duties. Their integrity may be proof against improper considerations immediately addressed to themselves; but they are apt to acquire a habit of looking with indifference upon the public interests, and of tolerating conduct from which an unpracticed man would revolt. Office is considered as a species of property; and Government rather as a means of promoting individual interests than as an instrument created solely for the service of the People. Corruption in some and in others a perversion of correct feelings and principles divert Government from its legitimate ends, and make it an engine for the support of the few at the expense of the many.[6]

Jackson's remedy relied upon the ballot box and frequent elections of all public officers to curb the evil he described and ensure that the popular will and popular government prevail.

Jacksonian democracy was based in part on the democratic theory that each candidate for elective office announces his policies and ethical standards and voters select the candidate reflecting their popular will. If an elected official does not implement popular policies or live up to ethical standards, the officer may be removed should he stand for reelection and be replaced by a person representing the views of the majority of the voters.

The recall, however, is designed to correct public officers' errors of commission and omission by removing them from office prior to the expiration of their terms of office. The reasons for the use of the recall are not limited to a *scandalum magnatum*, because the recall can be employed in most states for any reason, including disagreement on a policy issue. The

Michigan constitution, for example, stipulates "the sufficiency of any statement of reasons or grounds procedurally required shall be a political rather than a judicial question."[7]

The Nebraska Supreme Court in 1913 opined:

The policy of the recall may be wise or it may be vicious in its results. We express no opinion as to its wisdom with respect to the removal of administrative officers. If the people of the state find after a trial of the experiment that the provisions of the statute lead to capable officials being vexed with petitions for their recall, based upon mere insinuations or upon frivolous grounds, or because they are performing their duty and enforcing the law, as they are bound to do by their oath of office, or lead without good and sufficient reason to frequent and unnecessary elections, they have the power through their Legislature to amend the statute so as to protect honest and courageous officials.[8]

In upholding the constitutionality of a city charter providing for the recall, the Washington Supreme Court in 1909 explained:

Like the British ministry, an elective officer under the charter is at all times answerable to the people for a failure to meet their approval on measures of public policy.

Whether the interests of the city will be better subserved by a ready obedience to public sentiment than by a courageous adherence to the views of the individual officer . . . is a political and not a legal question.[9]

However, not all state supreme courts view the recall as a process involving only a political question, as will be revealed in the detailed analysis of the recall process in Chapter 2.

Are elected officers delegates or agents of the people? The delegate concept posits that elected officers will use their good judgment, based upon the facts they have gathered, to make decisions promoting the public good and that they are not bound by the wishes of their respective constituents. John F. Kennedy wrote a best selling book — *Profiles in Courage* — that praised certain decision makers for opting for a policy that was not popular with the citizenry yet was viewed by the decision makers as in the best interests of the polity.[10]

The agent concept posits that elected public officers must make decisions solely on the basis of the wishes of the electorate. Proponents are convinced that voting in periodic elections is an inadequate safeguard of the public weal and the ballot box must be continuously available to the electorate to enable them to enforce their will. The ultimate instrument available to the voters in certain states and local governments is the recall, which allows voters to circulate petitions calling for a special election to determine whether a named officer should be removed from office. If employed frequently, the recall would establish the principle that officers are agents of the voters, who have the right at any time to replace their agents. Chapters 3 and 4 explore the frequency of the use of the recall in the United States.

Supporters of the recall maintain that elected officers are agents of the voters who possess sovereign power to remove at any time an officer who fails to follow the public's will as expressed at the ballot box. They also maintain that all public officers are legally and morally responsible to the voters and that the recall permits voters to enforce the officers' responsibility.

Although the theory of the recall is premised on ensuring decision making in accord with the public's will, the recall also can be employed to remove a public officer accused of malfeasance, misfeasance, and nonfeasance, to deal with situations in which the officer is not removed by the impeachment process, the legislative address process (legislative directive to the governor to remove an officer), or direct gubernatorial action if authorized in the absence of a statute providing for the automatic vacating of an office when the incumbent is convicted of a felony. Due process of law guarantees and restrictions on the use of these removal methods typically make them relatively ineffective, long-drawn-out, and costly procedures, and, thus, the recall may be more effective.

Commenting on the recall in 1914, the Washington Supreme Court emphasized: "It cannot be questioned that the recall and its usual concomitant, the referendum, are wholesome means to the preservation of responsible popular government. They employed a principle as old as the English constitution. The frequent appeals of the English ministry from a vote of Parliament to a vote of the people on a given measure, requiring the members of Parliament to stand for reelection upon that measure as an issue . . . is obviously but a recall as to the personnel of the government and a referendum as to the given measure."[11]

Does a state or local government elected officer have a right to hold office guaranteed by the U.S. Constitution? The answer clearly is no, because courts have held that an election is not a contract and an elected officer has no property interest in the office. The U.S. Supreme Court in 1939 ruled that there is no U.S. constitutional guarantee — whether procedural due process or contract right — attached to the recall.[12] Similarly, the U.S. Court of Appeals for the Fifth Circuit in 1971 rejected a due process attack upon the use of the recall to remove a Florida local government officer.[13] In this case, the court opined: "Any governmental body is required to act fairly, but that is not true as to the voter. Insofar as the United States Constitution is concerned, an elector may vote for a good reason, a bad reason, or for no reason whatsoever. The principle applies to recall elections as it does to all other elections."[14]

ORIGIN OF THE RECALL

The term "recall" is associated directly with the word "democracy," which is an amalgamation of two Greek words meaning "power of the people." There was no need for a corrective device, such as the recall, in the historic New England open town meeting, because assembled voters enacted all bylaws. Elected administrators — selectmen, town clerks, fence viewers, cattle reeves, and so on — were not subject to recall but served a short term of one year and exercised little discretionary authority in carrying out the policies adopted by the annual and special (if any) town meetings.

Frank F. Abbott in 1915 traced the origin of the recall to ancient Rome in the year 133 B.C. when Tribune Octavius was removed from office by a vote of the people because he vetoed a senate bill.[15] Abbott quoted Plutarch's life of Tiberius as follows:

Octavius, however, would by no means be persuaded to compliance; upon which Tiberius declared openly, that, seeing the two were united in the same office, and of equal authority, it would be a difficult matter to compose their differences on so weighty a matter without a civil war; and that the only remedy which he knew, must be the deposing one of them from office. He desired, therefore, that Octavius would summon the people to pass their verdict upon him first, averring that he would willingly relinquish his authority if the citizens desired it. . . . The law for his deprivation being thus voted, Tiberius ordered one of his (Octavius) servants . . . to remove Octavius from the rostra. . . . This being done, the law concerning the lands was ratified and confirmed.[16]

The essential elements of a recall were employed in this case. A charge was made, there was no judicial procedure, and the tribune was removed from office by vote of the people.

The first authorization for the use of the recall in the United States is found in the Declaration of the Rights of the Inhabitants of the Commonwealth contained in the Pennsylvania Constitution of 1776: "VI. That those who are employed in the legislative and executive business of the state may be restrained from oppression, the people have a right, at such periods they may think proper, to reduce their public officers to a private station, and supply the vacancies by certain and regular elections."

The concept of the recall also was incorporated into Article 5 of the Articles of Confederation and Perpetual Union, effective in 1781, which provided that states could replace at any time their delegates to the Congress. The voters, however, participated in this type of recall only indirectly, because they lacked the direct power to replace delegates.

The origin of the movement for authorization of the recall of elected officers in the United States is traceable in general to the growing distrust of state legislatures in the nineteenth century and in particular to the populist and progressive movements in the later part of the century, which sought constitutional changes to empower voters to correct abuses of power by elected officers.

Distrust of State Legislatures

The framers of the constitutions of the original 13 states placed great trust in the legislative branch by granting it broad exercisable powers and subjecting it only to the prohibitions contained in the bills of rights.

However, the growth of Jacksonian democracy, as reflected in the election of most state and local government officers for short terms, in the 1830s and subsequent decades revealed growing voter distrust of government officers in general and state legislators in particular. Voters in New York state, for example, were distressed by the substantial state debt incurred as the result of state financial aid for canal and railroad construction and associated scandals and the result of pledges of state credit to private companies. Fear of a powerful governor, reflected in the 1777 state constitution, gave way to fear of an irresponsible state legislature by 1846.

The replacement fundamental document, drafted by a convention and ratified in an 1846 New York referendum, placed restrictions on the state legislature relative to state finance, corporations, and other matters. Jacksonian democracy was responsible for incorporation in the constitution of provisions for the election of judges, previously appointed by the governor with senate approval; popular election of the attorney general, canal commissioners, state comptroller, secretary of state, state engineer, surveyor, and inspectors of prisons; and a reduction of the term of office of senators from four to two years.[17] Members of the assembly, the lower house, continued to serve a one-year term. The new constitution also reflected distrust of the state legislature by directing that the question of whether a convention should be called to revise the constitution must appear automatically on the ballot every 20 years.[18]

New York voters in 1874 ratified six proposed constitutional amendments. Concern with pork-barrel appropriations led to the authorization of the governor to veto items in appropriation bills.[19] The second amendment forbade the state legislature to enact a local or private bill relating to 13 specified subjects, and a third amendment forbade the state legislature to audit or "allow any private claim or account against the state."[20]

Legislation by "reference" was eliminated by a fourth amendment, which stipulated that "no act shall be passed which shall provide that any existing law, or any part thereof, shall be made or deemed a part of said act, or which shall enact that any existing law, or any part thereof, shall be applicable, except by inserting it in such act."[21]

With respect to bills imposing, continuing, or reviving a tax or creating a debt, a fifth amendment provided that "the question shall be taken by yeas and nays, which shall be duly entered upon the journals, the three-fifths of all the members elected to either house shall, in all such cases, be necessary to constitute a quorum therein."[22]

The sixth limiting amendment forbade the state legislature to "grant any extra compensation to any public officer, servant, agent, or contract, or contractor."[23] The current New York state constitution contains the first five of these amendments.

A new state constitution, ratified by New York voters in 1894, sought to eliminate enactment of unprinted bills by stipulating that "no bill shall be passed or become law unless it shall have been printed and upon the desks of the members, in its final form, at least three calendar days prior to its final passage, unless the governor, or the acting governor, shall have certified to the necessity of its immediate passage."[24] Voters also decided to remove from the state legislature the power to incur long-term full faith and credit debt by stipulating that legislative proposals to contract such debt are subject to a voter referendum.[25] The current state constitution contains these provisions.

Although the New York constitution contains the largest number of prohibitions and restrictions upon the exercise of legislative powers, many other state constitutions were amended or replaced in the nineteenth century in order to restrict the power of the state legislature and generally to increase the power of the governor. These reforms, however, did not restore confidence in the state legislature in many states.

The continuing unrepresentative nature of many state and local governments and associated corruption generated several reform movements. Citizen dissatisfaction with certain statutes enacted by the state legislature and its failure to act on other bills desired by the electorate led to the ratification of a constitutional amendment in South Dakota in 1898 authorizing the voters by petitions to employ the protest referendum and the initiative.[26] The former allows voters by means of petitions to suspend a newly enacted statute until a referendum is held to determine whether the statute should be repealed.[27] The initiative authorizes the electorate to file petitions to place a proposed constitutional amendment or statute on the referendum ballot.

These citizen control devices quickly were found to be desirable by voters in several other states, who amended their respective constitutions to authorize the use of the protest referendum and the initiative. Nevertheless, ardent reformers were convinced that the voters needed what the reformers perceived to be the ultimate control device — the recall — which has a long history of use in Switzerland.

Cantonal law in Schaffhausen, for example, provides for petitions, signed by a minimum of 1,000 qualified voters of the canton, to be submitted to the president of the Communal Council of the commune in which each signer resides for a determination of the validity of each signature.[28] Insufficient petitions are returned to the circulators, who may collect additional signatures within a specified period. When the closing date is reached, the Executive Council ascertains whether the number of signatures is adequate and publishes its finding. If the petition contains the required number of signatures, the Executive Council must schedule a removal election within 30 days.

Agitation for the Swiss type of recall developed in the 1890s, and the 1892 and 1896 national platforms of the Socialist Labor Party and the platform of the Populist Party in several states called for adoption of the recall, which also was known as the "imperative mandate." No government, however, adopted the recall until voters approved a new city charter for Los Angeles on January 22, 1903.[29]

Populist-Progressive Roots

The United States underwent a dramatic metamorphosis between 1865 and the early decades of the twentieth century from a predominantly agricultural economy and society to one with large cities and the majority of the workforce engaged in industry and commerce. Mechanization of agriculture and the manpower needs of the growing industrial cities promoted an exodus from the land to the cities during a period when economic depressions and financial panics had an adverse impact upon farmers.

The socioeconomic transformation of the nation generated several popular movements, including the granger, populist, municipal reform,
administrative management, and progressive movements. The granger
movement was directed primarily against railroads, which often had a
monopoly on transportation and charged what the traffic would bear. This
movement achieved success in 1887, when Congress enacted the Interstate Commerce Act regulating railroad fares and routes.[30]

The populist movement included much more than the Populist Party.
Populists were in general sympathy with Jacksonian democracy, supported the movement to curb monopolies, and favored the silver standard, a
graduated income tax, women's suffrage, and the initiative, protest referendum, and recall. Eric F. Goldman commented: "In the spirit of Populism, progressives took up new proposals for direct democracy or the
advancement of lower-income groups, most notably popular primaries,
the recall of elected officials, workmen's compensation legislation, and
minimum-wage and maximum-hour laws."[31]

Richard Hofstadter noted that populism and progressivism arose during
a period of large-scale immigration from Europe of persons whose culture
and religion differed from those of the "Yankees," who generally were
protestants. He explained the system of political ethics of the immigrants
as follows: "The system . . . took for granted that the political life of the
individual would arise out of family needs, interpreted political and civic
relations chiefly in terms of personal obligations, and placed strong personal loyalties above allegiance to abstract codes of law or morals. It was
chiefly upon this system of values that the political life of the immigrant,
the boss, and the urban machine was based."[32]

Hofstadter also referred to the development of the agrarian myth, traceable to the farmer soldiers of the Revolutionary War and Jefferson's belief
in the yeoman farmer, which "encouraged farmers to believe they were
not themselves an organic part of the whole order of business enterprise
and speculation that flourished in the city, partaking of its character and
sharing in its risks, but rather the innocent pastoral victims of a conspiracy hatched in the distance."[33]

The conspiracy theory in particular colored the thinking of populists
who sought to improve the agricultural economy and establish popular
government. Writing in 1914, Albert M. Kales commented:

Unpopular government is, and indeed always has been a government of the few,
by the few, and for the few, at the expense and against the wish of the many.

If the extra-legal unpopular government by politocrats rests upon a condition of political ignorance on the part of the electorate, then it will be said that the obvious cure is to dissipate that ignorance by political education.[34]

Kales traced the movement for the recall to the realization by many citizens that the Jacksonian system of frequent elections did not prevent the "extra-legal government" from ensuring the election of its local supporters to office.[35] He was critical of the long ballot, which placed an undue burden upon the electorate to study the qualifications and records of numerous candidates for office, and also stressed that the recall could be employed by the "extra-legal government."[36]

The progressive movement developed as the populist movement was declining at the turn of the twentieth century. Whereas the latter movement was primarily agrarian based, the progressive movement was led by middle- and upper-middle-class leaders in cities and was a nationally based movement. In effect, the two movements became one in the early twentieth century. Hofstadter provides an interesting insight into the leaders of the progressive movement, described as of "the Mugwump type," who "were progressives not because of economic deprivations but primarily because they were victims of an upheaval in status that took place in the United States during the closing decades of the nineteenth and the early years of the twentieth century."[37] Hofstadter referred to the Mugwumps being bypassed by the newly rich and becoming "less important."[38]

The progressives were able to develop broad popular support in many regions of the nation, including the Midwest, West Coast, and Massachusetts. William Allen White, a famous Kansas City newspaper editor, commented in 1910 favorably on the adoption of the recall: "So the appearance of the recall, in the cities of a dozen states within a little over a year, should make those statesmen nervous who look forward to the time when the country will go back to the Good Old Days. For this tightening grip of the people upon their state governments . . . has been an intelligent, gradual, well-directed growth of popular power."[39]

A different perspective was provided in 1912 by Walter E. Weyl, who reported that the progressives sought to install popular control of governmental organizations and procedures and "to break the power of a politically entrenched plutocracy."[40] Weyl reported that legislators did not fear being defeated for reelection when opponents charged that their betrayal of the public trust would ensure they never would be reelected, because the legislators "interpreted the word 'never' in a Gilbertian Sense, as meaning 'hardly ever.'"[41]

Leaders of the progressive movement also were involved in other contemporary movements: municipal reform, national short ballot, and administrative management. The former movement was well-underway in the early 1890s and included the formation of the National Municipal League in 1894 under the leadership of New York City Police Commissioner Theodore Roosevelt and other reformers concerned about the corruption associated with boss-controlled cities.

Hofstadter was convinced: "The progressive leaders were the spiritual sons of the Mugwumps, but they were sons who dropped much of the ideological baggage of their parents. Where the Mugwumps had been committed to aristocracy . . . , the progressives spoke of returning government to the people. . . . The progressives had, on a substantial number of national issues, reliable allies in the very agrarian rebels for whom the Mugwumps had had nothing but contempt."[42] In his view, the progressives' campaign for adoption of the initiative, protest referendum, and recall "was, in effect, an attempt to realize Yankee-Protestant ideals of personal responsibility; and the progressive notion of good citizenship was the culmination of the Yankee-Mugwump ethos of political participation without self-interest."[43] Hofstadter described the progressives' attempt "to institutionalize a mood" as an impossible task.[44]

Progressive leader Robert M. La Follette was a strong advocate of the recall, which "enables the people to dismiss from public service those representatives who dishonor their commissions by betraying the public interest."[45] He emphasized that it was essential that voters must be given a means of stopping and reversing "the evils of misrepresentation and betrayal" if representative government is to be achieved in the United States.[46] Combined with the initiative and the protest referendum, the recall empowered the electorate to exercise absolute control of a government, according to La Follette.[47]

EARLY DEVELOPMENT OF THE RECALL

The state of California and the city of Los Angeles were controlled by the Republican Party at the beginning of the twentieth century. The party, in turn, took orders from the Southern Pacific Railroad. The migration of people to southern California produced a sharp increase in the population of Los Angeles during the last two decades of the nineteenth century and generated pressures for a reorganization of the city government.[48] There had been three failed attempts to revise the 1889 city charter by 1900, but pressure for revision continued. The city council called an election on July 17, 1900, for a board of freeholders to draft a new charter.

One of the 15 members of the board was John R. Haynes, an advocate of the initiative and referendum who drafted the first provision for a modern recall in the United States. He drafted provisions for the initiative and referendum and included a provision for the recall with the hope that it might be approved along with the other provisions. There was little opposition to the initiative and referendum provisions, because several cities had adopted such charter provisions. The recall, however, was an unknown device.

Surprisingly, there was little board opposition to the recall, and the small amount of press coverage was positive. Before a referendum could be held, the California Supreme Court ruled that the charter could be changed only by amendments submitted by the city council. The Los Angeles city council took no action on the proposed charter.

In 1902, a charter revision commission was formed, which recommended adoption of the initiative, referendum, and recall, and the city council referred these provisions, along with 12 others, to the voters to make a decision on December 1, 1902. Voters approved the initiative and referendum by a margin greater than six to one and the recall by a vote of four to one.

The state legislature traditionally approved home rule charter provisions submitted by cities, but there were strong attacks upon the Los Angeles charter provisions authorizing the initiative, referendum, and recall. Nevertheless, the charter amendments were approved on January 22, 1903. The recall provision was used immediately to remove a member of the city council who was considered to be a machine politician.

H. S. Gilbertson in 1912 referred to the political leaders who were responsible for the incorporation of the recall into the Los Angeles city charter and wrote that they probably lacked a political theory and were seeking to address a misrepresentative system in which elected officers often defied the will of the general public.[49] He added that the recall "was conceived in a spirit of optimism" relative to the ability of the average voter to exercise continuous oversight of elected officers.[50] Furthermore, he credited the framers of the device with the foresight of preventing "outbursts of passion" by requiring petition circulators to obtain valid signatures equal to 20 to 25 percent of those who voted in the preceding election.[51]

Twenty-five California municipalities adopted the initiative, referendum, and recall by 1911, when the state constitution was amended to authorize the recall of statewide elected public officers. This authorization was unusual in that a single petition, signed by the requisite number of voters, was sufficient to trigger a recall election for more than one officer.

The 1905 adoption of the recall by Pasadena, California, was unique. A city charter revision committee decided not to include the recall in a revised charter. Frustrated voters utilized the initiative to add a recall amendment to the charter.

Although Governor La Follette of Wisconsin in his 1905 message to the state legislature recommended that the recall of city officials be authorized, such a statute was not enacted until 1911.[52] It was not until 1926 that the Wisconsin constitution was amended to provide for the recall. The state legislature in 1911 for the first time approved a constitutional recall amendment and in 1913 approved the amendment for the second time. Voters in 1913, however, rejected the proposal. After a resurrected proposal was approved by the state legislature in 1923 and 1925, voters in 1926 ratified the amendment that currently is in effect.[53] An implementing statute, specifying procedures, was enacted by the state legislature in 1933.[54]

The first state to authorize the recall of elected state officials was Oregon, which adopted a recall constitutional amendment in 1908. The campaign for electoral reforms in Oregon was led by the People's Power League, which succeeded in 1902 in its efforts to have the state adopt the initiative and referendum and in 1904, the direct primary. The league in 1908 placed on the election ballot, via the initiative, a proposed constitutional amendment authorizing the recall, and the proposal was ratified by 62 percent of the voters.[55] Every elected public officer was made subject to the recall, which could be initiated by petitions containing signatures equal to 25 percent of the total vote for a supreme court justice in the previous election in the concerned district.[56] Over the next seven years, a total of 17 recall elections involving 34 elected officers were held, with 25 officers removed.[57]

By 1914, nine additional states — Arizona (1912), California (1911), Colorado (1912), Idaho (1912), Kansas (1914), Louisiana (1914), Michigan (1913), Nevada (1912), and Washington (1912) — had adopted a constitutional provision authorizing the recall, and the Illinois State Legislature in 1910 authorized use of the recall by statute.

It is interesting to note that, during the immediate post–World War I period, nine länder (states) in Germany during the Weimar Republic authorized voters in cities to employ the recall.[58] In common with the Swiss practice, the recall (with the exception of one city) could be employed by the electorate only to dissolve the entire council and to order new elections. Between 1919 and 1924, under a socialist government in Brunswick, voters were empowered to remove from office the Bürgermeister (mayor) and collectively or individually members of the Stadtmagistrat (council).[59] The recall, however, seldom was employed by the voters.

CURRENT STATUS

Today, the constitutions of 16 states authorize the electorate to employ the recall to remove all or specified elected public officers. Twenty additional states have sanctioned by statute the use of the recall to remove all or specified elected officers. Several states lacking a constitutional provision for the recall have a constitutional home rule provision that has been utilized by a number of general purpose local governments to draft charters providing for the recall or to amend charters to add a recall provision. As explained in Chapter 2, the state supreme courts in Connecticut and Pennsylvania have invalidated home rule charter recall provisions.

Support for the recall by the municipal reform movement, which sought to eliminate boss rule and corruption in cities and to have services provided in an economical and efficient manner, led to widespread incorporation of the recall in newly drafted commission and council-manager charters. Furthermore, the recall was added to a number of council-manager charters because opponents of the manager plan of administration maintained that a nonelected public officer should not possess the amount of authority typically delegated to a manager by the charter. When proponents of the plan pointed out that the manager can be removed at any time by a simple majority vote of the local legislative body, the opponents often replied that all the manager has to do to stay in office is to perform favors to keep a majority of the members of the governing body satisfied and they will vote to retain him. In response to this objection, proponents suggested the incorporation of a recall provision in the charter to allow voters to remove local legislators who do not vote to discharge an incompetent manager. As noted in Chapter 4, the recall in manager municipalities generally has been employed to remove a local legislator who voted to discharge the manager.

OPPOSITION TO THE RECALL

Not surprisingly, leaders of the major political parties and elected public officers typically opposed strongly the incorporation of a recall provision in the state constitution, state statutes, and local government charters. Relatively strong opposition quickly developed to the recall of state public officers, with the strongest opposition directed against the recall of judges. In 1911, the American Bar Association approved a resolution opposing the recall of judges.[60]

Congress is granted authority by the United States Constitution to admit territories to the union as states.[61] On occasion, Congress has attached conditions to the admission of a territory as a state. The United States Supreme Court has ruled that such conditions are judicially enforceable if they relate to federal government property in the new state or to grants of land or money to the state to be used for specific purposes.[62]

The provision in the proposed Arizona state constitution, approved by territory voters, that included elected state judges as public officers subject to the recall generated a national controversy. In admitting the Arizona territory to the union with a state constitution authorizing the recall of judges, Congress included in the joint resolution of admission a condition that a proposed amendment be submitted to the voters that would repeal authorization of the recall.[63]

President William H. Taft in 1911 vetoed the joint resolution of admission and wrote in his message of disallowance relative to the recall that: "its application to county and state judges, seems to me so pernicious in its effect, so destructive of independence in the judiciary, so likely to subject the rights of the individual to the possible tyranny of a popular majority, and, therefore, to be so injurious to the cause of free government, that I must disapprove a constitution containing it."[64] Arizona voters removed the recall provision from the proposed state constitution and promptly reinserted the provision, via a constitutional amendment, after duly gaining admission as a state. Earlier, New Mexico territory voters removed the recall provision in their proposed state constitution at the insistence of Taft.

Writing in 1912, Delos F. Wilcox — a leading proponent of the initiative, referendum, and recall — argued: "While the judges are bound to act in accordance with the established law and to interpret and apply that law to specific controversies, they ought to be just as responsible to the people for the manner in which they perform this function as the executive and the legislature are for the performance of their respective functions."[65] Wilcox added that judges either must "give up their policy-determining functions or" be subject to removal by the electorate.[66]

Taft, after leaving office, became Kent Professor of Law at Yale University, where he delivered a series of lectures in 1913 devoted to the initiative, the referendum, and the recall.[67] Taft advanced strong arguments against all three participatory devices and embellished the reasons in his veto message for opposing the recall. The recall, according to Taft, produced in public officers "a nervous condition of resolution as to whether he should do what he thinks he ought to do in the interest of the public, or should withhold from doing anything, or should do as little as possible, in order to avoid any discussion at all."[68] He strengthened his argument by referring to men — George Washington, Abraham Lincoln, and Grover Cleveland — who were subjected to vitriolic attack at the time of making decisions and later were recognized as great men.

The early decades of the twentieth century were a period of great fear of socialism. Taft buttressed his argument against the initiative, referendum, and recall by opining: "There is another basis for the movement today which gives strength to the proposal to put unrestrained and immediate control in the hands of a majority or minority of the electorate. It is in the idea that the unrestrained rule of the majority of the electors voting will prevent the right of property from proving an obstacle to achieving equality in condition so that the rich may be made poorer and the poor richer. In other words, a spur, conscious or unconscious, to this movement is socialistic."[69]

The American Bar Association appointed a committee to develop arguments in opposition to the judicial recall. The committee's 1914 report attacked socialist promoters of the recall who allegedly were seeking to replace the governance system and were advocating the recall "as an indirect instrument for achieving such change."[70]

The committee rejected the argument that the judicial recall is a remedial device and argued that it is subversive of a constitutional democratic system. In particular, the committee pointed out: "Any citizen, who is a lawyer or who has a judicial or lawyer-like mind, may be assumed to be able, without help, to reach an intelligent conclusion on this subject. Not so the average voter, who, . . . is easily led astray by fallacies so susceptible of subtle, insidious, and enticing presentations as those of the judicial recall."[71]

The committee noted that Ohio voters in 1912 had ratified a judicial constitutional amendment that is "less repugnant to our system of government than the recall."[72] Referred to as the Ohio plan, the amendment stipulates that a state statute can be declared unconstitutional only if six of the seven Supreme Court justices vote in the affirmative.[73]

Currently, constitutional recall provisions in Idaho, Louisiana, Michigan, and Washington exclude judges from the recall in order to immunize them from partisan political pressures and the passions of voters.

Opponents of the recall also argued that there was no need for the recall, because several means of removing such officers already existed. Writing in 1914, Charles Kettleborough identified seven methods of removal in addition to the recall.

(1) Impeachment, a quasi-judicial process, can be employed in all states except Oregon to remove officers, but the process is expensive and slow, and few officers have been removed.

(2) The governor is authorized to remove state and/or local officers in several states provided they are accorded their due process of law rights.

(3) Eleven states in 1914 authorized courts to remove certain officers if an action is brought against them. In certain states, the judge alone made the decision whether to remove an officer and in other states a jury made the decision.

(4) Specified officers in Iowa and Missouri in 1914 could be removed by the governor and senate acting jointly or by the state legislature.

(5) Statutes in Illinois, Indiana, and Ohio stipulated that a sheriff could be removed from office if a person in the sheriff's custody is lynched.

(6) The Arizona governor was authorized to remove a militia officer upon address (directive) of the state legislature or recommendation of the board of examination.

(7) New Jersey and Oregon statutes provided for the automatic vacating of office under specified circumstances. A New Jersey officer guilty of a misdemeanor involving moral turpitude forfeits his office and a member of an Oregon board or commission who fails to attend two consecutive meetings forfeits the office.[74]

In addition to the above removal methods, statutes in most states today provide for the automatic vacating of a public office if the incumbent is convicted of a felony. The Illinois constitution contains a broader list of grounds for vacating of a public office — conviction of bribery, felony, perjury, or other infamous crime.[75]

AN OVERVIEW

Declining voter turnout in most general elections and other indicia of voter alienation have rekindled interest in recent years in the populist-progressive direct democracy mechanism of the recall, as reflected in campaigns to recall the governor of Arizona, speaker of the California assembly, state legislators in Michigan and Wisconsin, mayors of Cleveland and San Francisco, and numerous other local government officers. The recall of Michigan and Wisconsin state legislators resulted in a change of party control of the senate in each state, a very significant political development.

Representative government continues to be criticized. Writing in 1984, political theorist Benjamin R. Barber noted: "A well-known adage has it that under a representative government the voter is free only on the day he casts his ballot. Yet even this may be of dubious consequence in a system where citizens use the franchise only to select an executive or judicial or legislative elite that in turn exercises every other duty of civic importance. To exercise the franchise is unhappily also to renounce it. The representative principle steals from individuals the ultimate responsibility for theory values, beliefs, and actions."[76] Barber specifically explained that the citizenry is subject to statutes made without participation by the governed and that this process allows representatives to "usurp" citizens' "civic functions and to deflect their civic energies."[77]

Barber's criticism of representative government is an overgeneralization, but it reflects the widely held popular distrust of legislators and the legislative process. His criticism is blunted in part by constitutional and statutory provisions in many states authorizing the use of one or more of the following correctives promoted by populists and progressives — protest referendum, initiative, and recall.

Chapter 2 examines in detail the constitutional and statutory recall provisions in 26 states and home rule provisions in other states authorizing voters in local governments to adopt and amend charters providing for the recall. As explained in the chapter, the state supreme courts in Connecticut and Pennsylvania have invalidated home rule recall charter provisions. The minimum number of verifiable voter signatures needed to trigger a recall election and other procedural requirements determine the degree of difficulty encountered by voters who wish to recall an elected public officer.

The use of the recall to remove a statewide elected public officer prior to the expiration of his or her term of office has been infrequent, in part because of the difficulty of collecting signatures on petitions. Nevertheless, the recall has been successfully utilized to recall statewide and district elected state public officers, as explained in Chapter 3.

Chapter 4 documents the considerably more frequent use of the recall to remove local government officers, which is not surprising when one considers the fact that the geographical area involved is relatively small compared with the area involved if a state legislator or a statewide elected officer is the target of a recall effort. Furthermore, decisions made by local government officers usually impact the voters more directly and immediately than decisions made by state officers.

Chapter 5 evaluates the five major arguments advanced by recall proponents that focus on keeping elected officers continuously responsible to the voter but also contend that the recall has auxiliary benefits in the form of reducing voter alienation and increasing voter education, removal of constitutional and statutory restrictions on legislative bodies, and lengthening of terms of office, which reduces election and campaign expenses.

The 12 major arguments of the opponents of the recall also are evaluated in Chapter 5. These arguments are more desirable removal methods exist, voters should not be allowed to make additional mistakes in the interim between general elections, use of the recall for undesirable purposes, unnecessary restraint of innovative and energetic public officers, deterrence of high-quality potential candidates, partisan use, increased governmental costs resulting from the holding of a special election(s), undesirable simultaneous elections, frivolous harassment of public officers, abuse by special interest groups, inadequate reason(s) for employing the device, and destruction of judicial independence.

Chapter 6 builds upon the findings and conclusions of Chapters 2 through 5 to develop a model constitutional or local government charter recall provision to guide state and local governments considering adoption of the recall or revision of an existing recall provision. According recognition to the fact that the recall alone will not guarantee that elected public officers will not abuse the public trust for private gain, the chapter recommends that the recall should be supplemented by the indirect initiative, the protest referendum, and various provisions designed to ensure that all governmental actions are ethical and that information to the extent practicable is available to the citizenry.

NOTES

1.   Joseph F. Zimmerman, *State-Local Relations: A Partnership Approach*, 2d ed. (Westport, Conn.: Praeger Publishers, 1995).

2.   *Popularly Elected Officials* (Washington, D.C.: U.S. Bureau of the Census, 1996), p. 1.

3.   Joseph F. Zimmerman, *The Massachusetts Town Meeting: A Tenacious Institution* (Albany: State University of New York, Graduate School of Public Affairs, 1967).

4.   For an interesting analysis of administrative due process, see Barbara R. Grumet, "Who is 'Due' Process?" *Public Administration Review* 42 (July–August 1982): 321–26.

5.   Paul L. Ford, ed., *The Writings of Thomas Jefferson*, Vol. 4. (New York: G. P. Putnam's Sons, 1894), p. 64.

6.   Henry S. Commager, ed., *The Era of Reform: 1830–1860* (New York: Van Nostrand Reinhold, 1960), p. 71.

7.   *Constitution of Michigan*, art. 2, § 8.

8.   *State ex rel. Topping v. Houston*, 94 Neb. 445, 143 N.W. 796 at 800 (Neb. 1913).

9.   *Hilzinger v. Gillman*, 56 Wash. 228 at 233, 105 P. 471 at 473-74 (Wash. 1909).

10. John F. Kennedy, *Profiles in Courage* (New York: Harper & Brothers, 1956).

11. *Stirtan v. Blethen*, 79 Wash. 10 at 14, 139 P. 618 at 620 (1914).

12. *Higginbottom v. City of Baton Rouge*, 306 U.S. 535 (1939).

⚔13. *Gordon v. Leatherman*, 450 2d 562 (5th Cir. 1971).

14. Ibid. at 567. The U.S. District Court rendered a similar opinion in *Roche v. Foulger*, 404 F. Supp. 705 (1975).

15. Frank F. Abbott, "The Referendum and the Recall Among the Ancient Romans," *The Swanee Review*, January 1915, pp. 92–94.

16. Ibid.

17. *New York Constitution of 1846*, art. 6, §§ 2-4, art. 3, § 2.

18. Ibid., art. 11, § 2 (1846).

19. Ibid., art. 4, § 9 (1874).

20. Ibid., art. 3, §§ 18–19 (1874).

21. Ibid., § 17 (1874).

22. Ibid., § 21 (1874).

23. Ibid., § 24 (1874).

24. *New York Constitution of 1894*, art. 3, § 14.

25. Ibid., art. 7, § 11 (1894).

26. *Constitution of South Dakota*, art. 3, § 1 (1898).

27. For details on the protest referendum and the initiative, see Joseph F. Zimmerman, *Participatory Democracy: Populism Revived* (New York: Praeger Publishers, 1986).

28. Margaret A. Schaffner, "The Recall," *Yale Review* 17 (August 1909): 206–9.

29. Frederick L. Bird and Frances M. Ryan, *The Recall of Public Officers: A Study of the Operation of the Recall in California* (New York: Macmillan, 1930), p. 22. Information in the following paragraphs is derived from this source. See also George E. Mowry, *The California Progressives* (Berkeley: University of California Press, 1951).

30. *The Act to Regulate Commerce of 1887*, 24 Stat. 379.

31. Eric F. Goldman, *Rendezvous with Destiny* (New York: Alfred A. Knopf, 1952), p. 76.

32. Richard Hofstadter, *The Age of Reform: From Bryan to F.D.R.* (New York: Alfred A. Knopf, 1955), p. 9.

33. Ibid., p. 55.

34. Albert M. Kales, *Unpopular Government in the United States* (Chicago, Ill.: University of Chicago Press, 1914).

35. Ibid., p. 122.

36. Ibid., p. 124.

37. Hofstadter, *The Age of Reform*, p. 135. The term "Mugwump" was first ascribed to a Republican who did not support James G. Blaine in 1884.

38. Ibid., p. 137.

39.   William Allen White, *The Old Order Changeth: A View of American Democracy* (New York: Macmillan, 1910), p. 60.

40.   Walter E. Weyl, *The New Democracy: An Essay on Certain Political and Economic Tendencies in the United States* (New York: Macmillan, 1912), p. 298.

41.   Ibid., pp. 304–5.

42.   Hofstadter, *The Age of Reform*, p. 167.

43.   Ibid., p. 259.

44.   Ibid., p. 264.

45.   Ellen Torelle, compiler, *The Political Philosophy of Robert M. La Follette* (Madison, Wisc.: Robert M. La Follette, 1920), p. 174.

46.   Ibid., pp. 175, 178.

47.   Ibid., p. 174.

48.   Information in this section is derived principally from Bird and Ryan, *The Recall of Public Officers*, pp. 22–33.

49.   H. S. Gilbertson, "Conservative Aspects of the Recall," *National Municipal Review* 1 (April 1912): 204.

50.   Ibid., p. 205.

51.   Ibid.

52.   *Wisconsin Laws of 1911*, chap. 635.

53.   *Constitution of Wisconsin*, art. 13, § 12.

54.   *Wisconsin Laws of 1933*, chap. 44.

55.   *The Historical Development and Use of the Recall in Oregon* (Salem: Legislative Research, 1976), pp. 1–2.

56.   *Constitution of Oregon*, art. 2, § 18.

57.   *The Historical Development and Use of the Recall*, p. 3.

58.   Roger H. Wells, "The Initiative, Referendum, and Recall in German Cities," *National Municipal Review* 18 (January 1929): 31.

59.   Ibid., p. 33.

60.   *Reports of the American Bar Association* 36 (1911): 231–32.

61.   *Constitution of the United States*, art. 4, § 3.

62.   *Sterns v. Minnesota*, 179 U.S. 223 (1900); *Ervien v. United States*, 251 U.S. 41 (1919).

63.   House Joint Resolution No. 14 of 1911.

64.   *Congressional Record*, August 15, 1911, p. 3964.

65.   Delos F. Wilcox, *Government by All the People* (New York: Macmillan, 1912), p. 218.

66.   Ibid., p. 223.

67.   William H. Taft, *Popular Government: Its Essence, Its Permanence, and Its Perils* (New Haven, Conn.: Yale University Press, 1913).

68.   Ibid., p. 83.

69.   Ibid., pp. 89–90.

70.   *Report of the Committee to Oppose Judicial Recall* (Washington, D.C.: American Bar Association, 1914), p. 8.

71. Ibid., p. 1.

72. Ibid.

73. Ibid., p. 4.

74. Charles Kettleborough, "Removal of Public Officers: A Ten-Year Review," *The American Political Science Review* 8 (November 1914): 623–29; see also *The Removal of State Public Officials from Office* (Madison: Wisconsin Legislative Reference Bureau, 1980).

75. *Constitution of Illinois*, art. 13, § 1.

76. Benjamin R. Barber, *Strong Democracy: Participatory Politics for a New Age* (Berkeley: University of California Press, 1984), p. 145.

77. Ibid., p. 147.

2

The Legal Foundation

The recall can be authorized directly or indirectly by the state constitution and similarly by statute (Table 2.1). An indirect authorization is a constitutional or statutory provision granting home rule to all or certain types of general purpose local governments by empowering their voters to draft, adopt, and amend local charters.[1] Numerous general purpose local governments in home rule states have taken advantage of such authorization to draft new charters that include provisions for the recall, and other local governments amended their charters to include the recall. The constitutionality of the recall provision of a city charter first was upheld in 1909 by the state of Washington Supreme Court, which declared the recall to be an inherent power of voters in the absence of a constitutional limitation.[2]

CONSTITUTIONAL PROVISIONS

Currently, employment of the recall to remove state officers is authorized by the constitutions or statutes of 16 states — Alaska, Arizona, California, Colorado, Georgia, Idaho, Kansas, Louisiana, Michigan, Montana, Nevada, New Jersey, North Dakota, Oregon, Washington, and Wisconsin. Judges are excluded from the recall by six of these state constitutions — Alaska, Idaho, Kansas, Louisiana, Michigan, and Washington.

TABLE 2.1
Constitutional and Statutory Recall Provisions, 1997

State	Constitutional Provision	Statutory Provision
Alabama	None	*Code of Alabama*, tit. 11, art. 9, §§ 11-44-134, 11-44E-168 (commission cities)
Alaska	art. 11, § 8	*Alaska Statutes*, §§ 14.08.081, 15.45.570-710, 15.60.010, 29.26.250-350
Arizona	art. 8, §§ 1–6	*Arizona Revised Statutes*, §§ 19-201–19-234
Arkansas	None	*Arkansas Code*, §§ 14-47-112, 14-48-114, 14-61-119, 14-92-209
California	art. 2, § 13; art. 23, § 1	*California Election Code*, §§ 27000–27104
Colorado	art. 21, § 1	*Colorado Revised Statutes*, §§ 1-12-101–1-12-122, 23-71-120.5, 31-4-501–31-4-505
Florida	None	*Florida Statutes Annotated*, § 100.361
Georgia	None	*Georgia Code Annotated*, §§ 21-4-1–21-4-21
Idaho	art. 6, § 6	*Idaho Election Laws*, §§ 34-1701–34-1715
Kansas	art. 4, §§ 3–5	*Kansas Statutes Annotated*, § 25-4301–25-4331
Louisiana	art. 10, § 26	*Louisiana Statutes Annotated*, §§ 18:1300–18:1300.17
Maine	None	*Maine Revised Statutes Annotated*, § 2602
Michigan	art. 2, § 8	*Michigan Compiled Laws Annotated*, Election Law, §§ 168.951–168.975
Minnesota	art. VIII, § 6	*Minnesota Statutes Annotated*, §§ 351.14–351.23 (county officers only)
Missouri	None	*Missouri Annotated Statutes*, §§ 77.650, 78.260

State	Constitution	Statutes
Montana	None	*Montana Code Annotated*, §§ 2-16-601–2-16-635
Nebraska	None	*Revised Statutes of Nebraska*, §§ 32-1301–32-1309
Nevada	art. 2, § 9	*Nevada Revised Statutes*, §§ 294A.006–294A.280, 306.15–306.130, 539.163–539.183
New Jersey	art. I, § 2	*New Jersey Revised Statutes Annotated*, §§ 19:27A-I –19:27A-18
New Mexico	art. 10, § 1 (county officers); art. 12, § 14 (school boards)	None
North Dakota	art. 3, §§ 1, 10	*North Dakota Century Code Annotated*, §§ 16.1-01-09, 44-08-21
Oregon	art. 2, § 18	*Oregon Revised Statutes*, §§ 249.865–249.880
South Dakota	None	*South Dakota Codified Laws Annotated*, §§ 9-13-29 –9-13-35 (first- and second-class cities)
Tennessee	None	*Tennessee Code Annotated*, § 6-31-301 (city school boards)
Washington	art. 1, §§ 33–34	*Washington Revised Code*, §§ 29.82.010– 29.82.220
Wisconsin	art. 13, § 12	*Wisconsin Statutes Annotated*, § 9.10

The constitutional recall provision may be self-executing or may require implementing legislation. The Wisconsin provision is self-executing and prevents legislative tampering with the recall by stipulating "no law shall be enacted to hamper, restrict, or impair the right of recall."[3] The Alaska provision, in contrast, is dependent for implementation upon the state legislature. There were doubts as to whether the 1908 Oregon constitutional recall provision could be employed in the absence of implementing legislation. The Oregon Supreme Court in 1914 held that the provision is self-executing.[4] In 1942, the Arizona Supreme Court ruled that the constitutional recall provision is self-executing and applies to precinct justices of the peace in the absence of a reference to precinct officials in the implementing statutes.[5]

Constitutional recall provisions may include considerable detail, as in California, or, as in Louisiana, simply stipulate "(t)he legislature shall provide by general law for the recall by election of any state, district, parochial, ward, or municipal official except judges of the courts of record."[6] The Arizona constitutional authorization, adopted in 1912, stipulates:

Every public officer in the state of Arizona, holding an elective office, either by election or appointment, is subject to recall from such office by the qualified electors of the electoral district from which candidates are elected to such office. Such electoral district may include the whole state. Such number of said electors as shall equal twenty-five per centum of the number of votes cast at the last preceding general election for all of the candidates for the office held by such officer, may by petition, which shall be known as a Recall Petition, demand his recall.[7]

The newest constitution with a recall provision — Alaska — simply provides "all elected public officials in the state, except judicial officers, are subject to recall by voters of the state or political subdivision from which elected. Procedures and grounds for recall shall be prescribed by the legislature."[8]

STATUTORY LOCAL OFFICER PROVISIONS

The states with a constitutional recall provision also authorize, by statute, all or certain local general purpose governments to employ the recall against all or specified local government officers. Although New Mexico lacks the recall for state government officers, the state constitution authorizes the employment of the recall to remove members of school boards.[9] Alabama restricts the recall to commission cities, and Minnesota restricts the recall to county elected officers.[10] In addition, 18 states authorize the recall of local officers by general law, special law, or a locally drafted and adopted charter.[11] The California constitution directs the state legislature to provide for the recall of local officers, but this directive does not affect cities and counties with home rule charters providing for the recall.[12] The California Supreme Court in 1935 sanctioned the use of the recall in the city of San Diego, which lacked a specific provision for the recall but incorporated the recall by reference to the general law recall provision.[13] The Florida Supreme Court in 1980 ruled that the Laurel Hill city charter, by referencing the statutes governing elections, had adopted the recall.[14]

The New Jersey Optional Municipal Charters Law stipulates "any elective officer shall be subject to removal from office for cause connected with his office, after he has served at least one year, upon the filing of a recall petition and the affirmative vote of a majority of those voting on the question of removal at any general, regular municipal, or special election."[15]

In Massachusetts, 52 locally drafted charters provide for the recall. The Billerica town charter stipulates "any person who holds an elected town office, but not including an elected town meeting member, with more than six months remaining of the term of office, may be recalled from office by the voters."[16] The Oxford town charter simply provides "any elective officer of the town may be recalled and removed from public office by the voters of the town as herein provided."[17] In Connecticut, 20 towns have recall provisions in their charters: 15 are contained in locally drafted and adopted charters, and 5 are special law provisions.

The locally drafted and adopted charters providing for a professional manager often include authorization for the recall because opponents of the manager plan of administration hold that a nonelected officer should not possess the amount of authority typically delegated to a manager appointed by the local legislative body. When proponents of the plan pointed out that the manager can be removed at any time by a simple majority vote of the local legislative body, the opponents often replied that all the manager has to do to stay in office is to perform favors to keep a majority of the members of the governing body satisfied and they will vote to retain him. In response to this objection, proponents suggested the incorporation of a recall provision in the charter to allow voters to remove local legislators who do not vote to discharge an incompetent manager.

JUDICIAL INTERPRETATION

Courts can influence the effectiveness of recall provisions by interpreting them narrowly or liberally. The California Court of Appeals in 1915 opined that recall statutes and constitutional provisions authorizing the statutes are to be construed liberally and that the power reserved to voters is not to be interfered with absent a clear showing of a violation of law.[18] In 1979, the Arizona Supreme Court ruled that the recall provision is to be interpreted liberally in favor of calling a recall election.[19] The Colorado Supreme Court in 1983 declared the recall to be a fundamental constitutional right that must be construed liberally, and the Wisconsin Supreme Court in 1989 issued a nearly identical ruling.[20]

Constitutional or statutory home rule provisions authorizing voters in general purpose local governments to draft, adopt, and amend charters in a few instances have been interpreted by courts to exclude the recall. The Connecticut Superior Court in 1973 ruled that recall provisions of a charter are not "basic and essential" features and that the state legislature had not explicitly authorized the recall.[21] In 1985, the Connecticut Supreme Court struck down home rule charter recall provisions on the ground that they lack constitutional or statutory authorization.[22] Five Connecticut municipalities, however, possess the power of recall because the state legislature by special laws authorized employment of the recall — Stratford (1921), Bristol (1939), New Haven (mayor only, 1952), Westport (1957), and Milford (1959).

OTHER VOTER INITIATED REMOVAL PROCEDURES

Ohio, Virginia, and Mississippi have unique removal provisions that are similar to a standard recall provision in that the removal process is initiated by voter petitions, but no recall election is held.

The Ohio constitution directs the state legislature to enact laws "providing for the prompt removal from office, upon complaint and hearing, of all officers, including state officers, judges, and members of the General Assembly, for any misconduct involving moral turpitude or for other cause provided by law."[23] State law authorizes citizens to file charges against an officer in the court of common pleas in the county where the officer resides, and removal proceedings will be commenced if the petition containing the charges is signed by at least 15 percent of the electorate who voted in the last gubernatorial election in the concerned jurisdiction. The removal proceedings are tried by a judge unless the officer subject to removal demands a jury trial, which must involve a 12-member jury; removal requires the approval of 9 members of the jury.[24] In 1948, the Ohio Supreme Court upheld the constitutionality of a city charter section providing for the recall of municipal officers without a complaint and hearing.[25] The court's decision was based on the constitutional grant of home rule powers to municipalities.[26]

Virginia voters, by means of petitions with signatures equal to 10 percent of the votes cast for the office in the last election, may initiate removal proceedings in the circuit court; the named officer may demand a trial by jury.[27]

Mississippi voters may petition the governor to remove a county officer from office for malfeasance, but the governor is not required to honor the request.[28]

RECALL OF MEMBERS OF CONGRESS

Can a U.S. representative or senator be recalled from office by voters? The Wisconsin constitution authorizes the voters in each congressional district to petition to recall any elected officer, which implies that the recall of a member of the U.S. House of Representatives is possible.[29] In 1979, the Wisconsin attorney general issued an opinion, in response to a request of the executive secretary of the state election board, that "in the event petitions for the recall of a United States Senator are presented to the election board, you should proceed to carry out your responsibilities under Wis. Const. Art. XIII, sec. 12, and sec. 9.10, Stats., unless and until directed otherwise by a court of law."[30] The attorney general admitted that there is a question as to whether the recall provision violates the U.S. Constitution but pointed out that the Wisconsin Supreme Court has issued decisions directing administrative bodies and officers to perform ministerial duties even if the result is of questionable constitutional validity.[31] The Michigan and New Jersey recall statutes specifically make members of the U.S. Senate and House of Representatives subject to the recall.[32]

It is clear, however, that the recall cannot be employed against a member of the U.S. Congress without a U.S. constitutional amendment authorizing the recall.[33] The Arizona statutes contain a provision for a "moral obligation" resignation by stipulating that candidates for the U.S. House of Representatives and Senate may file a preprimary pledge to resign their seats should they lose a recall election.[34]

RESTRICTIONS ON RECALL USE

Constitutional, statutory, and local charter provisions typically place restrictions on the exercise of the recall. The constitutions of Alaska, Idaho, Louisiana, Michigan, and Washington and statutes in Kansas and Michigan exclude judicial officers from the recall. Writing in 1914, Albert M. Kales emphasized: "A judge is one of the most helpless of all elective officers. He can run on no platform; he can have no political program. He cannot point dramatically to any achievements on behalf of the people. Whether he is a good judge or not is a matter of expert opinion that only a comparatively few persons are competent to pass upon. His reputation can be easily blasted by the circulation of false statements. He may even be hurt by the performance of his duty in a particular case."[35]

The Montana recall law is the only state law providing for the recall of appointed as well as elected officers subject to the stipulation that a public officer is not subject to the recall for performance of a mandatory duty or for failing to act if the action would subject the officer to prosecution for official misconduct.[36]

A number of municipal charters authorize the recall of appointed as well as elected officers. The City of Greeley, Colorado, has an unusual charter provision authorizing voters at an election held every six years to terminate the employment of the city manager.[37] The section of the charter of Long Beach, California, authorizing the recall of the city manager was repealed in 1972.[38]

Although the Ohio Supreme Court in 1922 held that the constitutional removal section provides for the removal of a public officer "only 'upon complaint and hearing,'"[39] the court in 1948 made an exception for charter cities by holding that such a city may provide for the recall in its charter without violating the constitutional removal provision because "it is not for the court to question the wisdom or desirability of provisions of such charters in respect to purely local affairs."[40] However, the Court of Common Pleas held in 1916 that the recall is not applicable to members of a board of education because a school district is not a municipal corporation and the statutory provision applies only to elected municipal officers.[41] In Oregon during the period 1965–76, 65 (41 percent) of the 159 recall petitions involved school board members.[42]

The charters of general purpose local governments with a recall provision typically exempt certain elected officials. In Massachusetts, elected town meeting members are exempted from the recall by the town charters in Billerica, Natick, and Saugus, and the Avon charter exempts public library trustees. In Minnesota, state law allows counties to employ the recall, but the charges against an officer must be malfeasance or misfeasance.[43]

California and Washington allow the recall process to be initiated as early as the day that the targeted state public officer assumes office. Constitutional and statutory provisions authorizing employment of the recall in other states prohibit its use during the first two months (Montana) to one year (New Jersey and Wisconsin) of an elected officer's term of office and during the last 180 days of an officer's term (Alaska, California,, Georgia, Kansas, and Minnesota).[44] Arizona, Colorado, and Oregon make an exception for members of the state legislature, who may be subject to the recall five days after the commencement of the legislative session.[45] The Georgia attorney general in 1992 advised that the prohibition of filing a recall petition during the first or last 180 days of a term does not apply to an officer appointed or elected to fill an unexpired term of another officer unless the attempted filing occurs during the first or last 180 days of the original term of office.[46] Arizona, Montana, and Nevada do not allow a second attempt to recall an officer during his or her term of office unless the petitioners reimburse the state for the cost of the first recall election.[47] Idaho, Kansas, Missouri, North Dakota, Oregon, Washington, and Wisconsin allow only one recall election for an officer during his or her term of office.[48]

The Arizona Constitution stipulates:

No recall petition shall be circulated against any officer until he shall have held his office for a period of six months, except that it may be filed against a member of the legislature at any time after five days from the beginning of the first session after his election. After one recall petition and election, no further recall petition shall be filed against the same officer during the term for which he was elected, unless petitioners signing such petition shall first pay into the public treasury which has paid such election expenses, all expenses of the preceding election.[49]

The recall may not be employed against a local government officer in California during the first 90 days and the last 6 months of a term of office or if the incumbent won a recall election during the previous 6 months.[50] The San Francisco home rule charter does not allow a recall election during the first six months of an officer's term of office.[51]

There are no restrictions on the use of the recall, other than time period or frequency, in California, North Dakota, Ohio, South Dakota, and Wyoming.

A POLITICAL OR A JUDICIAL PROCESS?

Constitutional and statutory provisions and courts differ as to whether the recall involves a political or a judicial process. If the recall is viewed as a political process, judicial guarantees protecting the rights of defendants do not apply because there is no requirement that an officer subject to the recall be charged with cause — malfeasance, misfeasance, nonfeasance, violation of oath of office. In contrast, impeachment is a judicial process with judicial guarantees.

A Political Process

The California constitution makes clear that the recall process involves a political question by stipulating that the grounds listed in a recall petition are not reviewable by the courts.[52] The Colorado constitution provides that "the registered electors shall be the sole and exclusive judge of the legality, reasonableness, and sufficiency of such ground or grounds assigned for such recall, and said ground or grounds shall not be open to review."[53] The Colorado Supreme Court in 1974 opined that the framers of the state constitution intended that the recall power is purely political in nature.[54]

The Michigan constitution declares "(t)he sufficiency of any statement of reasons or grounds procedurally required shall be a political rather than a judicial question."[55] The Michigan statutes authorize the county election commissions to "determine whether the reasons for recall stated in the petition are or are not of sufficient clarity to enable the officer whose recall is sought and the electors to identify the course of conduct which is the basis for the recall."[56] In 1979, the Michigan attorney general issued an opinion that the enactment into law of a bill limiting the grounds for the recall to misfeasance, malfeasance, or nonfeasance would be unconstitutional.[57] The Michigan Court of Appeals in the same year ruled that recall petitions merely alleging "administrative incompetence" did not meet the requirement that the petitions "shall state clearly the reason or reasons for recall," but, nevertheless, this defect did not invalidate the petitions.[58]

Alaska statutes clearly limit judicial review of the sufficiency of charges by providing that "a recall may not be held void because of insufficiency of grounds."[59] The Florida District Court of Appeals in 1973 voided as insufficient a recall petition that listed as grounds for recall that "all four said men have failed to obey or comply with the Charter of the City of Parker and the Law of the State of Florida" because "the charges must allege sufficient facts to identify to the electors the acts or failure to act without justification which are urged as misconduct in office."[60] The Missouri Court of Appeals in 1988 held that a court reviewing the sufficiency of allegations in recall petitions lacks authority to rule on the truth or falsity of the charges.[61]

The Arkansas recall statute simply stipulates "(t)he petition shall contain a statement of the grounds and reasons on which the removal is sought."[62] The Arizona Supreme Court in 1925 ruled that grounds for recalling a judge need not specify misconduct in office, because any ground is sufficient.[63] The Georgia Supreme Court in 1988 struck down the recall statute for failure to require specification of the grounds for the recall in violation of the constitutional requirement that the implementing statute must specify the grounds, procedures, and other matters relating to the recall.[64] The New Jersey Superior Court in 1964 refused to invalidate a recall petition that the plaintiffs alleged did not specify the reason for the recall and noted: "The courts throughout the United States have generally adopted the view that the power granted to electors of a municipality to remove certain public officers through recall procedure is political in nature and that it is for the people, and not the courts, to decide the truth and sufficiency of the grounds asserted for removal."[65]

The Nevada Supreme Court in 1965 ruled that the recall statute did not require specificity and opined that all that is required is that the reason for the recall be stated, regardless of whether the reason is a specific or a good one.[66] The court added that the merit of the reason as a ground for the recall of the officer is for the electorate to determine, because the reason involves a political issue to be resolved by a vote, not a legal question for the court to answer.

The Oregon constitution requires petitions only to "set forth in the petition the reasons for the demand."[67] The South Dakota statute contains a similar provision that "a specific statement of the grounds on which removal is sought" must be included in the petition.[68]

The Alaska constitutional authorization for the recall is implemented by a statute stipulating that an elected officer may be removed for "misconduct in office, incompetence, or failure to perform prescribed duties."[69] The statute was interpreted by the Alaska Supreme Court for the first time in *Meiners v. Bering Strait School District*, in which the court noted that "recall petitions will frequently be initiated by voters of limited means in districts of small population in remote parts of the state" and concluded that there should be a liberal construction of the statute.[70]

The court was reviewing the decision of the Alaska Superior Court in a case in which all parties to a recall action agreed that the first two paragraphs of a recall petition contained sufficient charges and also agreed that paragraph three did not contain sufficient grounds. In consequence, the Superior Court declared the entire petition to be invalid. On appeal, the Alaska Supreme Court reversed the decision by allowing the charges in the first two paragraphs to appear on the recall ballot.[71] The court continued by opining "(t)he purposes of recall are therefore not well served if artificial technical hurdles are unnecessarily created by the judiciary as parts of the process prescribed by statute."[72] Scolding the state legislature, the court added that "the need for judicial participation in the recall process could be decreased by more carefully drawn statutes."[73]

The Florida recall law lists the grounds for a recall of a public officer as malfeasance, misfeasance, neglect of duties, drunkenness, incompetence, permanent inability to perform official duties, and conviction of a felony involving moral turpitude.[74] In 1976, the Florida Court of Appeals held that, if any charge in a recall petition is sufficient, the entire list of allegations appears on the recall ballot even if the other allegations are insufficient.[75]

The Louisiana Superior Court in 1981 opined that the power of voters to recall public officers does not have to be based on malfeasance because the voters have the absolute right to recall a public officer for any reason or no reason because the state constitution stipulates that "the sole issue at a recall election shall be whether the official shall be recalled."[76]

A Judicial Process

The code of Georgia stipulates that grounds for recall are:

(A) that the official has . . . conducted himself or herself in a manner which relates to and adversely affects the administration of his or her office and adversely affects the rights and interests of the public; and (B) that the official: (i) has committed an act or acts of malfeasance while in office; (ii) has violated his or her oath of office; (iii) has committed an act of misconduct in office; (iv) is guilty of a failure to perform duties prescribed by law; or (v) has willfully misused, converted, or misappropriated, without authority, public property or public funds entrusted to or associated with the elective office to which the officer has been elected or appointed.[77]

The code continues that "(d)iscretionary performance of a lawful act or a prescribed duty shall not constitute a ground for recall of an elected public officer."[78]

Grounds for the recall of a public officer in Kansas are conviction of a felony, misconduct in office, incompetence, or failure to perform duties prescribed by law.[79] However, performance of a discretionary act is proscribed as a ground for the recall of a public officer.[80] In this respect, the Kansas Supreme Court in 1987 ruled:

The grounds stated in a recall petition must be specific enough to allow the official an opportunity to prepare a statement in justification of his or her conduct in office. Here, the charge is merely a general allegation that Unger and Temple violated the Open Meetings Act. Unless a particular allegation of the violation of the Open Meeting Act is stated, Unger and Temple have no opportunity to refute the charge. The petitions for recall of Unger and Temple do not contain a clear statement of the alleged act or acts constituting the grounds for recall.[81]

Justice Kay McFarland was the lone dissenter and stressed:

The majority has viewed the statutory recall of elected officials procedures from an improper perspective in determining the issue presented. . . . In criminal actions the rules are even more rigid. . . . It is not surprising that the majority would view the issue herein from the perspective of what is appropriate for a judicial adversary procedure. However, such perspective is, in my opinion, improper herein and has resulted in the majority incorrectly deciding the ultimate issue raised. Recall elections are so unlike judicial proceedings that they cannot be viewed from the same perspective or judged on the same standards.[82]

The Kansas Court of Appeals in 1995 was called upon to interpret a section of the recall statute directing the county or district attorney to "determine the sufficiency of the grounds stated in the petition for recall of a local officer."[83] The court referred to the Kansas Supreme Court's 1987 decision and a 1991 opinion of the attorney general holding that the truth or falsity of the recall grounds is to be determined by the voters and added "we agree."[84]

The Montana Recall Act stipulates that a public officer may be recalled for: "Physical or mental lack of fitness, incompetence, violation of his oath of office, official misconduct, or conviction of a felony offense. . . . No person may be recalled for performing a mandatory duty of the office he holds or for not performing any act that, if performed, would subject him to prosecution for official misconduct."[85] A petition was submitted in Montana alleging that the concerned sheriff "acted in a manner to bring discredit to himself and the Department by official misconduct stemming from an incident in Sweet Grass County on November 7, 1980."[86] The Montana Supreme Court concluded in 1982 that the statement "is deficient because it does not acquaint the public . . . with the alleged acts constituting misconduct, nor does it permit Sheriff Shaffer to respond and defend himself adequately against the allegation of misconduct in the event an election is required."[87]

In 1982, the Montana Supreme Court also emphasized the legal aspects of the recall by describing it as "special, extraordinary, and unusual" and a process that involves the "harsh" remedy of removing an officer prior to the expiration of the fixed term.[88] Hence, the court interprets statutory removal grounds narrowly in favor of the targeted officer, and any errors in recall procedures invalidate the recall effort.[89]

The Minnesota Supreme Court in 1959 ruled that the recall is a type of removal from office procedure and, hence, is governed by a constitutional provision limiting the recall to cases in which malfeasance or nonfeasance is charged.[90] The case involved an attempt to recall a councilman in the city of Fridley, which has a home rule charter provision for the recall as authorized by the state constitution and statute.[91] The court explained "that which constitutes malfeasance in an official capacity is not susceptible of an exact definition" but added: "To constitute malfeasance or nonfeasance the conduct must be such as affects the performance of official duties rather than conduct which affects the official's personal character as a private individual."[92]

The constitutions of New Mexico and Washington list the grounds for recall as malfeasance, misfeasance, and violation of oath of office.[93] The *Revised Code of Washington* expands upon the constitutional reasons for the recall in the following terms:

Whenever any legal voter of the state or of any political subdivision thereof, either individually or on behalf of an organization, desires to demand the recall and discharge of any elective public officer of the state or of such political subdivision, as the case may be, under provisions of sections 33 and 34 of Article 1 of the Constitution, he or they shall prepare a typewritten charge, reciting that such officer, naming him or her and giving the title of his office, has committed an act or acts of malfeasance, or an act or acts of misfeasance while in office, or has violated his oath of office, or has been guilty of any two or more of the acts specified in the constitution as grounds for recall. The charge shall state the act or acts complained of in concise language, give a detailed description including the approximate date, location, and nature of each act complained of, be signed by the person or persons making the charge, give their respective post office addresses, and be verified under oath that he or they believe the charge or charges to be true and have knowledge of the alleged facts upon which the stated grounds for recall are based.[94]

Washington's 1912 constitutional recall provision generated several court decisions with respect to the sufficiency of the charges against an officer and whether the court should conduct an examination beyond a review of the facial charges. The Washington Supreme Court first was faced with a case raising this issue in 1913. The plaintiff brought an action to enjoin the county auditor from acting on a recall petition until there was a determination of whether the charges were true. The superior court denied the petition for issuance of a writ of injunction, and the supreme court upheld the decision by opining that the role of the courts was limited to determining the sufficiency of the statement of charges; whether the charges were true was a political question to be determined by the voters.[95] The supreme court specifically noted: "It may be that the courts have jurisdiction to determine the sufficiency of the statement of the allegations made as a cause for removal if presented in a proper proceeding . . . but the trial of the question of whether such cause actually exists, and as to whether the officer shall be discharged shall be had before the tribunal of the people."[96]

In 1939, the Washington Supreme Court opined that the constitution and statutes of the state did not empower officers responsible for implementing the recall or courts to inquire into the truth of the alleged charges or the motives of the petitioners.[97] The court in 1967 upheld as constitutionally sufficient a charge that a water district commissioner was guilty of malfeasance and misfeasance by circulating a petition for the establishment of a new water district, which the petitioners maintained violated the commissioner's duty to operate and maintain the existing system.[98] The court's majority found that the advocating of the creation of a new district by the commissioner "is patently inconsistent with his duty" because a new district would compete for customers and reduce the revenues of the existing district.[99]

In 1968, the court identified in *State ex rel. LaMon v. Westport* two elements of a sufficient allegation — the charges must allege malfeasance or misfeasance, and the allegations must be sufficiently definite.[100] The court's definition of malfeasance was based upon its 1948 decision in *State v. Miller* involving a state action to recover money wrongfully received by a county clerk as the result of the employment of the clerk's wife in the county auditor's office.[101] In *Miller*, the Supreme Court defined malfeasance and misfeasance as "comprehensive which include any wrongful conduct affecting the performance of official duties."[102] The court in 1972 ruled that implementation by a school board of a mandatory busing system to eliminate *de facto* racial segregation did not constitute one of the three grounds for the use of the recall.[103]

The Washington Supreme Court in 1984 concluded that its construction of the constitutional recall provision during the previous 72 years had been wrong. The case involved a recall petition filed against members of the Shoreline school board, containing five charges. The Superior Court for King County examined the charges and the ballot synopsis and concluded that four of the charges were sufficient. On appeal, the supreme court reviewed the 1984 amendments to the recall statute and opined that the amendments "clearly disclose an intent by the legislature to limit the scope of the recall right to recall for cause and thereby free public officials from the harassment of recall elections grounded on frivolous charges or mere insinuations. . . . Such a rule is consistent with the original intent of the framers of the constitution's recall provision."[104] The court maintained that its ruling still allows voters to recall elected officers for cause, provided the charges are specific and definite, and added that courts lack authority to examine the truthfulness of the charges.[105]

In a strong dissent, Justice Fred H. Dore indicated that he would use the principles contained in previous decisions of the court and would find the four charges sufficient.[106] The first two charges related to the discretionary decision of the board to close a high school and two elementary schools. Dore opined: "The question of whether an act was an abuse of discretion is not something that should be left to this court to decide. Whether there has been an abuse of discretion, for recall purposes, is the prerogative of the voters, the reason being that whether someone has abused his discretion is a subjective question."[107]

In addition, Dore found the fourth charge — violation of the Open Public Meetings Act — sufficient, even though the charge did not specify the date of the violation, because the court in the past has ruled that "failure to comply with a statutory directive will not invalidate the recall unless the irregularity would affect the merits of the proceedings."[108] He also found the fifth charge — that the board employed an incompetent superintendent — sufficient because the court in four previous decisions found that such a charge was a sufficient ground for the recall.[109]

In 1989, the court held that an elected officer cannot be recalled for the appropriate exercise of discretion.[110]

OTHER ISSUES

Must the charges contained in recall petitions be restricted to action or inaction by a public officer during the current term of office, or can the charges relate to actions or inaction during a previous term of office? Constitutional and statutory recall provisions do not address this question. The

Washington Supreme Court, however, ruled in 1925 that the recall charges were not sufficient because the concerned officer, a sheriff, was serving a second term of office and "(t)here is nothing in the charges to show whether the acts complained of were committed during the first or second term of office."[111] In 1990, the Michigan Court of Appeals concluded that recall petitions based in part on the conduct of officers prior to holding elective office were invalid.[112]

Can recall petitioners be found guilty of slander or libel? In 1923, the Arizona Supreme Court determined that the charge "You are the most ignorant and incompetent County Recorder we ever had; you never do anything: this is one time you are going to do as I say" was not slanderous *per se* because the words meant the recorder was incompetent and guilty of dereliction of office.[113] On the other hand, the Washington Supreme Court in 1925 ruled that a voter's false and malicious charges contained in a recall petition constitute criminal libel even though the constitutional provision for recall elections, freedom of elections, and the suffrage right are similar to free speech rights.[114]

PETITION REQUIREMENTS

The recall is similar to the petition referendum and the initiative in that action originates with the voters. The first step in initiating voter removal of a state officer in eight states — Alaska, Arizona, California, Georgia, Idaho, Kansas, Oregon, and Washington — is the filing and publishing or posting of a notice of intent to circulate a recall petition (Figure 2.1).[115] A filing fee of $100 is required in Alaska and Kansas, but the fee is refunded if verified signatures equal to the number required for a recall election are filed by the deadline for the submission of petitions.[116]

In California, the notice must be served in person or by registered mail, and an affidavit of the manner and time of service must be filed with the secretary of state. This notice of intention must include the name and title of the officer sought to be recalled, a statement not exceeding 200 words of the reasons for the proposed recall, and the name and address of ten recall proponents. Within 7 days of receipt of the notice, the officer subject to the recall may file a response of up to 200 words with the secretary of state and must serve a copy of the response in person or by certified mail to one of the recall proponents named in the notice. After these formalities are complied with, official petitions are printed by the secretary of state and made available to proponents of the recall who filed the notice of intent.

FIGURE 2.1
Notice of Intention to Circulate a Recall Petition

TO THE HONORABLE (Name of Officer Sought to be Recalled)

Pursuant to Section 27020, California Elections Code, the undersigned, registered qualified voters of the (County/City/District) State of California, hereby give notice that we are the proponents of a recall petition and that we intend to seek your recall and removal of the office of (Title of Office), in (Name of County/City/District), California, and to demand election of a successor in that office.[1]

The grounds for the recall are as follows:

(STATE GROUNDS, 200 WORDS OR LESS)

The printed names, signatures, and business or residence addresses of the proponents are as follows:

(Name, Address, and Signature of Proponents. The least possible number of 10, however, more than 10 may be required by law.)

	NAME	ADDRESS	SIGNATURE
1.	_____		
2.	_____		

. . . .
. . . .
. . . .
10 or more.

Telephone number to contact proponents (optional) ( ) _____ [A copy of this notice and proof of service will be filed with the (Secretary of State, County Clerk, Secretary of District, as appropriate). Within 7 days after filing you may file with the (Secretary of State, County Clerk, Secretary of District, as appropriate) an answer, in not more than 200 words, to the statement of the proponents. If an answer is filed, a copy of it must also be served personally or by certified mail within that same 7 day period on one of the above proponents. The answer shall include the printed name, signature, and business or residence address of the officer sought to be recalled.][2]

---

[1]Omit the phrase "to demand election of a successor in that office" if it is a municipal recall. If it is the recall of an Appellate Justice, the request shall be that the Governor appoint a successor to the office.

[2]Note that the Notice of Intention must be published by proponents and proof of publication filed at the time of filing the two blank copies of the petition with the clerk or, in the case of a recall of a state officer, with the Secretary of State.

Although the statute implementing the Wisconsin constitutional recall provision contains a requirement that a reason(s) for the recall must be included in the petition, the attorney general issued an opinion in 1948 that an implementing statute could not impose an obligation on the electorate that expressly had been omitted from the constitutional provision.[117]

Each recall petition must contain a declaration by the circulator that each signature is a genuine one (Figure 2.2).[118] Petitions must be filed with a designated public officer within a stipulated number of days — ranging from 60 days in Wisconsin to 270 days for state officers and 180 days for other officers in Washington — after the certifying officer notifies proponents that the form and wording of the filed proposed petition are correct (Table 2.2).[119]

Successful collection of the required number of certified signatures on petitions results in a recall election, held in conjunction with a general election scheduled for the near future or held as a special election, to determine whether the named officer(s) shall remain in office until the expiration of his (their) regular term of office. In California, filing of the requisite number of signatures directs the governor to call a special recall election for a state officer within 60 days of certification of the sufficiency of the signatures.[120]

Within 14 days of receiving a certificate of signature sufficiency, a local governing body in California must issue an order that an election be held within 80 to 125 days after the governing body has issued the order for the election.[121] The San Francisco home rule charter, however, specifies that the recall election must be held within 60 to 75 days.[122]

The most common petition requirement is signatures equal to 25 percent of the votes cast for all candidates in the last general election for governor in the involved unit or the officer whose recall is sought (Table 2.2). Kansas has the highest statewide signature requirement, that is, 40 percent of the votes cast for the officer subject to recall at the last general election. The California signature requirements are the lowest statewide ones, that is, 20 percent for members of the boards of equalization, judges, and state legislators and only 12 percent of the votes cast for the other state officers in the last general election for the officer subject to the recall. The charter of the town of Methuen, Massachusetts, has a petition requirement of a minimum of 50 percent of the number of registered voters, and in contrast, the home rule charter of the city and county of San Francisco specifies that a recall election will be held if signatures equal to 10 percent of the registered voters are obtained on recall petitions and certified.[123] The charter of the city of South Portland, Maine, contains a

FIGURE 2.2
Petition for Recall

TO THE HONORABLE _____ *(Secretary of State, Clerk of* _____ *County,*
Board of Supervisors, etc.) _____ :

Pursuant to the California Constitution and California election laws, we the undersigned registered and
qualified electors of the _____ *(County/City/District)* _____ of _____ *(Name of County/City/District)* ,
California, respectfully state that we seek the recall and removal of _____ *(Name of Recallee)* ,
holding the office of _____ *(Name of Office)* _____ , in _____ *(Name of County/City/District)* ,
California.

We demand an election of a successor to that office.[1]

The following Notice of Intention to Circulate Recall Petition was served on _____ *(Date)* _____
to _____ *(Name of Recallee)* _____ :

(Insert complete text of Notice of Intention)

The answer of the officer sought to be recalled is as follows:

(Insert Statement—200 words or less)
(If no answer, so state.)

Each of the undersigned states for himself/herself that he or she is a registered and qualified elector of the
_____ *(County/City/District)* _____ of _____ *(Name of County/City/District)* _____ , California.[2]

			THIS COLUMN FOR OFFICIAL USE ONLY
Petition must be set in at least 6-point type.	PRINT YOUR NAME 1.	RESIDENCE ADDRESS ONLY	
	YOUR SIGNATURE AS REGISTERED TO VOTE	CITY ZIP	
	PRINT YOUR NAME 2.	RESIDENCE ADDRESS ONLY	
	YOUR SIGNATURE AS REGISTERED TO VOTE	CITY ZIP	

DECLARATION OF PERSON CIRCULATING SECTION OF RECALL PETITION

I, _____ *(Print Name)* _____ declare:

1. My residence address is _____
_____ , in _____ County, California,
and I am a registered voter in _____ *(County/City/District of officer sought to be recalled)* _____ ;

2. I personally circulated the attached petition for signing;

3. I witnessed each of the appended signatures being written on the petition and to my best information and belief,
each signature is the genuine signature of the person whose name it purports to be; and .

4. The appended signatures were obtained between the dates of _____ and
_____ , inclusive.

I declare under penalty of perjury under the laws of the State of California that the foregoing is true and
correct.

Executed on _____ *(Date)* _____ at _____ *(Place of Signing)* _____ .[3]

_____ *(Complete Signature of Petition Circulator)*

1. In case of city officer, the phrase "demand an election of a successor" should be replaced by the phrase "demand an election to
determine whether (name of officer sought to be recalled) shall be removed from office." In case of Appellate Court Justice, request
shall be that the Governor appoint a successor.

2. It is suggested that petitions be printed on 8 1/2" x 14" paper in order to maximize the number of signature spaces you can print on
a sheet of paper.

3. If signature spaces are printed on both sides of a sheet of paper, the above information, except for the declaration of circulator,
must appear on each side of the paper.

similar requirement.[124] A low signature threshold obviously encourages employment of the recall.

California and Georgia have a geographical requirement relative to the minimum number of petition signatures for the recall of an officer elected on a statewide basis. The California constitution stipulates that the required 12 percent of the last vote for a state office must include signatures equal to at least 1 percent of the last votes cast for the office in each of five counties.[125] The Georgia Recall Act of 1989 stipulates that "at least one-fifteenth of the number of electors necessary to petition the recall of the officer must reside in each of the United States congressional districts in the state as said congressional district may now or hereafter exist."[126] Similarly, city charters typically require that a specified number of signatures must be collected in each voting precinct or ward.

Circulators of initiative, protest referendum, and recall petitions in various states may be volunteers or paid workers. The use of paid petition circulators is a common practice in California. Fear has been expressed that wealthy special interests, with the assistance of paid petition circulators, will be able to initiate legislation or veto statutes. To guard against this possibility, the Colorado State Legislature enacted a statute providing: "Any person, corporation, or association of persons who directly or indirectly pays to or receives or agrees to pay to or receive from any other person, corporation, or association of persons any money or other thing of value in consideration of or as an inducement to the circulation of an initiative or referendum petition or in consideration of or as an inducement to the signing of any such petition commits a class 5 felony and shall be punished as provided in section 18-1-105, C.R.S. (1973)."[127]

Initiators of an initiative petition removing motor carriers from the jurisdiction of the Colorado Public Utilities Commission concluded that they would need the assistance of paid petition circulators if they were to obtain the required number of certified petition signatures within the allowable time for signature collection. They brought a section 1983 action under the Civil Rights Act of 1871 in the U.S. District Court against Colorado, seeking a declaratory judgment that the statutory prohibition of paid circulators violated their First Amendment rights under the U.S. Constitution.[128]

The district court upheld the statute because it did not place any restrictions on the petitioners' ability to express their opinions and they could use their funds to advance their position on the issue through advertising. Furthermore, the court agreed with Colorado that the statute was designed to ensure that there was broad-based grass-roots support for placing the

TABLE 2.2
State Recall Provisions: Applicability to State Officials and Petition Circulation

State or other jurisdiction	Officers to whom recall is applicable[a]	Number of times recall can be attempted	Recall may be initiated after official has been in office	Recall may not be initiated with days remaining in term	Basis for signatures[b]		Maximum time period allowed for petition circulation[c]
					Statewide officers	Others	
Alabama	—	—	—	—	—	—	—
Alaska	All but judicial officers	—	120 days	180 days	25% VO	25% VO	—
Arizona	All	[d]	6 mos.–5 days legislators	—	25% VO	25% VO	120 days
Arkansas	—	—	—	—	—	—	—
California	All	[e]	No limit	—	12% VO, 1% from 5 counties	20% VO	160 days
Colorado	All	[f]	6 mos.–5 days general assembly	—	25% VO	25% VO	60 days
Connecticut	—	—	—	—	—	—	—
Delaware	—	—	—	—	—	—	—
Florida	—	—	—	—	—	—	—
Georgia	All	—	180 days	180 days	15% EV[g], 1/15 from each congressional district	30% EV[g]	90 days
Hawaii	—	—	—	—	—	—	—
Idaho	All but judicial officers	[d]	90 days	—	20% EV[g]	20% EV	60 days
Illinois	—	—	—	—	—	—	—
Indiana	—	—	—	—	—	—	—
Iowa	—	—	—	—	—	—	—
Kansas	All but judicial officers	1 time	120 days	200 days	40% VO	40% VO	90 days

State	Officers subject to recall						
Kentucky	—	—	—	—	—	—	—
Louisiana	All but judicial officers of record	h	—	6 mos.	33-1/3% EV[i]	33-1/3% EV[i]	180 days
Maine	—	—	—	—	—	—	—
Maryland	—	—	—	—	—	—	—
Massachusetts	—	—	—	—	—	—	—
Michigan	All but judicial officers of record	—	6 mos.	6 mos.	25% VG	25% VG	j
Minnesota	—	—	—	—	—	—	—
Mississippi	—	—	—	—	—	—	—
Missouri	—	—	—	—	—	—	—
Montana	All public officers, elected or appointed	d	2 mos.	—	10% EV	k	3 mos.
Nebraska	—	—	—	—	—	—	—
Nevada	All public officers	d	6 mos.[l]	—	25% EV in given jurisdiction	25% EV in given jurisdiction	60 days
New Hampshire	—	—	—	—	—	—	—
New Jersey	All elected officials	—	—	—	—	—	—
New Mexico	—	—	—	—	—	—	—
New York	—	—	—	—	—	—	—
North Carolina	—	—	—	—	—	—	—
North Dakota	All but U.S. Congress	1 time	—	—	25% EVg	25% EVg	—
Ohio	—	—	—	—	—	—	—
Oklahoma	All but U.S. Congress	d	—	—	15%[m]	15%[m]	90 days
Oregon	6 mos.–5 days general assembly						
Pennsylvania	—	—	—	—	—	—	—
Rhode Island	Governor, Lieutenant Governor, Secretary of State, Attorney General, and Treasurer	—	6 mos.	1 yr.	15%[n]	—	90 days

47

Table 2.2, continued

State or other jurisdiction	Officers to whom recall is applicable[a]	Number of times recall can be attempted	Recall may be initiated after official has been in office	Recall may not be initiated with days remaining in term	Basis for signatures[b]		Maximum time period allowed for petition circulation[c]
					Statewide officers	Others	
South Carolina	—	—	—	—	—	—	—
South Dakota	Municipal only (1st and 2nd class)	—	—	—	—	15% EV	—
Tennessee	—	—	—	—	—	—	—
Texas	—	—	—	—	—	—	—
Utah	—	—	—	—	—	—	—
Vermont*	—	—	—	—	—	—	—
Virginia	—	—	—	—	—	—	—
Washington	All but judges of courts of record	—	IM	180 days	25% VO	35% VO	°
West Virginia	—	—	—	—	—	—	—
Wisconsin	All	1 time	1 yr.[p]	—	15% VG[q]	25% VP[r]	60 days[s]
Wyoming	—	—	—	—	—	—	—
U.S. Virgin Islands	All	—	1 yr.	1 yr.	30% VO	30% VO	—

Notes:

*State election administration offices, except where noted by * where data are from *The Book of the States 1994–1995*.

—, not applicable; All, all elective officials; VO, number of votes cast in the last election for the office or official being recalled; EVg, number of eligible voters in the last general election for governor; EV, eligible voters; VG, total votes cast for the position of governor in the last election; VP, total votes cast for position of president in last presidential election; IM, immediately.

[a]An elective official may be recalled by qualified voters entitled to vote for the recalled official's successor. An appointed official may be recalled by qualified voters entitled to vote for the successor(s) of the elective officer(s) authorized to appoint an individual to the position.

[b]Signature requirements for recall of those other than state elective officials are based on votes in the jurisdiction to which the said official has been cleared.

48

c The petition circulation period begins when petition forms have been approved and provided to sponsors. Sponsors are those individuals granted permission to circulate a petition and are, therefore, responsible for the validity of each signature on a given petition.

d Additional recall attempts can be made provided that the state treasury is reimbursed the cost of the previous recall attempt(s).

e Must wait until 6 months after the first recall attempt.

f If signatures are obtained equal in number to at least 50% of those voting in the last general election.

g Eligible voters for office at last general election to fill office.

h Must wait at least until 18 months after the first recall attempt.

i Basis for signatures 33-1/3% if over 1,000 EV; 40% if under 1,000 EV.

j In Michigan, signatures dated more than 90 days prior to the filing deadline are ruled invalid.

k 15% EV for district or county officials; 10% EV for municipal or school officials.

l Six months or 10 days after legislative session begins for legislators.

m 15% of the total votes cast in the public officer's electoral district for all candidates for governor at the election next preceding the filing of the petition at which a candidate for governor was elected for a four-year term.

n In Rhode Island, a recall may be instituted by filing with the state board of elections an application for issuance of a recall petition against said general officer that is signed by duly qualified electors equal to 3% of the total number of votes cast at the last preceding general election for that office. If, upon verification, the application is determined to contain signatures of the required number of electors, the state board of elections shall issue a recall petition for circulation among the electors of the state. Within 90 days of issuance, recall petitions containing the signatures of duly qualified electors consisting of 15% of the total number of votes cast in the last preceding general election for said office must be filed with the state elections board.

o Statewide officials 270 days; others 180 days.

p Petition may be filed after official has been in office one year.

q State, congressional, judicial, legislative, and county offices.

r For city, village, town, and school district elected officials.

s For statewide offices, 30 days for local offices (city, town, and village).

Source: The Book of the States 1996–1997 (Lexington, Ky.: Council of State Governments, 1996), pp. 221–22. Copyright 1996–1997 The Council of State Governments. Reprinted with permission from *The Book of the States*.

question on the ballot and to protect the integrity of the petition process by eliminating the temptation that paid circulators would have to file fraudulent signatures.

A divided U.S. Court of Appeals initially upheld the district court decision but reversed it after a rehearing. Basing its decision upon the U.S. Supreme Court decision in *Buckley v. Valeo* striking down a congressional limit on the amount of a candidate's own funds that could be spent in a campaign, the court of appeals rejected the arguments that the prohibition was necessary to protect the general public from fraud by paid circulators and that the ban was necessary to ensure that there was broad public support for an initiative proposition. This decision was upheld by the U.S. Supreme Court in 1988 for the following two reasons."First, it limits the number of voices who will convey appellee's message and the hours they can speak and, therefore, limits the size of the audience they can reach. Second, it makes it less likely that appellee will garner the number of signatures necessary to place the matter on the ballot, thus limiting their ability to make the matter the focus of statewide discussion."[129] This decision equally applies to paid circulators of recall petitions.

Petition certifying officials are required to complete the certification process in a time period ranging from 10 days in Idaho, Louisiana, Oregon, and Washington to 75 days in Arizona (Table 2.3). Filers of rejected petitions may appeal to the courts for a reversal of the rejection and placement of the recall question on the ballot.

In North Dakota, the secretary of state is directed to "conduct a representative random sampling of the signatures contained in such petitions by use of questionnaires, post cards, telephone calls, personal interviews, or other accepted information techniques, or any combination thereof, to determine the validity of the signatures."[130] The North Dakota Supreme Court has ruled that a qualified elector can sign a recall petition if he or she did not vote in the preceding election, but a voter who signed a petition could not withdraw his or her signature after the filing of the petition and before the calling of the election.[131] Oregon law provides that petitions requiring more than 15,000 signatures may be verified through statistical sampling.[132]

In 1980, Barrow County (Georgia) Probate Judge Laurie Bramlette rejected recall petitions presented to her because signatures matching voting records did not total 30 percent of the registered voters. Although her decision was upheld by the Georgia Superior Court, the Georgia Supreme Court reversed the lower courts' decisions on the basis of the voters' "intent" to sign the petitions in spite of the fact the recall statute stipulates "the elector shall sign his name as it appears on the registration books."[133]

The Louisiana Court of Appeals in 1965 stressed that the recall enabling statute is "designed for prompt action following the circulation of a recall petition" and "the jurisprudence by which this court is bound holds that a recall petition is deemed abandoned by laches when the recall petitioners do not actively pursue their remedy so as to require substantial compliance with the mandatory statutory requirements that recall elections be held expeditiously within a limited period of time after the recall petition is first presented for processing to government authorities."[134] The case involved the question of whether the plaintiff was entitled to enjoin the transmission to the appropriate state officer of a recall petition filed with the parish registrar approximately five and one-half months earlier. The petition was filed on June 26, 1964, and the trial court granted a preliminary injunction enjoining the registrar from transmitting the petition. No appeal was made for several months.

Petition fraud is a danger involved with the three participatory democracy mechanisms — initiative, protest referendum, and recall. The 1908 Oregon constitutional recall provision contained no penalties for petition fraud, and the state legislature enacted no implementing legislation until 1923, when criminal penalties were provided for misrepresenting or uttering false statements about the petition to convince voters to sign it, knowingly circulating or filing a petition containing false signatures, and employing the recall in an attempt to extort money from the targeted public officer.[135] Filing of a falsified petition is a misdemeanor in Alaska and Arizona and a felony in Oregon and Washington. Specific penalties are provided in certain states for filing falsified petitions, for example, a $1,000 fine and 12 months in jail in Georgia, a $5,000 fine and two years in jail in Idaho, and a $10,000 fine and up to ten years in prison in Nevada.

The Oregon State Legislature in 1933 established procedures for filing a recall petition that require sponsors to complete and file reports identifying contributors and expenditures.[136] In addition, the statute restricts the petition circulation period to 90 days in order to prevent sponsors from obtaining the specified number of petition signatures and holding the petition as a "Sword of Damocles" over the head of the targeted public officer (rather than filing the signatures) in order to persuade the officer to support the policy objectives of the sponsors.

Writing in 1930 with reference to the California recall, Frederick L. Bird and Frances M. Ryan concluded:"The courts have proved so dependable a haven of refuge for several officials whose recall has been sought, that some authorities have been led to declare that any public official, by retaining the services of a clever attorney, can almost completely

TABLE 2.3
State Recall Provisions: Petition Review, Appeal, and Election

State or other jurisdiction	Signatures verified[a] by	Days to amend or appeal a petition that is: Incomplete[b]	Days to amend or appeal a petition that is: Not accepted[c]	Penalty for falsifying petition (denotes fines, jail time)	Days allowed for petition to be certified[d]	Days to step down after certification[e]	Voting on the recall[f]: Election held after certification	Voting on the recall[f]: Election type	Days to contest election results[g]
Alabama*	—	—	—	—	—	—	—	—	—
Alaska	Director of elections	20	30	Class B misdemeanor	30	—	60–90 days	SP, GE, or PR	5
Arizona	SS, county recorder	—	—	Class 1 misdemeanor	75	5	100–120 days	SP	5
Arkansas	—	—	—	—	—	—	—	—	—
California	County clerk or registrar of voters	—	—	—	—	—	60–80 days	SP	—
Colorado	SS	60	—	$1,000, 1 yr.	36–60	5	60–90 days	SP or GE	—
Connecticut	—	—	—	—	—	—	—	—	—
Delaware	—	—	—	—	—	—	—	—	—
Florida	—	—	—	—	—	—	—	—	—
Georgia	Election supervisor	Not allowed	10	$1,000, 1 yr.	30–45	—	30–45 days	SP, PR, or GE	5
Hawaii	—	—	—	—	—	—	—	—	—
Idaho	County clerk	30	10	$5,000, 2 yrs.	10	5	45+ days[h]	SP or GE[h]	20[i]
Illinois	—	—	—	—	—	—	—	—	—
Indiana	—	—	—	—	—	—	—	—	—

State								
Iowa	—	—	—	—	—	—	—	—
Kansas	County election officer	—	Class B misdemeanor	30	—	60–90 days	SP or GE	30
Kentucky	—	—	—	—	—	—	—	—
Louisiana	Registrar of voters	—	$100–1,000, 30–90 days	10	—	—	SP	30
Maine*	—	—	—	—	—	—	—	—
Maryland	—	—	—	—	—	—	—	—
Massachusetts	—	—	—	—	—	—	—	—
Michigan	City and township clerks[k]	—	—	35	—	w/i 60 days	SP	2[i]
Minnesota	—	—	—	—	—	—	—	—
Mississippi	—	—	—	—	—	—	—	—
Missouri	—	—	—	—	—	—	—	—
Montana	County clerk, recorder	20	$500, 6 mos.	30	5	3 mos.	SP or GE	—
Nebraska	—	—	—	—	—	—	—	—
Nevada	County clerk, registrar	—	$10,000, 1–10 yrs.	20–50	5	—	SP	10
New Hampshire	—	—	—	—	—	—	—	—
New Jersey	—	—	—	—	—	—	—	—
New Mexico	—	—	—	—	—	—	—	—
New York*	—	—	—	—	—	—	—	—
North Carolina	—	—	—	—	10[n]	—	—	—
North Dakota	SS	20[m]	—	35	—	—	SP, GE, or PR	14[o]
Ohio	—	—	—	—	—	—	—	—
Oklahoma	—	—	—	—	—	—	—	—
Oregon	SS or county clerk	—	Class C felony (possible)	10	5	w/i 40 days	SP	40

53

Table 2.3, continued

State or other jurisdiction	Signatures verified[a] by	Days to amend or appeal a petition that is: Incomplete[b]	Not accepted[c]	Penalty for falsifying petition (denotes fines, jail time)	Days allowed for petition to be certified[d]	Days to step down after certification[e]	Voting on the recall[f] — Election held after certification	Voting on the recall[f] — Election type	Days to contest election results[g]
Pennsylvania	—	—	—	—	—	—	—	—	—
Rhode Island	—	—	—	—	—	—	—	—	—
South Carolina	—	—	—	—	—	—	—	—	—
South Dakota	Municipal finance officer	—	—	—	—	—	–	SP	—
Tennessee	—	—	—	—	—	—	—	—	—
Texas	—	—	—	—	—	—	—	—	—
Utah	—	—	—	—	—	—	—	—	—
Vermont*	—	—	—	—	—	—	—	—	—
Virginia	—	—	—	—	—	—	—	—	—
Washington	SS, county auditor	—	10[p]	Felony	w/i 10	IM	45–50 days	SP	3
West Virginia	—	—	—	—	—	—	—	—	—
Wisconsin	Filing offices[q]	5	7[r]	Not more than $10,000	31	10	6 weeks	SP[s]	3[t]
Wyoming	—	—	—	—	—	—	—	—	—
U.S. Virgin Islands	—	—	—	—	60	—	—	GE	7

Notes:

*State election administration offices, except where noted by * where data are from *The Book of the States 1994–1995.*

—, not applicable; SS, secretary of state; SP, special election; PR, primary election; GE, general election; IM, immediate and automatic removal from office; w/i, within

[a]The validity of the signatures, as well as the correct number of required signatures, must be verified before the recall is allowed on the ballot.

[b]If an insufficient number of signatures is submitted, sponsors may amend the original petition by filing additional signatures within a given number of days. If the necessary number of signatures has not been submitted by this date, the petition is declared void.

[c]In some cases, the state officer will not accept a valid petition. In such a case, sponsors may appeal this decision to the supreme court, where the sufficiency of the petition will be determined. When this is declared, the recall is required to be placed on the ballot.

[d]A petition is certified for the ballot when the required number of signatures has been submitted by the filing deadline and the signatures are determined to be valid.

[e]The official to whom a recall is proposed has a certain number of days to step down from his or her position before a recall election is initiated, if he or she desires to do so.

[f]A majority of the popular vote is required to recall an official in each state.

[g]Individuals may contest the results of a vote on a recall within a certain number of days after the results are certified. In Alaska, an appeal to courts must be filed within five days of the recount.

[h]In Idaho, the dates on which elections may be conducted are the first Tuesday in February, the fourth Tuesday in May, the first Tuesday in August, and the Tuesday following the first Monday in November. In addition, an emergency election may be called upon motion of the governing board of a political subdivision. Recall elections conducted by any political subdivision shall be held on the nearest of these dates that falls more than 45 days after the clerk of the political subdivision orders that the recall election shall be held.

[i]After election is certified.

[j]The election must be held on the next available date of six dates per year allowed by the election committee.

[k]In Michigan, all petition signatures are verified by the city and township clerks. The Board of State Canvassers certifies the petition as having adequate number of valid signatures. Both of these procedures fall under the auspices of the secretary of state.

[l]In Nevada, a recall election is held 10–20 days after the court determines a recall election is to be held. In South Dakota, a recall election is held 30–50 days after the governing board orders a recall election. The governing board must meet within 10 days after the petition is filed.

[m]Only signatures already collected can be amended such as adding addresses or correcting some other flaw that makes the signatures unverifiable.

[n]After petition is filed with the secretary of state.

[o]Fourteen days after the canvas board has certified the results.

[p]In Washington, a petition that is not accepted may be appealed in 10 days.

[q]Where declaration of candidacy is filed.

[r]After certificate.

[s]May be held on general election but is still considered special election.

[t]Business days.

Source: *The Book of the States 1996–1997* (Lexington, Ky.: Council of State Governments, 1996), pp. 223–24. Copyright 1996–1997 The Council of State Governments. Reprinted with permission from *The Book of the States*.

immunize himself from the process."[137] Experience since 1930 does not support this conclusion.

THE RECALL ELECTION

Collection of the requisite number of certified petition signatures does not always guarantee that a recall election will be held in certain states, because the concerned officer is given five days to resign from office after certification of signatures in Arizona, Colorado, Idaho, Montana, Nevada, and Oregon and ten days in North Dakota and Wisconsin (Table 2.3). Furthermore, the Arizona attorney general issued an opinion that an officer cannot be recalled if there is no opposing candidate, and the Arizona Supreme Court in 1988 ruled that the state was not estopped from canceling the recall election of the governor after his impeachment and removal from office.[138]

The Arizona constitution stipulates that the failure of the targeted public officer to resign within five days of the certification of the recall petition signatures requires the issuance of an order for a special election to be held within 100 to 120 days after the issuance of the order.[139] Under provisions of the New Jersey optional municipal charters law, a municipal officer subject to recall must be notified by the municipal clerk of the sufficiency of the recall petition within two days of verification of the signatures, and the clerk must order the holding of a recall election within 60 to 90 days of the filing of the petitions if the officer does not tender his or her resignation within five days after the service of the notice.[140] A similar provision is contained in the charter of the town of Billerica, Massachusetts.[141]

The reasons advanced in support of the recall of a public officer are printed on the recall ballot, but the number of words is limited; 200 is the most common synopsis limit (Figure 2.3).[142] A 1976 Oregon report maintained that the reasons advanced in support of the recall "could best be described as subjective and emotional."[143] The officer whose recall is sought may submit a statement of justification of conduct in office typically limited to 200 words. San Francisco publishes a voter information pamphlet containing a sample ballot, the proponents' statement of reasons for the proposed recall, the targeted officer's reply to the reasons, and paid advertisements. The 24-page pamphlet issued for the special recall election of Mayor Dianne Feinstein in 1983 contained 49 paid advertisements — 37 in favor of the mayor and 12 in favor of recall.[144]

FIGURE 2.3
Sample Recall Ballot

S A M P L E

A. V. INSTRUCTION BALLOT

OFFICIAL BALLOT

CITY OF HIGHLAND PARK

COUNTY OF WAYNE, STATE OF MICHIGAN

SPECIAL MUNICIPAL RECALL ELECTION

Saturday, February 19, 1977

REASON FOR DEMANDING RECALL

1. We charge that Jesse P. Miller is incompetent (and unfit) to administer the affairs of this City as detailed below . . .

   a. Miller failed to curtail the $2 million budget deficit.
   b. Miller spent taxpayers' money making political pay-offs.
   c. Miller lied by promising to stop pornography, while accepting $1,000 from the owner of the Celebrity House.
   d. Miller failed to curb crime.
   e. Miller, as a member of the Hospital Board of Managers, and most recently as Mayor, has sacrificed Highland Park General Hospital and 250 jobs.
   f. Miller's incompetence is threatening future funding of Federal, State and County programs.
   g. Miller lied by refusing to keep his pledge to return the $10,000 salary increase to the City Treasury.
2. We charge that Jesse P. Miller has violated 8 different sections of the City Charter, as detailed below . . .

   a. Sec. 7-20 — hiring non-residents
   b. Sec. 7-13 (3) — failure to follow bidding requirements resulting in $300,000 loss at hospital
   c. Sec. 17-18 (4) — paying unearned sick benefits
   d. Sec. 7-8 (4) — improper disposal of hospital assets
   e. Sec. 5-6 and 5-7 — operating under an illegal budget
   f. Sec. 7-5 (1) — preventing City Attorney from advising Council
   g. Sec. 14-1 and 14-2 — entering into contracts illegally
   h. Sec. 7-5 (4) — failure to prosecute charter and ordinance violations

THE ELECTED OFFICIAL'S JUSTIFICATION OF HIS CONDUCT IN OFFICE

The charges made in this ballot are a mixture of misleading half-truths and deliberate vicious lies by the political group that brought chaos and near bankruptcy to our City and were repudiated last year by the voters.

My administration inherited, from this group, a budget deficit of $2,000,000.00. I fought to keep Highland Park Hospital open, but because of years of neglect and mismanagement by former administrations, the State of Michigan closed it for building deficiencies.

My pay raise is in escrow and will be repaid upon completion of my first year.

Some accomplishments of my administration include:

   (a) closing all model studios and bringing about 30 pornography cases to Court.
   (b) razing neglected homes on East Grand Avenue and building new housing.
   (c) breaking ground for an $11 million, 330 unit housing development.
   (d) rehabilitating Ives Field and Hackett Field House recreation facilities.
   (e) obtaining extended funding for police programs.
   (f) negotiating to reopen Highland Park Hospital as a private, modern facility employing 600-700 persons.

In summary, in one year, despite the crushing burdens of mismanagement from former administrations and the lack of cooperation from Council, we are progressing toward our goals.

SHALL JESSE P. MILLER BE RECALLED FROM THE
OFFICE OF MAYOR OF THE CITY OF HIGHLAND PARK.

                             YES ⎯ 18 ➡
                             NO ⎯ 19 ➡

S A M P L E

ABSENT VOTERS INSTRUCTION BALLOT

PLEASE NOTE:

Punch the black dot just above the Number of YES or NO that you wish to Vote For.

YES – To Recall   NO – Not To Recall

TREMON McDERMOTT
City Clerk

The Michigan recall statute admirably stipulates: "The statement 'Vote no on the recall' or 'Vote yes on the recall' or words of similar import shall not be permitted on the ballot. A part of the reason for demanding the recall of the officer or the officer's justification of conduct in office shall not be emphasized by italics, underscoring, or in any other manner."[145]

Depending upon the state, the recall election may be a special election, as in Arizona and California, or the election may be held in conjunction with a primary election or a general election, as in Alaska, Georgia, and Ohio. In common with a regular election, the results of a recall election can be contested provided a challenge to the results is filed with the specified officer within the stipulated time limit, which ranges from 3 business days in Wisconsin to 40 days in Oregon (Table 2.3).

As noted, the 1908 Oregon constitutional provision was the first one authorizing the recall to be employed statewide. This provision, however, did not clarify whether the question of a replacement officer should appear on the recall ballot in the event that the targeted public officer was recalled. The Oregon Supreme Court in 1914 ruled that two distinct questions should appear on the ballot.[146] This decision created a problem in that a majority of the voters may favor recall and a plurality of the voters may reelect the recalled officer. Oregon voters in 1926 approved a constitutional amendment stipulating that the only question to appear on the ballot should be whether the public officer should be recalled and that a replacement should be elected under current statutes governing the filling of a vacancy in a public office.[147]

In nine states, voters in a recall election simply vote on the question of whether the public officer should be removed from office immediately. A majority affirmative vote *ipso facto* removes the officer from office in most jurisdictions. However, the charter of the town of Oxford, Massachusetts, stipulates that "a majority vote of the electorate to recall such elective officer is not effective unless a total of at least fifty percent of the electors entitled to vote on the question shall have voted, and unless the number of votes cast in favor of recall shall exceed the number of votes he received on the last occasion he was elected to office."[148]

A separate election on the question of recalling a public officer has the advantage of allowing voters to concentrate on the question of the removal of the incumbent without having their attention diverted by the claims of other candidates but suffers from the disadvantage of increasing governmental costs if a special election is held to fill the vacancy should the officer be recalled.

Where the two questions appear on the same ballot, proponents of the recall typically recruit and endorse a replacement candidate and campaign for his or her election. In the only judicial recall election in Wisconsin, recall proponents in 1977 did not endorse a replacement candidate for fear of dividing voters favoring the recall of Judge Archie Simonson of Dane County.[149]

Absentee voting is permitted in recall elections as in other elections and may play an important role in determining the outcome of the recall effort (Figure 2.4). California law facilitates absentee voting, and this fact was reflected in the 1983 recall election of San Francisco Mayor Feinstein, where absentee ballots accounted for in excess of 36 percent of the total number of ballots cast.[150]

The recall of statewide elected public officers, as explained in Chapter 3, is an infrequent occurrence. North Dakota voters in 1921 removed Governor Lynn J. Frazier, the attorney general, and the commissioner of agriculture from office. Interestingly, Frazier won the Republican nomination for U.S. Senator in 1922 and was elected but lost his Republican Party membership in 1924, when he supported the candidacy of Robert M. La Folette for president.

Frazier's recall was the first and only successful recall of a governor. Theodore C. Sharpe reported that the charges against Frazier did not involve corruption or dereliction of duties but focused on "the wisdom of certain policies of the Bank of North Dakota with regard to issuance of bonds, high risk loans to farmers, and partisan policies regarding redeposits by the Bank of North Dakota in small banks within the state."[151]

Arizona voters in 1988 successfully filed petitions containing an adequate number of certified signatures to trigger a special recall election of Governor Evan Mecham, which was scheduled for May 17. The Arizona Senate, however, on April 4, convicted the governor of two charges of misconduct and removed him from office after an impeachment trial by a vote of 21 to 9.[152] He had been impeached by the House of Representatives, by a vote of 45 to 14, on February 5.

Sponsors of a recall petition to remove the governor of Louisiana challenged in 1992 a provision of the state's recall statute providing for a 600-foot-radius campaign-free zone at polling places.[153] The statute applies to nonballot passive speech, including campaign T-shirts and buttons. The U.S. District Court rejected the challenge, and an appeal was made to the U.S. Court of Appeals for the Fifth Circuit, which in 1993 rejected the First and Fourteenth Amendments challenges and opined that the state has a compelling interest in providing for a campaign-free zone around polling places.[154]

If a recall attempt fails, proponents can initiate another recall attempt in five states — Arizona, Idaho, Montana, Nevada, and Oregon — provided

FIGURE 2.4
Example of Absentee Ballot for a Recall Election

ABSENT VOTER

OFFICIAL BALLOT

CITY OF ROY
PIERCE COUNTY, WASHINGTON

SPECIAL ELECTION—MAY 25, 1976

INSTRUCTIONS: To vote for or against a proposition place "X" in appropriate ☐ following the proposition

PROPOSITION NO. 1

RECALL—MAYOR GARY ROUSH

Shall Gary Roush, the elected Mayor of the City of Roy, be recalled on the following charge which alleges malfeasance, misfeasance or violation of his oath of office: He utilized Pierce County Manpower Program employees (Ralph D. Craddock, Jeffery B. Craddock, Michael W. Cooper) to perform manual yard work services at the Mayor's personal property during summer 1975?

FOR the Recall of
Gary Roush, Mayor
of the City of Roy .... ☐

AGAINST the Recall
of Gary Roush, Mayor
of the City of Roy .... ☐

Source: Pierce County Board of Elections.

the proponents reimburse the state for the costs incurred in conducting the previous recall attempt. Although reimbursement is not required in California and Louisiana, proponents may not launch another recall attempt for 6 months and 18 months, respectively. Colorado allows a second attempt only if the number of certified signatures is equal to 50 percent of those voting in the previous general election, a percentage twice as high as the one required to launch the first recall attempt. Idaho, Kansas, Missouri, North Dakota, Oregon, Washington, and Wisconsin specifically allow only one additional recall attempt to remove a public officer during a given term of office.

RESTRICTIONS ON APPOINTIVE OFFICE

To prevent an officer subject to the recall from resigning from office and being appointed to the same office, state laws and local government charters typically prohibit the appointment of the officer to the same or similar office for a period of years, most commonly two. Federal and state case law makes clear that such a provision does not violate the equal protection of the laws clause of the Fourteenth Amendment to the U.S. Constitution.

Michigan law not only forbids a recalled officer to be a candidate to fill the vacancy caused by the successful employment of the recall but also prohibits a recalled officer from being "appointed to fill a vacancy in an elective office in the electoral district or governmental unit from which the recall was made during the term of office from which the officer was recalled."[155] Similarly, an officer resigning after a recall petition has been filed against him or her is ineligible for appointment to a public office "during the term of office from which the officer was recalled."[156]

CAMPAIGN FINANCE

A recall election can be expensive for the public officer subject to the recall and to the government involved. Feinstein of San Francisco raised in excess of $344,000 in a campaign to defeat a 1983 attempt to recall her from office, and the cost to the city and county of San Francisco to conduct the recall election was approximately $450,000.[157] The California corrupt practices act does not apply to the recall.[158]

The Oregon recall law requires the sponsors of a recall petition to file with it "a sworn statement by one of them giving the name and address of all contributors and members of their recall organization" prior to circulation of the petition to voters for their signatures.[159] The Washington recall statute prohibits corrupt practice acts defined, among other things, as "any consideration, compensation, gratuity, reward, or thing of value or promise thereof" designed "to induce a voter to sign or refuse to sign a recall petition."[160]

The Georgia Recall Act applies the Ethics in Government Act to recall elections as well as other elections.[161] Washington law requires the organizers of a recall campaign to submit a report on their expenses when filing recall petitions and makes a recall campaign subject to the state's corrupt practices act.[162]

A public officer subject to a recall election is not limited in spending his or her money by a state corrupt practices act in campaigning for the defeat of the recall petition. The United States Supreme Court in *Buckley v. Valeo* in 1976 ruled "that the limitations on campaign expenditures, on expenditures by individuals and groups, and on expenditures by a candidate from his personal funds are constitutionally infirm."[163]

As noted, the California constitution authorizes reimbursement of the campaign expenses of a state officer who defeats a recall attempt. The Colorado statutes authorize a municipality to repay the incumbent for campaign expenditures if he or she is not recalled or the petitions are insufficient.[164] In 1989, the Colorado attorney general issued an opinion that a public officer who challenges successfully a recall petition is not entitled to payment of incurred expenses, because no recall election is held.[165] The charter of the city and county of San Francisco also authorizes reimbursement of the election expenses of an incumbent officer who is retained in office by a recall election.[166]

LOCALLY DRAFTED CHARTERS

Local government charter recall procedures generally are similar in nature to state constitutional and statutory recall procedures and involve the filing of an affidavit or petition signed typically by ten voters with a specified local government officer, listing the name of the officer whose recall is sought, grounds for the recall, and a request for the scheduling of a recall election upon the filing of the requisite number of certified signatures by the filing deadline.

A state legislature may incorporate a recall provision in a special charter enacted for a local government, authorize a specific local government to draft and enact a recall ordinance, authorize all general purpose local governments to adopt a state recall statute, and grant home rule powers to general purpose local governments to draft and adopt charters including a provision for the recall. Relative to the third method, the Florida Supreme

Court in 1980 upheld as valid a city of Laurel Hill charter provision that includes a provision adopting the recall by simply referencing the state statute.[167] New Hampshire did not authorize cities and towns to incorporate a recall provision in their charters until 1991, and currently, five towns — Bedford, Derry, Durham, Hooksett, and Newmarket — have charters containing recall provisions, which have not been employed to date.[168]

The question often is raised of whether a state recall statute or other election statute preempts a home rule charter recall provision. The California Election Code provides a clear answer to this question by stipulating that the recall provision in the election code "does not supersede the provisions of a city or county charter, or ordinances adopted pursuant to a city charter or county charter, relating to the recall."[169]

The Washington Supreme Court addressed the constitutionality of a home rule charter provision in 1909 and opined:

The people of the City of Everett in framing the charter intended that their representatives should be held strictly amenable to both the existing and changing public sentiment on all local measures, and that if the official conduct of any elective officer failed at any time to so respond, he was subject to recall if the majority of the electorate in his district so determined. The (plaintiff) accepted the trust subject to this power in his constituency, and the duration of his term of office is dependent upon the wish of the majority as expressed at the polls. The removal sought is not of the character provided for in the constitution. Whether the interests of the city will be better subserved by a courageous adherence to the views of the individual officer on questions of public concern is a political, and not a legal question.[170]

The Michigan state constitution and recall statutes lack a clear statement with respect to the applicability of the state recall provisions to home rule cities, and the courts were called upon to clarify whether home rule recall charter provisions are preempted. In 1949, the Michigan Supreme Court held that the recall provisions of the *Michigan Compiled Laws* relative to the recall were paramount and nullified a home rule charter containing different recall provisions.[171]

In a 1959 decision, the Minnesota Supreme Court upheld the constitutionality of a home rule charter recall provision but noted that such a provision must require the petitioners to list grounds for recall that constitute malfeasance or misfeasance in office.[172]

In 1971, Judge Robert J. Testo of the Connecticut Superior Court ruled that the section of the Westport charter governing recall elections does not

apply to school board members because they are agents of the state and
not municipal officers.[173] Four years later, the Georgia Supreme Court
ruled that the language in the state constitution mandating removal of an
officer under specified circumstances was not preemptive and did not pre-
clude the employment of the recall.[174]

The Florida attorney general in 1976 issued an opinion that the state
recall act was limited to members of the governing body of a municipality and in 1979 concluded that the act provides procedures for the recall of
governing bodies of all municipalities and charter counties except Dade
County.[175] In 1982, the Florida attorney general issued an opinion that the
state recall act applies to each municipality within Dade County and prevails over a conflicting section of a municipal charter.[176]

The Massachusetts Home Rule Procedure Act provides that "no change
in the composition, mode of election or appointment, or terms of office (of
those offices) may be accomplished by by-law or ordinance."[177] Several
cities and towns, however, have provided for the recall by incorporating it
in a home rule charter or charter amendment.

In reporting that 33 cities and towns in Massachusetts have charters
authorizing the employment of the recall, the Massachusetts Legislative
Research Council raised the question of whether such charter provisions
violate a provision of the home rule constitutional amendment forbidding
"regulating elections by local charter."[178] The report noted:

There are no cases interpreting this provision although it was the basis for one of
the arguments recently used to strike down an ordinance of the City of Boston
limiting campaign expenditures. . . . However, the Elections Division of the Secretary of State's office has interpreted section 7(1) in the past to forbid only the
regulation of voting rights and the details of election administration, in other
words, matters which are regulated by statutes. . . . It is therefore assumed that
recall provisions established by a home rule charter subject to certain standards
established by the legislature are valid, although the matter will not be completely free from doubt until some authoritative judicial determination is made.[179]

A similar question was raised relative to recall provisions in Connecticut municipal charters. Some ambiguity surrounded aspects of the constitutional grant of discretionary authority to cities and towns in this state.
Twenty municipal charters provide for the recall of local officers. Five
recall provisions were authorized by special act charters approved by the
general assembly or other special acts, and consequently, the legal status
of these provisions is clear. Fifteen locally drafted and adopted charters,
however, contain recall provisions, and their validity has been questioned

by local government experts because the enabling statute implementing the constitutional grant of local discretionary authority stipulates that "no provision of this chapter shall be deemed to empower any town, city, or borough to draft, adopt, or amend a charter which shall affect matters concerning qualifications and admission of electors . . . ; conduct of and procedures at elections; election contests."[180]

In 1985, the Connecticut Supreme Court unanimously invalidated the recall provision in the locally drafted and adopted charter of Watertown by noting that the general assembly had delegated specific powers to municipalities and "a fortiori, if the legislature had intended to confer the recall power on municipalities it would have done so explicitly."[181]

The most major court decision involving the constitutionality of the home rule recall charter provision was issued by the Pennsylvania Supreme Court in 1976 and invalidated the provisions of the Philadelphia home rule city charter that had been employed by opponents of Mayor Frank L. Rizzo.[182] The court's majority based its decision on varying interpretations of a section of the commonwealth's 1874 constitution specifying how public officers can be removed.[183]

The Philadelphia city charter authorized the holding of a recall election if petitions were signed by a number of electors equal to 25 percent of the number who voted for mayor in the last election.[184] A total of 145,448 certified signatures were required to trigger a recall election. Proponents of the recall of Rizzo collected and submitted 210,806 signatures to the board of elections, which rejected 121,902 signatures; 115,818 signatures were rejected because the notarization was by 16 individuals who were recall proponents. Instead of restricting its ruling to the question of the sufficiency of the number of petitions submitted, the Pennsylvania Supreme Court's majority extended its ruling to invalidate Philadelphia's home rule charter provisions for the recall, thereby invalidating all home rule recall charter provisions in the commonwealth.

Interestingly, the challenge to the constitutionality of the charter recall provision was brought by the mayor, who, on two inaugural occasions, had sworn to uphold the city charter containing the recall provision. In contrast to the Pennsylvania court ruling, the Tennessee Court of Appeals in 1957 opined that a mayor could not challenge the constitutionality of a home rule charter recall provision.[185]

Jefferson B. Fordham, a former dean of the University of Pennsylvania Law School, wrote an article that was highly critical of the Pennsylvania Supreme Court decision. In 1977, he maintained: "Since the 1922 home rule amendment is amendatory of the constitution, it must, as an elementary rational matter, be regarded as controlling over the provisions of the

Constitution of 1874 with which it is inconsistent. . . . The opinion of the court and the concurring opinions do not even cite the 1968 amendment, let alone refer to its text and consider the meaning and effect of its language with specific reference to the nature and scope of home rule powers directly granted by this constitutional amendment."[186]

LOSS OF A QUORUM

The successful employment of the recall can result in the inability of a municipal legislative body to take action should a quorum be lacking because of the removal of public officers. The problem, of course, will not occur if state law or the local charter provides for the simultaneous election of replacements for officers recalled or the appointment of sufficient replacements to achieve a quorum.

The Kansas legislature addressed this potential in 1978 by stipulating "(t)he number of local officers serving on the same governing body which may be subject to recall at the same time shall not exceed a majority of the members of the governing body minus one."[187] In addition, state law and local charters commonly authorize a local council to coopt members to fill vacancies on the council. However, cooptation typically is not possible unless a quorum exists on the council.

In Washington, the recall of all three Yakima County commissioners in 1916 created a most unusual situation. The action of the governor in appointing three replacements was challenged, but the Washington Supreme Court upheld the validity of the appointments by referring to an 1890 statute providing that the governor was empowered "to see that all offices are filled, and the duties thereof performed."[188]

Arcadia, California, in 1939 was faced with a lack of a quorum on its five-member council because two members had been recalled and one member resigned subsequent to the recall election. Existing California law authorized the voters at the recall election either to authorize the council to fill the vacancies or to call a special election. Because the voters did not call a special election, the court ruled that the two remaining members of the council constituted a quorum for the purpose of filling the vacancies, regardless of the fact that state law stipulated a majority of the council constitutes a quorum.[189] Earlier, the Kentucky Supreme Court ruled that a statute stipulating that vacancies on a school board shall be filled by the remaining members was valid even in the absence of a quorum, absent contrary statutory provisions.[190]

In 1970, voters in Tacoma, Washington, recalled five of the nine members of the city council who had been charged with conspiracy to hire an unqualified city manager and to award a cable television franchise to the Tacoma Cable Company without seeking expert advice.[191] Because the four remaining council members did not constitute a quorum, they were unable to employ the city charter provision allowing the council to fill a vacancy in its membership by cooptation. In deciding how to fill the vacancies, the assistant city attorney advised the city manager that the state constitution authorizes the governor to fill vacancies in state offices if no other provision for filling vacancies exists and state law directs the governor to "see that all offices are filled."[192] *Per consequens*, the city petitioned Governor Daniel J. Evans to appoint a member to the council to bring its members up to a quorum; Governor Evans appointed Allan R. Billett to fill a vacancy.[193]

SUMMARY AND CONCLUSIONS

Voters are authorized to use the recall in various state and local governments by the state constitution or statutes in 26 states to remove all elected officers, state officers only, or all or specified local officers only. In addition, constitutional or statutory home rule provisions in several states lacking a specific authorization for the recall enable all or certain general purpose local governments to draft and adopt charters providing for the recall. As noted, the supreme courts in Connecticut and Pennsylvania invalidated home rule charter recall provisions.

The constitutional recall provision in several states is not self-executing, and its implementation is dependent upon a cooperative state legislature enacting an implementing statute. State courts have played an important role in determining whether the recall is a political or legal process. Where the courts have ruled that the recall is a legal process, voters typically experience greater difficulty in removing a public officer by means of the recall.

Many constitutional and statutory provisions contain restrictions by excluding judges or other named officers, prohibiting the use of the recall during an initial grace period — typically the first six months of a term — and during the period immediately preceding a general election, and allowing only one recall attempt during a given term of office. The success of a recall campaign is influenced heavily by the threshold petition signature requirement. A restrictive threshold, particularly a high percentage of registered voters, may pose an insurmountable barrier to recall proponents compared with a less restrictive threshold, such as 10 percent of those who voted in the previous election for the office.

In common with the initiative and protest referendum, petition fraud and campaign finance irregularities are potential problems associated with the recall. Nevertheless, experience reveals that such problems have not been major ones in most recall campaigns. Chapter 3 examines the use of the recall in attempts to remove state officers and facilitates an evaluation of the recall as a participatory democracy device.

NOTES

1. See, for example, *Constitution of the State of New York*, art. 9, § 2.
2. *Hilzinger v. Gillman*, 56 Wash. 228, 105 P. 471 (1909).
3. *Constitution of Wisconsin*, art. 13, § 12.
4. *State v. Harris*, 114 P. 109 (1914).
5. *Miller v. Wilson*, 59 Ariz. 403, 129 P.2d 668 (1942).
6. *Constitution of Louisiana*, art. 10, § 26.
7. *Constitution of Arizona*, art. 8, § 1.
8. *Constitution of Alaska*, art. 11, § 8.
9. *Constitution of New Mexico*, art. 12, § 14.
10. *Code of Alabama*, §§ 11-44E-168, 11-44-134; *Minnesota Statutes*, §§ 351.15–351.22.
11. Arkansas, Florida, Georgia, Hawaii, Massachusetts, Minnesota, Mississippi, Missouri, Nebraska, New Jersey, New Mexico, New York, Ohio, Pennsylvania, South Dakota, Tennessee, West Virginia, and Wyoming.
12. *Constitution of California*, art. 2, § 19.
13. *Muehleisen v. Forward*, 4 Cal.2d 17, 46 P.2d 969 (1935). A similar decision was rendered by the state's appeals court in *Becker v. Council of City of Albany*, 47 Cal.App.2d 702, 118 P.2d 924 (1941).
14. *City of Laurel Hill v. Sanders*, 392 So.2d 33 (Fla. App. 1980).
15. *New Jersey Laws of 1950*, chap. 210; *New Jersey Statutes Annotated*, § 40.69A-210.
16. *Town of Billerica (Massachusetts) Charter*, art. VI, § 6-4.
17. *Town of Oxford (Massachusetts) Charter*, chap. 7, § 6.
18. *Laam v. McLaren*, 28 Cal.App. 632, 153 P. 985 (1915).
19. *Johnson v. Maehling*, 123 Ariz. 15, 497 P.2d 1 (1979).
20. *Groditsky v. Pinckney*, 661 P.2d 279 (1983); *Matter of Recall of Redner*, 153 Wis.2d 383, 450 N.W.2d 808 (1989).
21. *Canavan v. Messina*, 31 Conn. Sup. 447 at 450, 334 A.2d 237 (1973).
22. *Simons v. Canty*, 195 Conn. 524 (1985).
23. *Constitution of Ohio*, art. 2, § 38.
24. *Ohio Revised Code*, § 3.08.
25. *State ex rel. Hackley v. Edmonds*, 150 Ohio St. 203 (1948).
26. *Constitution of Ohio*, art. 8, §§ 3, 7.

27.   *Virginia Laws of 1975*, chap. 515, 595; *Code of Virginia*, §§ 24.1-79.5, 24.1-79.7.

28.   *Constitution of Mississippi*, § 139; *Mississippi Code Annotated*, § 25-5-7.

29.   *Constitution of Wisconsin*, art. 13, § 12.

30.   68 OAG (Wisconsin) 148 (1979).

31.   Ibid., at 146. See also *State ex rel. Martin v. Zimmerman*, 233 Wis. 16, 288 N.W. 454 (1939).

32.   *Michigan Public Acts of 1954*, Number 116; *Michigan Compiled Laws Annotated*, §§ 168.121, 168.149 (1967). A U.S. Senator or Representative from New Jersey may not be recalled during the first year of the incumbent's term of office. *New Jersey Laws of 1995*, chap. 105, § 2.

33.   *Constitution of the United States*, Art. 1, §§ 5–6 and Fourteenth Amendment, § 3. See also *Keogh v. Horner*, 8 F.Supp. 933, D. Ill., (1934); *Burchell v. State Board of Election Commissioners*, 252 Ky. 823, 68 S.W. 427 (1934); *State ex rel. 25 Voters v. Selvig*, 170 Minn. 406, 212 N.W. 604 (1927).

34.   *Arizona Laws of 1973*, chap. 159; *Arizona Revised Statutes*, §§ 19-221, 19-222.

35.   Albert M. Kales, *Unpopular Government in the United States* (Chicago, Ill.: University of Chicago Press, 1914), p. 125.

36.   *Montana Laws of 1977*, chap. 364; *Revised Code of Montana*, § 2-16-603(3).

37.   *Greeley (Colorado) City Charter*, § 4.3.

38.   Letter to author from Long Beach City Attorney Robert W. Parkin dated March 28, 1984.

39.   *State ex rel. Hoel v. Brown*, 105 Ohio St. 479 at 487 (1922).

40.   *State ex rel. Hackley v. Edmonds*, 150 Ohio St. 203 at 218 (1948).

41.   *Dayton v. Thomas*, 28 Ohio Dec. 261, 20 Ohio N.P.(n.s.) 539 (1916).

42.   *The Historical Development and Use of the Recall in Oregon* (Salem: Legislative Research, 1976), p. 13.

43.   *Minnesota Statutes Annotated*, §§ 351.15–351.22.

44.   *Montana Code Annotated*, § 2-16-613(2); *New Jersey Statutes Annotated*, § 40:69A-168; *California Election Code*, § 11007; *Code of Georgia*, § 21-4-5; *Kansas Statutes Annotated*, § 25-4323; *Minnesota Statutes Annotated*, § 351.16; *Constitution of Wisconsin*, art. 13, § 12; *Alaska Statutes*, § 15.45.550.

45.   *Constitution of Arizona*, art. 8, § 5; *Constitution of Colorado*, art. 21, § 4.

46.   *Georgia Attorney General Opinion No. 92-12* (1992).

47.   *Arizona Revised Statutes Annotated*, § 19-202(B); *Revised Code of Montana*, § 2-16-613(3); *Constitution of Nevada*, art. 2, § 9.

48.   *Idaho Code*, § 34-1713(2); *Kansas Statutes Annotated*, § 25-4311; *Missouri Statutes*, § 77.650(2); *Constitution of North Dakota*, art. 3, § 10; *Constitution of Oregon*, art. 1, § 1; *Constitution of Washington*, art. 13, § 12(6); *Constitution of Wisconsin*, art. 13, § 12.

49. *Constitution of Arizona*, art. 8, § 5.

50. *California Laws of 1976*, chap. 271, § 1; *California Elections Code*, §§ 27007-7008. For details on the recall procedure in California, see *Procedure for Recalling State and Local Officials* (Sacramento: California Secretary of State, 1994). The California Court of Appeals ruled that an officer elected at a special recall election was subject to recall. See *Magoon v. Health*, 79 Cal.App. 632, 250 P. 583 (1926).

51. *Charter of the City and County of San Francisco*, § 9.108.

52. *Constitution of California*, art. 2, § 14(a).

53. *Constitution of Colorado*, art. 21, § 1.

54. *Bernzen v. City of Boulder*, 186 Colo. 81, 525 P.2d 416 (1974).

55. *Constitution of Michigan*, art. 2, § 8.

56. *Michigan Compiled Laws Annotated*, § 168.952(3).

57. *Opinions of the Michigan Attorney General*, No. 5556 (1979).

58. *Noel v. Oakland County Clerk*, 92 Mich.App. 181, 284 N.W.2d 761 (1979). The appeals court in 1990, however, rejected petitions based on the conduct of officials before they entered elective office. See *Bronkowski v. Macomb County Election Committee*, 185 Mich.App. 288, 460 N.W.2d 308 (1990).

59. *Alaska Statutes*, § 15.45.710.

60. *Gilbert v. Morrow*, 277 So.2d 812 (Fla. Dis. App. 1973).

61. *State ex rel. Gladstone v. Yeaman*, 768 S.W.2d 103 (Mo. 1988).

62. *Arkansas Code*, § 14-61-119(b)(2).

63. *Abbey v. Green*, 28 Ariz. 53, 235 P. 150 (1925).

64. *Mitchell v. Wilkerson*, 372 S.E.2d 431 (Ga. 1988).

65. *Westpy v. Burnett*, 82 N.J. Super. 239 at 246, 197 A.2d 400 at 404 (1964). The decision was affirmed by the New Jersey Supreme Court, 41 N.J. 554, 197 A.2d 857 (1964).

66. *Batchelor v. District Court*, 81 Nev. 629, 408 P.2d 239 (1965).

67. *Constitution of Oregon*, art. 1, § 18(3).

68. *South Dakota Codified Laws*, § 9-13-29.

69. *Constitution of Alaska*, art. 11, § 8; *Alaska Statutes*, § 39.38.140.

70. *Meiners v. Bering Strait School District*, 687 P.2d 287 at 295-96 (Alaska 1984).

71. Ibid.

72. Ibid. at 303.

73. Ibid. at 296.

74. *Florida Statutes Annotated*, § 100.361(1)(b).

75. *Wolfson v. Work*, 326 So.2d 90 at 91-92 (Fla.App. 1976).

76. *Ponds v. Treen*, 407 So.2d 671 (La. Sup., 1981); see also *Constitution of Louisiana*, art. 10, § 26.

77. *Code of Georgia*, § 21-4-3(7).

78. Ibid.

79. *Kansas Statutes Annotated*, § 25-4302.

80. Ibid.

81. *Unger v. Horn*, 240 K. 740 at 741, 732 P.2d 1275 at 1276 (Kan. 1987).

82. Ibid., at 747-48.

83. *Kansas Statutes Annotated*, § 25-4302.

84. *Kansas Attorney General Opinion No. 91-59*; *Cline v. Tittel*, 20 Kan.App. 695 at 701 (1995).

85. *Revised Code of Montana*, § 2-16-603(3).

86. *Steadman v. Hallard*, 197 Mont. 45, 641 P.2d 448 (Mont. 1982).

87. Ibid.

88. *State ex rel. Palmer v. Hart*, 655 P.2d 965 (Mont. 1982).

89. *Kotar v. Zupan*, 658 P.2d 1095 (Mont. 1982).

90. *Jacobensen v. Nagel*, 255 Minn. 300, 96 N.W.2d 596 (1959); see also *Constitution of Minnesota*, art. 13, § 2.

91. *Charter of the City of Fridley*, §§ 5.13–5.18; *Constitution of Minnesota*, art. 13, § 2; *Minnesota Statutes Annotated*, §§ 410.04–410.07 (1959).

92. *Jacobensen v. Nagel*, 255 Minn. 300 at 304, 96 N.W.2d 596 at 600 (1959).

93. *Constitution of New Mexico*, art. 12, § 12; *Constitution of Washington*, art. 1, § 33.

94. *Revised Code of Washington*, § 29.82.010.

95. *Cudihee v. Phelps*, 76 Wash. 314, 136 P. 367 (1913).

96. Ibid., 76 Wash. at 330-31, 136 P. at 373.

97. *Roberts v. Millikin*, 200 Wash. 60, 93 P.2d 393 (1939).

98. *Danielson v. Faymonville*, 72 Wash.2d 854, 435 P.2d 963 (1967).

99. Ibid., 72 Wash. 854 at 860, 435 P.2d 963 at 967.

100. *State ex rel. LaMon v. Westport*, 73 Wash.2d 255, 438 P.2d 200 (1968).

101. *State v. Miller*, 32 Wash.2d 149, 201 P.2d 136 (1948).

102. Ibid.

103. *Citizens Against Mandatory Busing v. Brooks*, 80 Wash.2d 121, 492 P.2d 536 (1972).

104. *Cole v. Webster*, 692 P.2d 799 at 802 (Wash. 1984).

105. Ibid., at 803–4.

106. Ibid. at 805.

107. Ibid.

108. Ibid., at 806.

109. Ibid.

110. *In re Zufelt*, 112 Wash.2d 906, 774 P.2d 1223 (1989).

111. *Gibson v. Campbell*, 136 Wash. 467 at 469, 241 P.2d 21 at 23 (1925).

112. *Bronkowski v. Macomb County Election Committee*, 185 Mich.App. 288, 460 N.W.2d 308 (1990).

113. *Vinson v. O'Malley*, 25 Ariz. 552, 220 P. 393 (1923).

114. *State v. Wilson*, 137 Wash. 125, 241 P. 970 (1925); see also Sam B. Warner, "Criminal Responsibility for Statements in Recall Charges," *National Municipal Review* 15 (February 1926): 118–22.

115. For an example of a statutory requirement, see *California Elections Code*, § 27020.

116. *Alaska Laws of 1960*, chap. 83; *Alaska Statutes*, § 15.45.480; *Kansas Laws of 1976*, chap. 179; *Kansas Statutes Annotated*, § 25-4306.

117. *37 Opinions of the Attorney General* (Wisconsin) 91 (1948); see also *Constitution of Wisconsin*, art. 13, § 12; *Wisconsin Laws of 1933*, chap. 44; *Wisconsin Laws of 1965*, chap. 666; *Wisconsin Laws of 1977*, chap. 403; *Wisconsin Statutes Annotated*, § 9.10(2)(a).

118. For an example of this requirement, see the *Constitution of Arizona*, art. 8, § 2.

119. See *Revised Code of Washington*, § 29.82.025.

120. *Constitution of California*, art. 2, § 15.

121. *California Laws of 1976*, chap. 1437; *California Election Code*, §§ 27230–7231.

122. *Charter of the City and County of San Francisco*, § 9.111.

123. *Charter of the Town of Methuen (Massachusetts)*, § 8-6(b); *Charter of the City and County of San Francisco*, § 9.11. Prior to voter approval of Proposition A in November 1983, the signature requirement was 10 percent of the votes cast for the office in the last election.

124. *Charter of the City of South Portland, Maine*, § 1013.

125. *Constitution of California*, art. 2, § 14(b); *California Elections Code*, § 27211(b).

126. *Georgia Code Annotated*, § 21-4-4.

127. *Colorado Revised Statutes*, § 1-40-110.

128. *Civil Rights Act of 1871*, 17 Stat. 13, 42 U.S.C.A. § 1983.

129. *Myer v. Grant*, 486 U.S. 414 at 421 (1988).

130. *North Dakota Laws of 1981*, chap. 241, § 1; *North Dakota Century Code*, § 16.1.01-10. The New Jersey recall statute also authorizes the use of a random sample to verify petition signatures. *New Jersey Laws of 1995*, chap. 105, § 12a(1).

131. *State ex rel. Riedman v. Baillie*, 62 ND 705, 245 NW 466 (1932); *Coghlan v. Cuskelly*, 62 ND 275, 244 N.W. 39 (1932).

132. *Oregon Laws of 1957*, chap. 608; *Oregon Revised Statutes*, § 249.008.

133. *Segards v. Bramlett*, 245 Ga. 386, 265 S.E.2d 297 (1980).

134. *Cloud v. Dyess*, 172 So.2d 528 (La. App. 1965).

135. *Oregon Laws of 1923*, chap. 247.

136. *Oregon Laws of 1933*, chap. 381.

137. Frederick L. Bird and Frances M. Ryan, *The Recall of Public Officers: A Study of the Operation of the Recall in California* (New York: Macmillan, 1930), p. 193.

138. *Arizona Attorney General Opinion No. 180-208* (1980); *Greene v. Osborne*, 157 Ariz. 363, 758 P.2d 138 (1988).

139. *Constitution of Arizona*, art. 8, § 3.

140. *New Jersey Laws of 1950*, chap. 210; *New Jersey Statutes Annotated*, §

40.69A-171.

141.   *Town of Billerica (Massachusetts) Charter*, § 6-4.

142.   For example, see *Michigan Public Acts of 1978*, Public Act 533, § 1; *Michigan Compiled Laws Annotated*, § 168.966(1).

143.   *The Historical Development and Use of the Recall in Oregon*, p. 11.

144.   *San Francisco Voter Information Pamphlet: Special Recall Election, April 26, 1983* (San Francisco, Calif.: Registrar of Voters, 1983).

145.   *Michigan Compiled Laws Annotated*, § 168.966(3).

146.   *State v. Barbur*, 144 P. 126 (1914).

147.   *Constitution of the State of Oregon*, art. 2, § 18. Justice William Rehnquist of the U.S. Supreme Court, as a circuit justice in 1985, refused to stay an order of the Hawaii Supreme Court precluding two recalled city councilmen from being candidates in the election scheduled for the day after Rehnquist's ruling. See *Republican Party of Hawaii et al. v. Patsy Mink et al.*, 474 U.S. 1301 (1985).

148.   *Town of Oxford (Massachusetts) Charter*, § 7-6-3.

149.   "Winner in War Over Judge's Words," *New York Times*, September 9, 1977, p. B1.

150.   *California Elections Code*, § 1006; see also "Absentee Ballots Over 36% in San Francisco Recall," *Election Administration Reports* 13 (May 2, 1983): 5, 7.

151.   Theodore C. Sharpe, *Recall* (Grand Forks: University of North Dakota, Bureau of Governmental Affairs, 1971), p. 41.

152.   Lindsey Gruson, "Mecham of Arizona is Convicted by His State's Senate and Ousted," *New York Times*, April 5, 1988, pp. 1, A16.

153.   *Louisiana Statutes Annotated*, § 18-1462.

154.   *Schirmer et al. v. Edwards*, 2 F.3d 117 at 121 (5th Cir. 1993).

155.   *Michigan Public Acts of 1978*, Act 533; *Michigan Compiled Laws Annotated*, § 159.974(1).

156.   Ibid., § 169.974(2).

157.   Wallace Turner, "Bid to Oust San Francisco Mayor Polarizes Splinter Groups," *New York Times*, March 26, 1983, p. 6; "Absentee Ballots Over 36% in San Francisco Recall," pp. 5, 7.

158.   *California Government Code*, §§ 83100–122.

159.   *Oregon Laws of 1979*, chap. 190, § 136; *Oregon Revised Statutes*, § 249.865.

160.   *Washington Laws of 1965*, chap. 9; *Revised Code of Washington*, § 29.82.070.

161.   *Georgia Code Annotated*, § 21-4-16.

162.   *Washington Revised Code*, §§ 29.82.070, 29.82.220.

163.   *Buckley v. Valeo*, 424 U.S. 1 at 143 (1976).

164.   *Colorado Revised Statutes*, § 31-4-504.5(1).

165.   *Opinion of the Colorado Attorney General No. OLS8803872/AOR* (1989).

166.   *Charter of the City and County of San Francisco*, § 9.113.

167. *City of Laurel Hill v. Sanders*, 392 So.2d 33 (Fla. 1980).

168. *New Hampshire Revised Statutes*, § 49C:13.

169. *California Election Code*, § 11000.

170. *Hilzinger v. Gillman*, 56 Wash. 228, 105 P. 471 (1909).

171. *Amberg v. Welsh*, 325 Mich. 285, 38 N.W.2d 304 (1949).

172. *Jacobsen v. Nagel*, 255 Minn. 300, 96 N.W.2d (1959).

173. *Sherman v. Kemish*, 29 Conn. Sup. 198, 279 A.2d 571 (1971).

174. *Smith v. Abercrombie*, 235 Ga. 471, 221 S.E.2d 802 (1975).

175. *Opinion of the Florida Attorney General No. 076-232* (December 8, 1976); *Opinion of the Florida Attorney General No. 079-38* (April 18, 1979).

176. *Opinion of the Florida Attorney General No. 082-11* (March 2, 1982).

177. *Massachusetts General Laws*, chap. 43B, § 13.

178. *Report Relative to Recall of Local Officials* (Boston: Massachusetts Legislative Research Council, 1979), pp. 8, 32. Thirty-one municipalities have drafted and adopted home rule charters, 15 other municipalities operate under provisions of special laws authorizing the recall, and 6 municipalities have special charters providing for the recall. See *Recall of Elected Officials in Massachusetts Municipalities* (Boston: Massachusetts Executive Office of Communities and Development, 1982).

179. *Report Relative to Recall of Local Officials*, p. 32.

180. *Connecticut General Statutes*, chap. 99, § 192a (1969).

181. *Simons v. Canty*, 195 Conn. 524 at 532 (1985); see also *Statutory Authority Under Home Rule for Recall* (Hartford: Connecticut Office of Legislative Research, 1974), pp. 2–3.

182. *Citizens Committee to Recall Rizzo v. The Board of Elections*, 470 Pa. 1,367 A.2d 232 (1976); see also *Philadelphia Home Rule Charter*, §§ 9-100, 9-101.

183. *Constitution of the Commonwealth of Pennsylvania*, art. 6, § 7. The original section 4 was renumbered by a 1966 constitutional amendment as section 7.

184. *City of Philadelphia Charter*, §§ 9-100–9-101 (1976).

185. *Roberts v. Brown*, 43 Tenn. App. 567, 210 S.W.2d 197 (1957).

186. Jefferson B. Fordham, "Judicial Nullification of a Democratic Political Process —The Rizzo Recall Case," *University of Pennsylvania Law Review* 126 (November 1977): 14, 17.

187. *Kansas Laws of 1978*, chap. 147, § 6; *Kansas Statutes Annotated*, § 25-4323 (c).

188. *Gilbert v. Dimmick*, 89 Wash. 182, 154 P. 163 (1916).

189. *Nesbitt v. Bolz*, 13 Cal. 677, 91 P.2d 879 (1939).

190. *Douglas et al. v. Pittman et al.*, 239 Ky. 548, 39 S.W.2d 979 (1931).

191. "Tacoma, in Recall Election, Votes Five Councilmen Out of Office," *New York Times*, September 17, 1970, p. 30.

192. City of Tacoma Interdepartmental Communication from Assistant City Attorney Geoffrey C. Cross to City Manager Marshall McCormick dated August

25, 1970; *Constitution of Washington*, art. 3, § 13; *Revised Code of Washington*, § 43.06.010(2) (1981).

193. "Minutes of Special Meeting of the Tacoma City Council," September 29, 1970, p. 1.

3

Recall of State Officers

As noted in Chapter 2, charges may have to be included in recall petitions. In several states, the charges, whether true or false, must constitute legal cause for removal — malfeasance, misfeasance, or nonfeasance — or recall petitions will be rejected. Sponsors of a recall may not include the real reason(s) for the recall in the petitions. The charge may be misfeasance but the real reason may be that the opposition party or candidate is seeking a second chance to win the office. Furthermore, the official sponsors of the recall may not be the real sponsors of the recall. In other states, the charge(s) may involve simply a disagreement over policy or the manner in which a public officer treated constituents, such as with rudeness or arrogance. The officer subject to the recall is entitled to include a statement — typically 200 words maximum — on the ballot, refuting the charges.

A review of the few state recall election campaigns and a sample of the more numerous local government recall election campaigns, described in Chapter 4, will facilitate the evaluation of the desirability of the recall by highlighting its associated advantages and disadvantages.

The recall, somewhat surprisingly, has been little used to remove state officers from office prior to the expiration of their terms. This fact is attributable in part to the need for a statewide organization to collect signatures if a statewide elected official — such as the governor or lieutenant governor — is the object of recall petitions. More surprisingly, the recall

has been utilized relatively seldom to remove a district-based state legislator. The most controversial use of the recall has involved the removal of
judges from office.

There are other reasons why the recall is not employed often at the state
level, and these reasons are the alternative methods of removal —
impeachment conviction and removal, legislative address (legislative resolution directing the governor to remove a named officer), and a state law
providing for automatic vacating of office upon conviction of a felony. In
addition, state legislatures in proposing a constitutional recall amendment
or in enacting a statutory recall provision in 22 states restricted the recall
to local government officers. Charles Press and Lawrence Sych advanced
another reason for the relatively infrequent use of the recall involving
state officials: "A vote in favor of recall, even signing a petition, is more
than repudiation of an official — it is also a rejection of his or her party.
And recallers may expect that if the official still has solid party support,
the party organization will mount a defense campaign against the recall."[1]
Many state legislative districts, of course, are larger than numerous local
governments, and collection of petition signatures is more difficult in such
districts compared with a small local government.

The recall of state officers other than the governor or a state legislator
is extremely rare. The Oregon constitution simply provides that recall
petitions must set forth "the reasons for the demand."[2] In 1922, Oregon
voters recalled two members of the State Public Utility Commission
because of dissatisfaction with those members for voting in favor of rate
increases.[3] Commenting on this recall, James T. Young in 1936 maintained "there was no responsible ground for recall action. Were the
removal of public service commissioners to be frequently indulged in, the
independence of these semi-judicial officials would be entirely
destroyed."[4]

Press and Sych surveyed the secretary of state office in each state and
reported in 1987 that only 16 recent recall elections involving state officers had been held — 1 judge, 2 public utility commissioners, and 13 state
legislators.[5] Eight officials faced recall elections between 1908 and 1922,
and seven of the remaining eight officials faced recall elections between
1971 and 1985.[6] It should be noted that a recall threat occasionally is
made against a state officer, but either recall petitions are not filed or
sponsors are unable to obtain the required number of certified signatures.

RECALL OF GOVERNORS

A total of 16 governors have been impeached, and 7 have been convicted on impeachment charges. Only three governors convicted on impeachment charges have been removed from office: Lynn J. Frazier of North Dakota in 1921, Henry S. Johnston of Oklahoma in 1919, and Evan Mecham of Arizona in 1988. Johnston was found guilty of cooperating with the Ku Klux Klan.

The constitution of North Dakota is silent relative to the grounds for employment of the recall, and, hence, any reason is a sufficient ground to employ the recall.[7] The recall first was employed on the state level in 1921 to remove from office the members of the North Dakota Industrial Commission, whose members were the governor, attorney general, and commissioner of agriculture and labor.[8] This recall was an unusual one and grew out of a dispute involving the Nonpartisan League and establishment of state-owned companies. Frazier, although recalled, was elected a U.S. senator in 1922. The league, an advocate of a state-owned grain elevator, controlled the Republican Party in 1916, whose candidates were elected to statewide offices. The attorney general, a Nonpartisan League candidate, opposed the governor in the 1920 election and lost. Voters in a referendum in the same year added the recall to the state constitution.

The Arizona constitution requires only that a recall petition contain a general statement of the grounds supporting the petition.[9] In 1972, the United Farm Workers of America (UFW), women's rights organizations, environmentalists, and certain members of the Democratic Party announced that they were launching a petition campaign for a recall election against Arizona's Republican Governor John R. Williams.[10]

The origin of that recall campaign is traceable to a controversial farm labor bill — House Bill 2134 — which was enacted by the 1972 state legislature and signed into law by the governor within two hours of receiving the bill.[11] This action by the governor did not trigger immediately the recall effort. Critics claimed the bill was pro-grower and anti-farm labor, with several critics maintaining that the bill was class or racial legislation, because most of the farm workers were Mexican-Americans.

The UFW members particularly were upset by the governor's action in quickly signing the bill into law, because such a signing deprived the union of an opportunity to attempt to persuade the governor to veto the bill. UFW president César Chávez appeared at a rally on the grounds of the capitol the next day and commenced a fast in protest. Shortly thereafter, union leaders decided to attempt to recall the governor.

Recall petitions in Arizona are not restricted to legal cause, and sponsors of the recall action included other charges against the governor in their petitions — holding him responsible for environmental degradation, overtaxation, failure to protect the rights of citizens — in order to appeal to other voters with grievances against the governor.

If the ground for initiating a recall petition drive to remove Williams from the office involved only the farm labor bill, the conclusion follows that the sponsors chose the wrong participatory corrective. The protest referendum should have been utilized in an attempt to repeal the farm labor law instead of attempting to remove the officer who merely signed a bill into law.

After analyzing the views of proponents and opponents of the attempt to recall Williams, Harry G. Matthews and C. Wade Harrison concluded:

This survey of political elites in Arizona in 1973 supports the view that recall as a process does not evoke attitudinal cleavages along liberal-conservative or Democrat-Republican lines. Although more liberals than conservatives felt that recall can be justified by public disgruntlement, it was a conservative member of the state legislature who shouted during an interview that recall should be a process where if you don't like the son-of-a-bitch, you can throw him out! Nevertheless, partisan and ideological leanings do seem important whenever people talk about a specific recall effort such as that against Governor Williams in 1972–73.[12]

Arizona recall supporters filed 177,000 signatures, but Attorney General Gary Nelson ruled that the petitions, containing more than 26,000 signatures circulated by deputy voter registrars, were not valid unless signers submitted statements to the effect that they had not been forced to sign the petitions as a condition for being registered as voters.[13] In addition, 68,000 signatures were found to be invalid by the secretary of state, who ruled that only 81,658 valid signatures had been filed; the required minimum number was 103,000.[14]

Attempts were made in 1983 and 1991 to recall the governor of Michigan. A petition seeking the recall of Governor James Blanchard in 1983, containing the statement "Send Blanchard the Message: We are Fed Up with High Taxes," was circulated but not filed with the secretary of state. The charge in the petition was "He originated and then signed into law the 38% State Income Tax Increase."

The sponsor of the 1991 attempt to recall Governor John M. Engler was informed on September 11, 1991, by the director of elections of the Michigan Department of State that there was a signature deficiency in that there were only 336,525 signatures as against the total of 641,141 valid signatures required by section 168.961 of the Michigan Consolidated Laws.[15] Petitions also were circulated unsuccessfully in 1991 for the recall of Governor Walter J. Hickel of Alaska.[16]

Mecham was successful in 1986 in his fourth attempt to win the governorship of Arizona. However, he, almost immediately after his inauguration, became controversial when he cancelled plans to declare the birthday of Martin Luther King, Jr., a state holiday and, furthermore, in June 1987 addressed the John Birch Society and made derogatory comments about blacks, homosexuals, and women.[17] The founder of the Mecham Recall Committee, Ed Buck, was a 33-year-old millionaire who had retired from the insurance business in 1987 and announced his homosexuality.[18]

The committee was successful in collecting 388,988 signatures, including 301,032 valid signatures, which exceeded the required 216,746 valid signatures. On January 26, 1988, Secretary of State Rose Mofford informed the governor that the petitions charged him as follows:

In his first 180 days as governor of the state of Arizona, Evan Mecham has demonstrated his lack of knowledge, vision, and unifying leadership necessary to govern the citizens of this state.

He has embarrassed Arizonans nationally through his insensitive and demeaning statements about women and minorities as well as his appointment of individuals who are not qualified to appropriately respond to the state's severe environmental problems.[19]

The governor had five days during which he could decide to resign. Failure to resign within this period automatically results in a recall election in which the governor is a candidate to replace himself in the event that he is removed from office. The governor notified the secretary of state on January 30, 1988, that he would not resign and declared, "I don't for a minute think that the people of this state are going to turn out a record of accomplishment for a bunch of vague promises on people who have no record of accomplishment in the field they're talking about."[20] Mofford scheduled the recall election for May 17, 1988.

Mecham had other troubles to worry about in addition to the scheduled recall election. The Arizona constitution authorizes the impeachment by a majority vote of the house of representatives of a member of the executive branch or judicial branch for "high crimes, misdemeanors, or malfeasance." On January 8, 1988, Mecham was indicted by a grand jury on six felony charges, including three counts of perjury, two counts of fraud, and one count of filing a false report on campaign contributions and expenditures. The charges were related to a controversial joint loan of $350,000 from a lawyer and developer. The Arizona house of representatives on February 5, 1988, by a vote of 46 to 14, impeached the governor by a resolution reporting that investigations and hearings by the house of representatives "revealed to the satisfaction of a majority of the members in this house that Governor Evan Mecham has, by his conduct in office, committed high crimes, misdemeanors, or malfeasance of office, and that the state of Arizona would be improved by the removal of Evan Mecham as governor of the state of Arizona."[21] Subsequently, the house transmitted to the senate 23 impeachment articles.[22] Conviction of a governor on a charge requires a two-thirds vote of the senate.

The impeachment trial of Mecham was the first one held since Governor Henry Horeton of Tennessee was impeached in 1931 but acquitted. On April 4, 1988, the senate, by a vote of 21 to 9, convicted Mecham of obstructing justice by attempting to impede a state police investigation into charges that an aide had made a death threat against a witness who appeared before a grand jury and, by a vote of 26 to 4, convicted the governor on the charge that he misused a state fund by loaning $80,000 to his automobile dealership.[23] The senate, by a 17 to 13 vote, rejected a motion to prohibit their former governor from holding any public office in the future.[24]

Considerable legal confusion existed in Arizona subsequent to the conviction of Mecham on impeachment charges. Arizona Attorney General Bob Corbin issued an opinion that, legally, the recall election must be held but that Mecham should not be allowed to be a candidate for election to the governorship in the recall election because he had not filed petitions to have his name placed on the ballot and the removal from office was for the remainder of his term of office.[25]

The legal confusion was removed on April 12, 1988, when the Arizona Supreme Court, by a four to one vote, opined that the constitutional provision for an acting governor has precedence over a recall election of the governor.[26] In consequence, the court ordered the acting secretary of state to cancel the scheduled recall election.

RECALL OF STATE LEGISLATORS

In states authorizing the use of the recall against state officers, the participatory control device seldom is employed against state legislators. As noted, the recall in 22 states is limited to local government officers.

California

The California constitution contains a liberal provision for the use of the recall and stipulates that "sufficiency of reason is not reviewable."[27] The recall was used for the first time in California in 1913 to remove Senator Marshall Black from office; he was treasurer of the failed Palo Alto Building and Loan Association and had been accused of embezzlement.[28] Later in the same year, an attempt was made to recall Senator James C. Owens on the ground that he had not fulfilled campaign pledges. The attempt, led by organized labor, failed, as had an earlier attempt against Owen when he was a Richmond councilman.[29]

A third recall campaign was launched in 1913 against Senator E. E. Grant, led by cigar dealer Andrew Einsfeldt. The petition charged that Grant: "had noted to make the World's Fair 'dry,' that he had voted against a bill to prevent the solemnizing of marriages until at least five days after the issuance of the license, and that he had opposed a measure giving California authors and publishers preference in the publication of school books."[30] According to Frederick L. Bird and Frances M. Ryan, Einsfeldt wanted Grant removed because he "had actively supported the Redlight Abatement Act, that he was a prohibitionist, and that he had refused to collaborate with his colleagues on Sundays in concluding the work of the legislative session."[31] A total of three recall petitions were filed against the senator. The first petition was burned in a fire, the second petition contained numerous fraudulent signatures, and the third petition was certified. Eligible voters totalled 16,090; 4,672 voted for recalling Grant in 1914, and 4,141 voted to retain him in office.[32]

Anti-gun control groups failed in their 1994 attempt to recall senate President *pro tempore* David Roberti, but Republican voters in 1995 were successful in recalling two assembly members who had been elected as Republicans in 1994.

The November 1994 elections appeared to give the Republican Party control of the assembly, effective in January 1995, when 41 Republicans and 39 Democrats would assume office. It was anticipated that Willie Brown, Jr., a Democrat from San Francisco who had been speaker for 14 years, would be replaced in January 1995 by a Republican speaker. Nevertheless, Republicans did not gain control of the assembly until voters recalled two Republican assembly members who were described as renegades.

The first renegade was Paul Horcher of West Covina, who won the 1990 Republican primary for Assembly District 60 with 18 percent of the vote.[33] In 1993, the Republican caucus wanted Dean Andal of Stockton appointed vice-chairman of the ways and means committee. Brown, however, declined to appoint Andal and offered the post to other Republican members, who rejected the appointment. Finally, the post was offered to Horcher, who accepted and was punished by being excluded from the Republican caucus. Voters became very upset with Horcher in December 1994 when he changed his party affiliation from Republican to independent and "cast the deciding vote for Brown's speakership."[34]

The Democrats attempted to save Horcher from being recalled by sponsoring signs and advertisements stating that firefighters, nurses, and teachers were opposed to the recall because the Republicans would enact laws injurious to the welfare of workers. Nevertheless, he was recalled from office on May 16, 1995, by a 63 percent to 37 percent margin and was replaced by Republican Gary Miller. Absentee ballots were approximately 53 percent of the total ballots cast and favored Horcher's recall by a margin of 69 percent to 31 percent.

Sacramento Bee columnist William Endicott in 1996 commented on the Horcher recall aftermath as follows:

San Francisco Mayor Willie Brown, as we learned last week, is doing his part to trim the state's unemployment rolls.

Brown plucked an old political ally — Paul Horcher — off the streets of Diamond Bar in Southern California and installed him in a $70,000 job as a liaison between the mayor's office and the San Francisco Board of Supervisors.

It was Horcher whose renegade vote blocked fellow Republicans from ousting Democrat Brown as speaker of the assembly in December 1994, a move that ultimately led to Horcher's recall from office.

There was no *quid pro quo* for Horcher's support of Brown, both he and Brown insisted at the time, so I guess we can assume Horcher got his new job strictly on merit.[35]

Andal resigned his assembly seat after being elected to the board of equalization in 1994, and his seat in the assembly was won by Democrat Michael Machado of Stockton with a 1,764 vote margin. Republicans in 1995 launched a recall campaign against Machado, charging that he stated during the election campaign that he was not committed to voting for Brown as speaker but subsequently voted for Brown. Don Parson, a leader of the recall campaign, maintained that Machado "knows that if he had campaigned differently, he wouldn't have won."[36]

Laureen Lazarovici of *cjWeekly* suggested prior to the recall election that it had a closer connection to the senate than to the assembly.

Sen. Rob Hurtt (R-Garden Grove) and the Allied Business PAC have together donated $30,000 to the effort. Assm. Larry Bowler (R-Elk Grove) is regarded as an Allied ally, and Bowler, not coincidentally, is nested with Machado in the senate district now represented by Sen. Pat Johnston (D-Stockton). He also is active in the Machado recall campaign. Johnston is considered marginally vulnerable in the 1996 election, and Bowler would raise his profile in the part of the senate district that he does not represent if he can spearhead the effort to knock out Machado. Even if the recall doesn't succeed, it could sufficiently weaken Machado and set him up for defeat by some other Republican in 1996. All this plays itself out against a backdrop of a state senate where the Democrats hold the slimmest of majorities.[37]

On August 22, 1995, Machado survived the recall attempt by a margin of 63 percent to 37 percent, with an approximate 28 percent turnout of registered voters. Brown no longer was speaker on the day of the recall vote, and voters were aware that Republican senate minority leader Rob Hunt and Republican Larry Bowler of the neighboring assembly district raised a sizeable proportion of the $200,000 spent by recall proponents. Following the recall election, former Assemblyman Andal commented "the Democrats spent $1.3 million to keep what they had. That's $1.3 million they would have for assembly seats next year."[38]

According to Charles M. Price, Machado's recall was sought by Republican assembly leaders who concluded that "his removal would provide personal gain for the recall leaders — Assemblyman Larry Bowler (R-Elk Grove); Dean Andal, a member of the board of equalization who formerly represented Machado's district in the assembly; and senate minority leader Rob Hunt (R-Garden Grove), who provided seed money for the recall's signature drive."[39]

A 1976 amendment to the California constitution stipulates: "A state officer who is not recalled shall be reimbursed by the state for the officer's recall election expenses legally and personally incurred."[40] Price reported that three legislators since 1911 were eligible for reimbursement: Owens in 1914, Roberti in 1994, and Machado in 1995.[41] The first two did not seek reimbursement, but Machado has requested the California Board of Control to reimburse him for the $889,000 spent to defend his seat.

The third recall election in 1995 involved former Assembly Speaker Doris Allen of Cypress, who, along with two other Republican members of the assembly, were redistricted into the same district in 1992, and she won the primary election.[42] Subsequently, conservative Republicans learned that the California Teachers' Association, which generally supports Democrats, had assisted her primary election campaign. Her relations with fellow Republicans deteriorated after she entered a special election for a seat in the state senate against Assemblyman Ross Johnson, who was backed by Republican leaders. According to A. G. Block of the *California Journal*, Johnson's "eventual victory left Allen feeling bitter and abused."[43]

With the Republicans beginning to solidify their control of the assembly, Brown engineered an agreement with Allen that Democratic assembly members would vote for her as speaker. Block reported: "she could accomplish two supreme acts of revenge: snag the speakership for herself and thereby stiff assembly GOP Leader Jim Brulte (R-Rancho Cucamonga), whom she blamed for not keeping the caucus neutral during the senate campaign; and assume control over all things Republican in the assembly, including committee assignments, staffing, and allocation of precious resources."[44] Allen became the first woman to become speaker and the first Republican speaker in 20 years.

Enraged Republicans, including Governor Pete Wilson and other party leaders, called for her recall. Because of California's term limit, she could serve only another 13 months if not recalled and consequently was unable to raise significant campaign funds. On September 13, 1995, Allen resigned as speaker and threw her support to another renegade Republican — freshman Brian Setencich — who was elected speaker for the remaining two days of the 1995 session. She stated "it is in the best interest of my constituents and party to step aside and hand the speaker's gavel to another fair-minded Republican."[45]

Although Republicans outnumbered Democrats by 52 percent to 35 percent, Democrats concluded that their candidate could win if four strong Republican candidates split their party's vote. Complicating the Democrats' plan was the entry of Laurie Campbell, a legal secretary, as a Democratic candidate. Democrats sued to have her name removed from the recall ballot as a candidate by alleging she was sponsored in fact by Orange County Republicans. Superior Court Judge James Ford in October removed her name from the ballot because the 43 required petition signatures had not been personally collected, although she signed a statement that she had collected them personally.[46]

Four Republican candidates entered the race to replace Allen if she was recalled — former mayor of Huntington Beach Don McAlister, Huntington Beach Planning Commissioner Haydee Tillotson, school board member Shirley Carey, and Scott Baugh, an attorney. Two of the candidates — Baugh and Tillotson — were viewed as strong candidates who could split the Republican vote and allow former Huntington Beach Mayor Linda Moulton-Patterson to win the seat with a plurality of the votes in a state with no provision for a runoff election between the two top vote-getters. Block reported that Baugh and Tillotson and their respective allies attacked each other strenuously, with the former's supporters comparing Tillotson with Allen and with Baugh being accused of "padding his political resume and of having taken no interest in local GOP politics prior to being recruited as a candidate."[47]

Under strong pressure from leading Republicans, including Wilson, Tillotson on November 16 withdrew as a candidate and stated "the campaign was taking a more negative tone and we were heading for a collision course, and I couldn't continue to divide the party."[48] She spent $175,000 of her own money in the quest for the assembly seat.[49] On November 28, 1995, Allen was recalled by a 65 percent to 35 percent margin in an election with a turnout of slightly less than 26 percent of registered voters.[50]

In January 1996, the Republicans finally gained control of the assembly as Curt Pringle was elected speaker and Republicans were appointed chairs of committees with lopsided Republican majorities. Almost immediately, a flood of Republican bills dealing with important policy issues were approved by the assembly.[51] Control of the assembly does not ensure enactment of all Republican Party–sponsored bills because Democrats retain control of the senate with a slim majority. Furthermore, certain important bills, including appropriations ones, require 54 affirmative votes for approval in the assembly.

Idaho

Although the Idaho constitution is silent relative to the reasons for employment of the recall, the implementing statute requires that reasons for the recall be contained in the petition without specifying whether cause is required.[52] Prior to a vote on a salary increase for state legislators in Idaho in 1971, the senator and three representatives from the Idaho Falls area conferred with constituents and discovered that they were opposed to the proposed salary increase. The senator and two of the representatives voted for the bill, and recall petitions were circulated against the senator and one representative; both were recalled.[53]

Michigan

The constitution of Michigan directs the state legislature to enact statutes providing "for the recall of all elective officers except judges of courts of record" but does not specify grounds for recall.[54] Michigan statutes, however, authorize "the board of county election commissioners to consider the clarity of each reason."[55]

Upon assuming office in January 1983, Governor James Blanchard was informed by the state budget director that there was a budget deficit of $900 million. In response, the governor proposed a 38 percent increase in the income tax rate over a period of five years. The bill incorporating the proposal was approved quickly by the house of representatives, which was controlled solidly by the Democratic Party. Senate Democrats had only a two vote majority, and one Democratic senator announced his opposition to the tax increase. Shortly thereafter, a Republican senator announced that he would vote for the bill, and it was approved by one vote.

A recall drive was launched by an unsuccessful Republican candidate for various offices against the governor and 12 Democratic senators and the one Republican senator who had voted for the tax increase. A total of approximately 760,000 valid signatures would be required for a gubernatorial recall election, and approximately 20,000 valid signatures would be required for a recall election of a senator. Under the Michigan state constitution, recall petition charges may be political and do not have to constitute legal cause. Petition circulators have 90 days to collect the required number of signatures. Democrats maintained that the recall campaigns were organized by the Republican Party, which was seeking control of the senate.

Petition circulators were unable to collect the required number of valid signatures to force a recall election of Blanchard, but did collect the required number of signatures for the recall elections of Senator Philip O. Mastin and Senator David M. Serotkin.

On November 22, 1983, Mastin was recalled by a vote of 60 percent to 40 percent.[56] On November 30, 1983, Serotkin was recalled by a vote of 64 percent to 36 percent.[57] Voter turnout in the two recall elections was approximately 56 percent and 54 percent, respectively, of the number of voters casting ballots in the 1982 general election.

Senator Gary G. Corbin, Democratic majority floor leader, reported that only 19 percent of the electorate recalled the two senators and that the recall was "an attack on representative government" and a "signal to the public that the best way to get something done is to begin a recall procedure."[58] Serotkin maintained that the recall device was used by "extreme right wing elements" to further their goals, which involve more than taxation, and added "many people still think the tax bill resulted in a thirty-eight percent increase in taxes."[59] In fact, taxes increased only 1.75 percent, although the increase in the tax rate was 38 percent.

Special elections were held on January 31, 1984, to select replacements for the two recalled senators, who were ineligible to seek reelection during the remainder of their original terms ending on December 31, 1986. As the result of the election, control of the senate passed from Democrats to Republicans, because Republican candidates won the two special elections in which turnout of voters was approximately 37 percent and 46 percent of the number of voters participating in the 1982 general election.[60] Republicans assumed the chairmanship of senate committees, occupied offices in the capitol building with Democratic senators moved to an annex, and fired 22 Democratic staff members. In addition, Blanchard responded to the success of the recall drives by proposing that the income tax increase be rolled back "in October if revenues warrant — some three months before the rollback was to go into effect. He also submitted the state's first 'no increase' budget."[61]

Wisconsin

The constitution of Wisconsin contains a self-executing and mandatory recall section that authorizes the state legislature to enact laws "to facilitate its (recall) operation but no law shall be enacted to hamper, restrict, or impair the right of recall."[62]

A tax dispute, similar to the one in Michigan, generated in late 1995 a campaign to recall Republican Senator George Petak of Wisconsin, who twice voted against a bill establishing a taxing district for the new Milwaukee Brewers' stadium but switched his vote at 5 A.M. on October 6, 1995, thereby ensuring approval of the bill.[63] Racine voters were infuriated at their county being included in the taxing district and organized the No More Petak Recall Committee. The senator originally opposed the stadium bill because it included a sales tax in Racine County. Republicans at the time held a one vote majority in the senate. The recall election had no effect on the tax because it was enacted by the state legislature and was not the object of a protest referendum signature campaign.

In common with the Michigan senatorial recall campaigns, Petak alleged that the state Democratic Party was behind the attempt to recall him and signed a contract with a Racine temporary employment agency to hire petition solicitors.[64]

The recall committee submitted 15,060 signatures, and the election board tentatively certified 14,204 signatures, with 11,577 certified signatures being necessary for a recall election. Petak challenged 6,452 signatures on three major grounds and several technical grounds.[65] First, the senator alleged that petitions were circulated prior to the end of his first year in office in violation of the state constitution. According to the senator, the committee registered with the state on November 2, 1995, and began collecting signatures on December 15, 1995. Second, he maintained that the signatures were not collected during the 60-day collection period, which he maintained commenced on November 2, 1995, when the committee registered. Elizabeth Erven, coordinator of the committee, responded that the committee had registered as a political action committee on November 2, 1995, but amended its registration form on December 15, 1995, to list December 15 as the registration date for the start of the 60-day signature collection period. Third, the senator contended that the committee did not report receiving a financial contribution from the Democratic Party of Wisconsin and, hence, paid signature collectors should be disqualified as agents of the Democratic Party, which is not a resident of Racine.

A relatively large number of signatures were challenged on various grounds — 1,817 signatures of persons whose residences could not be verified, 951 signatures on petitions that were not notarized, 373 signatures on petitions with incomplete or illegible names of notary publics, 287 duplicate signatures, 286 signatures with apparent alterations, 238 signatures collected on 26 petitions by a circulator who used two addresses, 211 signatures collected by felons, 200 signatures of nonresidents of the senatorial district, 156 signatures lacking complete information, 85 groups of names written in the handwriting of a single person, and 65 names collected by non–Racine County circulators.[66]

Nevertheless, the requisite number of valid signatures were certified, and a recall election was held on June 4, 1996. Petak lost the election by a vote of 21,045 to 19,318 to Democrat Kimberly M. Plache.[67] In common with the 1984 senate recall elections in Michigan, control of the Wisconsin senate shifted parties as the Democrats gained a 17 to 16 majority.

Sych investigated the March 1990 recall election involving a Wisconsin assemblyman to determine whether partisanship, voter apathy on the part of supporters of the assemblyman, or conversion of supporters to opponents best explains the result of the election.[68]

The recall attempt was triggered by the Democratic assemblyman supporting a plan, negotiated by Republican Governor Thomas G. Thompson, providing for the ten-year lease of Chippewa Indians' rights to fish, hunt, and harvest timber and food on nonreservation public lands under treaties ceding the northern section of the state to the federal government. The plan was designed "to help settle the escalating confrontations between tribal and nontribal factions."[69] Supporters of the recall drive were associated with tourism, including sports fishing. The targeted officer was not recalled, because only 39.9 percent of those voting favored his removal from office in an election with a voter turnout of 38.3 percent. Sych's analysis reveals that conversion of former supporters to favor recall was the major explanatory factor and that party affiliation and voter turnout were not major influences.[70]

RECALL OF JUDICIAL OFFICERS

As noted in Chapter 2, constitutional provisions authorizing the recall typically exclude judicial officers. Where authorized, the most controversial use of the recall involves judges. The number of judicial recall elections is small, although the filing of notices of intent to seek the recall of judges is more common.

In Wisconsin, a recall campaign was launched in 1977 against Dane County Judge Archie Simonson when the transcripts of his remarks at a May 25 hearing for a 15-year-old boy, who pleaded no contest to a second-degree sexual assault charge, were made public by a circuit court judge.[71] In response to a complaint by an assistant district attorney that the judge's comments at the hearing were "particularly sexist," Simonson responded:

You bet it is. I can't go around exposing my genitals like they can their mammary glands.

Even in open court, we have people appearing — women appearing without bras, and with the nipples fully exposed, and they think it is smart, and they sit here on the witness stand with their dresses up over the cheeks of their butts, and we have this type of thing in the schools.

It really is wide open, and are we supposed to take an impressionable person 15 or 16 years of age, who can respond to something like that, and punish that person severely because they react to it normally?[72]

The judge's remarks, particularly the reference to the boy reacting normally, sparked a recall drive by the Committee to Recall Judge Archie Simonson that collected more than 35,000 signatures. Feminists played a major role in collecting signatures and in mobilizing voter support for the recall of the judge.[73] Sponsors of the recall maintained that the real issues were the judge's lack of qualifications and judicial incompetence. Prior to becoming a judge, he had been a fencing coach at the University of Wisconsin and an attorney.

The judge was a candidate for reelection in the event that he was recalled, and he ran against five other candidates. The winner of the recall election was Moria Krueger, the only woman candidate, who defeated the judge by an 8,809 vote margin — 27,244 to 18,435.[74] He became the first judge in Wisconsin to be recalled. Voter turnout in the recall election was approximately 48 percent of those eligible.

In 1982, Circuit Judge William L. Reinecke survived a recall attempt in Lancaster, Wisconsin, by winning 50.85 percent of the votes.[75] The recall campaign was sparked by his comment that a five-year-old female sexual assault victim was "unusually promiscuous."[76] The judge promised that he would be more careful in the wording of his comments in the future.

A notice of intent to recall Chief Justice Rose E. Bird of the California Supreme Court was filed in 1982.[77] Appointed to the court in 1977 by Governor Edmund G. Brown, Jr., the chief justice became controversial because of her votes overturning death sentences imposed by trial courts in the 61 capital crime cases that came before the supreme court after her appointment to the court. A total of 731,244 signatures of registered voters were necessary to force a recall election. Although a recall election was not held, the chief justice was defeated for election to the supreme court on November 4, 1986, along with two other supreme court justices.[78] The three jurists were the first ones removed from a court by voters since the state constitution was amended in 1934 to mandate that appointed appellate justices were subject to periodic confirmation elections.

SUMMARY AND CONCLUSIONS

Evidence presented in this chapter reveals that the fear of the opponents of the recall that it would be used often and disrupt representative government has proven to be unfounded on the state level. The recall seldom has been employed to remove state officers in the states that authorize its use for this purpose. Not surprisingly, the recall has been employed successfully on only three occasions — Governors Frazier of North Dakota in 1921, Johnston of Oklahoma in 1929, and Mecham of Arizona in 1988 — to remove statewide elected officers. The explanation for the infrequent use is simple. The voter signature threshold is high, and a statewide organization is essential if the requisite number of signatures is to be obtained. In addition, there are other methods that can be employed for removing a statewide elected officer in whom the voters have lost confidence — impeachment process, defeat of the incumbent in a reelection bid, and a state law providing for automatic vacating of office of any official convicted of a felony. Available evidence leads to the conclusion that

Mecham would have been removed from office via a recall election if he had not been convicted on impeachment charges by the state senate and removed from office.

Although signature collection is less difficult for those seeking the recall of a state legislator, few recall drives have been successful. The recall was employed successfully in California in 1913 to recall two senators and in 1995 to recall two representatives. Two Idaho legislators were recalled in 1971, two senators were recalled in Michigan in 1983, and one senator was recalled in Wisconsin in 1996. The latter recalls were politically significant, because control of the Michigan senate passed from the Democrats to the Republicans.

The recall of a state judge is a rarity. As noted, Simonson was recalled in 1977. A second Wisconsin judge survived a 1982 recall election, and an unsuccessful attempt was made to recall California Chief Justice Bird in the same year.

Chapter 4 examines the more numerous attempts to recall local government officers and the charges against them.

NOTES

1. Charles Press and Lawrence Sych, "Participation in State Recall Elections," paper presented at the annual meeting of the American Political Science Association, Chicago, Illinois, September 3–6, 1987, p. 6.

2. *Constitution of Oregon*, art. II, § 18.

3. James D. Barnett, "Fighting Rate Increases by the Recall," *National Municipal Review* 11 (July 1922): 213–14.

4. James T. Young, *The New American Government and Its Work*, 3rd ed. (New York: Macmillan, 1936), p. 854.

5. Press and Sych, "Participation in State Recall Elections," pp. 3–4.

6. Ibid., p. 4.

7. *Constitution of North Dakota*, art. III, § 10.

8. Robert Morlan, *Political Prairie Fire* (Minneapolis: University of Minnesota Press, 1955), pp. 315–35; Bruce Nelson, *Land of the Dakotahs* (Minneapolis: University of Minnesota Press, 1946), pp. 284–98.

9. *Constitution of Arizona*, art. VIII, § 2.

10. "Recall Bid Faces Delay in Arizona," *New York Times*, January 21, 1973, p. 30.

11. Information on the recall is derived from Harry G. Matthews and C. Wade Harrison, *Recall and Reform in Arizona, 1973* (Tucson: University of Arizona, Institute of Government Research, 1973).

12. Ibid., pp. 33, 35.

13. "Campaign to Recall Arizona Governor Proves a Failure," *New York Times*, October 7, 1972, p. 64.

14. Ibid.

15. Letter to Jacqueline Shrader from Director of Elections Christopher M. Thomas of the Michigan Department of State, dated September 11, 1996.

16. Brian S. Akre, "Recall Effort: Group Says Alaskan Governor Abusing Power," *Times Union*, October 16, 1991, p. B-10.

17. Lori K. Weinraub, "Arizona Governor Officially Told to Resign or Face Recall Vote," *Schenectady Gazette*, January 27, 1988, p. 2; Thomas J. Knudson, "Arizona Governor Dismissive of Foes," *New York Times*, July 13, 1987, p. A18.

18. Gail D. Cox, "The Trials of Gov. Evan Mecham," *National Law Journal* 10 (March 28, 1988): 8.

19. Weinraub, "Arizona Governor Officially Told to Resign or Face Recall Vote," p. 2.

20. "Arizona's Governor Won't Quit," *New York Times*, February 1, 1988, p. A28.

21. "Amid Impeachment, Mecham Maintains He'll be Vindicated," *Knickerbocker News*, February 6, 1988, p. 2A.

22. Lindsey Gruson, "Arizona Senate Begins Impeachment Trial of Mecham," *New York Times*, March 1, 1988, p. A13.

23. Lindsey Gruson, "Mecham of Arizona is Convicted by His State's Senate and Ousted," *New York Times*, April 5, 1988, pp. 1, A16.

24. Lindsey Gruson, "Arizona is Facing a Legal Question," *New York Times*, April 6, 1988, p. B7.

25. Ibid.

26. "Arizona Court Blocks a Special Vote on Governor," *New York Times*, April 14, 1988, p. A32.

27. *Constitution of California*, art. II, § 14(a).

28. Frederick L. Bird and Frances M. Ryan, *The Recall of Public Officers: A Study of the Operation of the Recall in California* (New York: Macmillan, 1930), pp. 271–72.

29. Ibid., pp. 272–75.

30. Ibid., p. 276.

31. Ibid.

32. Ibid., pp. 278–79.

33. Laureen Lazarovici, "Horcher Recalled Emphatically," *cjWeekly*, May 22, 1995, p. 11.

34. Laureen Lazarovici, "Machado Recall May be Headed for Ballot," *cjWeekly*, May 8, 1995, p. 5.

35. William Endicott, "A Turn Around Political Track," *Sacramento Bee*, February 3, 1996, p. A3.

36. Lazarovici, "Machado Recall May be Headed for Ballot," p. 5.

37. Laureen Lazarovici, "Machado Foes Say They Have Enough Signatures," *cjWeekly*, May 29, 1995, p. 6.

38.   Laureen Lazarovici, "Machado Recall Fails," *cjWeekly*, August 28, 1995, p. 12.

39.   Charles M. Price, "Paying the Tab for Recall Elections," *California Government & Politics Annual* (1996–1997): 77.

40.   *Constitution of California*, art. 2, § 18.

41.   Price, "Paying the Tab for Recall Elections," pp. 77–78.

42.   A. G. Block, "A Twisted Tale of Revenge," *California Journal* 27 (January 1996): 36.

43.   Ibid.

44.   Ibid.

45.   "GOP Leader Quits California Post," *Times Union*, September 15, 1995, p. A-6.

46.   A. G. Block, "Democrat Bounced from Allen Recall Ballot," *cjWeekly*, November 6, 1995, p. 5.

47.   Block, "A Twisted Tale of Revenge," p. 40.

48.   Ibid., p. 41.

49.   Ibid.

50.   "California Voters Recall Ex-Speaker of the Assembly," *New York Times*, November 30, 1995, p. A14.

51.   Mary L. Vellings, "Assembly GOP, Long Subservient, Relishing Chance to Rule," *Sacramento Bee*, January 29, 1996, p. A 6.

52.   *Constitution of Idaho*, art. VI, § 6; *Idaho Code*, § 34-1703.

53.   Press and Sych, "Participation in State Recall Elections," pp. 10–11.

54.   *Constitution of Michigan*, art. II, § 8.

55.   *Michigan Compiled Laws Annotated*, § 168.952(e)(4).

56.   "Michigan Ouster Votes Threaten Democratic Control in Legislature," *New York Times*, December 2, 1983, p. A22.

57.   Ibid.

58.   Candace Romig, "Two Michigan Legislators Recalled," *State Legislatures* 10 (January 1984): 5.

59.   "Michigan Voters Recall Backers of Tax Hike," *Public Administration Times* 6 (December 15, 1983): 1.

60.   Charles Press and Kenneth VerBurg, "Recall Reverses Party Composition of Michigan Senate," *Comparative State Politics Newsletter* 5 (April 1984): 7–8.

61.   Ibid., p. 7.

62.   *Constitution of Wisconsin*, art. XIV, § 12.

63.   Mary Balousek, "2-Week Reprieve for Petak," *Wisconsin State Journal*, February 21, 1996, p. 1.

64.   Joseph A. Scolaro, "Petak: Dems Involved in Recall," *Racine Journal Times*, February 2, 1996, p. 1.

65.   Joseph A. Scolaro, "Petak, GOP Question Over 6,400 Signatures," *Racine Journal Times*, March 7, 1996, p. 1.

66.   Ibid.

67. "Statement of Board of State Canvassers for State Senator, District Twenty-One Recall Election, June 4, 1996," Madison, Wisconsin, June 12, 1996.

68. Lawrence Sych, "State Recall Elections: What Explains Their Outcomes?" *Comparative State Politics* 17 (October 1996): 7–25.

69. Ibid., p. 9.

70. Ibid., p. 8.

71. "Judge Who Suggested Boy in Rape Reacted 'Normally' Draws More Ire," *New York Times*, August 26, 1977, p. A14.

72. Ibid.

73. Laura R. Woliver, *From Outrage to Action: The Politics of Grass-Roots Dissent* (Urbana: University of Illinois Press, 1993), pp. 30–60.

74. "Winner in War Over Judge's Words," *New York Times*, September 9, 1977, p. B1.

75. "Judge Beats Recall," *Knickerbocker News*, May 12, 1982, p. 2A.

76. Ibid.

77. Wallace Turner, "California's Chief Justice is Facing a Recall Move," *New York Times*, October 15, 1982, p. A13.

78. Robert Lindsey, "Deukmejian and Cranston Win as 3 Judges are Ousted," *New York Times*, November 6, 1986, p. A30.

4

Recall of
Local Government Officers

The procedures and requirements for the recall of local government officers are similar to those for state officers. Not surprisingly, the charges against local officers in recall petitions cover a variety of subjects not found in recall petitions for state officers. Charges include firing the city or town manager, interference by a councillor with the police department, firing of the police chief, interference with the zoning board of appeals, violation of the state open meetings law, rudeness, tax increases, felony indictment of an officer, promoting school integration, ethnic slurs, acceptance of contributions from the owner of a topless, bottomless bar, voting to create a county police department, voting for a gun control ordinance, changing party affiliation, dispute over the location of a new courthouse, profligate spending of public funds, nonresponsiveness to the electorate, mismanagement of city funds, conducting council business prior to entering the council chambers, conduct unbecoming a municipal officer, using county employees to do work at the officer's home, and failure to respond to a letter from the state water pollution control commission. Proponents of the recall of an officer often failed to collect the required number of signatures, as illustrated by the filing of only 162 of the 808 signatures necessary to call a recall election of Kethikan Gateway Borough, Alaska, Mayor James Carlton in 1996.

EARLY RECALL ELECTIONS

The city of Los Angeles, which adopted a city charter in 1903 authorizing use of the recall, held the first recall election in the United States. A member of the city council was charged with being a tool of the liquor interests and accepting money in exchange for his vote to allow a slaughter house in his district.[1] Although the councilman was recalled, he was successful in obtaining, on technical grounds, the issuance by a court of a writ of mandamus directing the city council to seat him. A second recall election, however, was called, and he was recalled for the second time and removed from office.

The recall of a mayor first occurred in 1909, when Mayor A. C. Harper of Los Angeles was recalled.[2] Elected in 1906, the mayor commenced to make appointments that appeared to be payments to political supporters seeking public offices instead of appointments made to promote the public interest. Furthermore, a grand jury reported that the city was not enforcing the antivice ordinances yet did not return a true bill because the ordinances had been enforced since the jury commenced its investigation. A minority of the jurors accused the mayor and police officials of failing to perform their duties, and the Municipal League, a civic organization, organized a successful recall campaign.

Shortly thereafter, the recall was employed to remove two school trustees in Dallas who had discharged the principal and a teacher in a high school without filing charges against them and without a public hearing.[3]

In Seattle, Mayor Hiram C. Gill was recalled in 1910. He was accused of opposing the establishment of a garbage crematory, supporting the local electric light utility company, and failing to eliminate gambling and other forms of vice.[4] Disgruntled citizens in Tacoma in 1911 attempted to recall the entire city commission. Voters had adopted the commission form of government but quickly became dissatisfied with the mayor and other commission members. The mayor was hostile to the commission form, and factional disputes broke out on the commission, which allegedly led to a sharp increase in governmental costs. The mayor and two other commissioners were removed from office. During the same time period, a movement developed in Huron, South Dakota, to remove the entire city commission because of the increased tax rate, but voters retained all members of the commission.

The recall also was employed in 1911 in Wichita, Kansas, and the issue involved public policy; the charge was that the mayor and another commissioner sought to have the city purchase a private water company at a price exceeding its value.[5] They were removed from office. An attempt to recall an Alameda County, California, supervisor failed in 1915 because an inadequate number of valid signatures were filed. Commenting on this recall attempt in 1916, F. Stuart Fitzpatrick of Columbia University highlighted abuses of the petition procedure and noted that safeguards were inadequate "to prevent unscrupulous men from taking advantage of the manifold opportunities for misrepresentation and fraud, not to speak of forgery and bribery, that present themselves in circulating a petition. . . . The professional solicitor is not made of the staunchest stuff, leaving out of account the 'amateur' who hires him."[6]

Shortly thereafter, an attempt was made by a former mayor and his chief of police to recall Mayor George Wixom of San Bernardino, California, who was charged with extravagance and inefficiency. These charges apparently masked the real issue, which involved whether the town would be an open town that would tolerate illegal activities. Voters retained the mayor.[7]

The Atlanta Board of Police Commissioners — composed of the mayor, one councilman, and five others — in 1915 removed the police chief, who had served the city for 26 years without a reprimand. The charges were incompetence, inefficiency, and insubordination, but the evidence did not support the first two charges, and the third charge apparently was the result of the chief attempting to enforce the liquor law.[8] Recall petitions were filed, and the members of the board survived the January 5, 1916, recall election, apparently because the three city newspapers convinced the voters that the removal of the chief would not result in nonenforcement of the liquor law. Observers concluded that the recall election had a deterrent effect on the board in the future.

J. Otis Garber of the University of Toledo in 1925 posted a questionnaire on the use of the recall to all 149 city manager cities with a charter recall provision and received replies from 121 cities.[9] The recall had been used on 27 occasions in 24 of the cities; seven petitions contained an insufficient number of signatures, officers were not recalled in 13 elections, and officers were recalled in 7 elections (Table 4.1). Garber concluded that the recall had not been overused and quoted a city officer who maintained the greatest value of the recall "lies in the fact that it gives the public a sense of confidence in itself. The people feel that at any time they can 'turn the rascals out' if they misbehave in office."[10]

Frederick L. Bird and Frances M. Ryan examined the use of the recall in California through 1929 and reported results of its use in cities under 20,000 population, between 20,000 and 100,000 population, and over 100,000 population — Oakland, Los Angeles, and San Francisco.[11] Collecting data was difficult because there is no statute requiring each city to

TABLE 4.1
Employment of the Recall in 40 Cities, 1903–25

State and City	Petition Failed	Election Failed	Recall Successful
Alabama*			
Mobile		1	
California			
Bakersfield		1	
Colton		1	1
Long Beach			1
Los Angeles	2		1
Oakland	1	2	
Richmond		2	
Riverside			1
San Bernardino		1	1
San Diego			1
San Francisco	1		3
San Jose	1		
Santa Cruz			1
Tulare		1	
Vallejo	1		
Visalia			1
Colorado			
Colorado Springs	1	1	
Denver		1	
Connecticut			
Stratford			1
Georgia			
Atlanta		1	
Illinois			
Springfield	1		
Waukegon		1	
Iowa			
Marshalltown	1	1	
Sioux City		1	
Kansas			
Cherryville	1		
Hayes	1		
Lawrence		1	
Pratt		1	
Salina	1		1
Wichita			1
Louisiana			
Shreveport			1
Maine			
Portland			1
Massachusetts			
Boston		2	
Lawrence			1
Mansfield		2	
Salem			1
Michigan			
Albion	1		
Bay City			1

100

Michigan (continued)				
Kalamazoo	2			
Munising			1	
Pontiac	1			
Minnesota				
Morris	1			
Missouri				
Joplin	1			
Nebraska				
Nebraska City	1			
New Jersey				
Long Branch			1	
Wildwood	1			
New Mexico				
Alberquerque	1			
North Carolina				
Charlotte	1			
North Dakota				
Mandan	1			
Minot	2			
Ohio				
Sandusky	1			
Oklahoma				
Ardmore	1			
Bartlesville				
Duncan	1			
Guthrie	2			
Oklahoma City	2			
Oregon				
Junction City				1
Portland				1
South Carolina				
Beaufort		1		
Columbia	2			
South Dakota				
Aberdeen		1		
Huron		1		
Rapid City		1		
Sioux Falls		1		1
Tennessee				
Nashville		1		1
Texas				
Dallas		2		2
Virginia				
Norfolk	1			
Portsmouth		1		
Wisconsin				
Janesville	1			
Superior		1		
Washington				
Escatada				1
Everett				1
Hoquiam				1
Seattle				1
Tacoma	2			2
Walla Walla	1			2
Total	28	36	36	36

*The supreme court of Alabama declared the recall unconstitutional.

Source: J. Otis Garber, "The Use of the Recall in American Cities," *National Municipal Review* 15 (May 1926): 261.

report recall elections to a state office. Bird and Ryan secured information from 172 of the 245 small cities and reported that the remaining municipalities were scattered throughout the state and each had a population under 2,000. Table 4.2 reveals that recall petitions had been filed in 50 cities and involved 103 public officers. Nineteen petitions did not result in recall elections because petitions were insufficient, elections were avoided as the result of court suits, and targeted officers resigned prior to the scheduled elections. Seventy-four elections, involving 191 officers, were held, with 81 officers recalled in 36 elections. Bird and Ryan reported: "The most unique plan for the avoidance of recall elections was evolved by a councilmanic majority of the city of Watts. The 'ins' conceived the scheme of waiting until a petition for the recall of some of their number was about to be filed and then of accepting their resignations and filling the vacancies by appointment with others of their own faction."[12]

TABLE 4.2
Summary of Recall Movements in
Cities under 20,000 Population

Summary Statement	Number	Number of Officials Involved
Number of cities from which information secured	172	
Number of cities in which recall petitions filed	50	
Number of times recall petitions filed	103	264
Number of times held insufficient	17	46
Number of times election averted by litigation	10	23
Number of times election averted by resignation	2	4
Number of times election held	74	191
Number of times recall successful	36*	81

*In two cases that are included in this number, certain officials were sustained and others removed.

Source: Frederick L. Bird and Frances M. Ryan, *The Recall of Public Officers: A Study of the Operation of the Recall in California* (New York: Macmillan, 1930), p. 111.

Relative to cities with populations of 20,000 to 100,000, voters in Bakersfield, Riverside, and San Diego each employed the recall four times, voters in Long Beach and San Bernadino each utilized the recall on three occasions, voters in each of four cities used the device twice, and voters in five cities employed it once.[13] Table 4.3 presents summary data on the use of the recall.

TABLE 4.3
Summary of Recall Movements in
Cities of 20,000–100,000 Population

Summary Statement	Number	Number of Officials Involved
Number of cities in 20,000–100,000 group	22	
Number of cities in which recall petitions filed	14	
Number of times recall petitions filed	31	58
Number of times held insufficient	3	3
Number of times election averted by litigation	6	11
Number of times election held	22	44
Number of times recall successful	9*	14
Number of times recall failed	12*	30

*The results of one election were divided, five councilmen being sustained and two being removed.

Source: Frederick L. Bird and Frances M. Ryan, *The Recall of Public Officers: A Study of the Operation of the Recall in California* (New York: Macmillan, 1930), p. 193.

Of the 22 cities in the population group, 31 recall petitions were filed in 14 cities, 22 recall elections were held, and public officers were recalled in 9 elections. The issues in these recall elections were similar to the issues in the recall elections in the small cities — "(1) the machinations of some faction or interest, (2) malfeasance in office, (3) inefficiency, (4) failure to respond to the will of the electorate."[14]

Four recall elections were held in Los Angeles between 1904 and 1928 and resulted in the removal of a member of the council in 1905 and 1928 and of Harper in 1909.[15] San Francisco voters employed the recall on four occasions — a police judge was removed in 1913, a court terminated an attempt to recall the city attorney in 1916, an attempt to recall the district attorney in 1918 was unsuccessful, and two police judges were recalled in 1921.[16] Oakland voters frequently circulated recall petitions, but only a small number of petitions contained the required number of signatures, because the circulation period was limited to 40 days. Six petitions resulted in recall elections involving three attempts to remove the mayor and three attempts to remove members of the council; none was successful.[17]

The recall was adopted, commencing in 1918, by nine German länder (states) — Baden, Bavaria, Bremen, Brunswick, Lippe, Mecklenburg-Schwerin, Oldenburg, Saxony, and Thuringia.[18] In contrast to the recall in the United States, the recall in these länder could be employed only to dissolve the entire council and to replace its members with new members. There is no similar recall provision in the United States, but separate petitions providing for the recall of each member of a governing body can be filed.

Voters in Pasadena, California, utilized the recall in 1931 to remove all members of the board of city directors (city council).[19] One-half of the directors were elected biennially for a four-year term. Four new directors, elected in May 1931, were pledged to firing the city manager, who subsequently was persuaded to resign. Prior to his resignation, the manager discharged an employee in the office of the city comptroller who had furnished information to the new directors. The directors were deadlocked for weeks relative to the hiring of a new city manager. Various demands were made that the employee be rehired, but the new city manager took no action, because he did not want to become involved in a factional fight. Public opinion was turning against the directors when an ordinance was enacted allowing one director to be termed "mayor," even though the city charter did not provide for such an office.

The new city manager soon discovered that decisions were being made by the directors without his knowledge and advice, and items placed on the agenda by the manager often were not acted upon. William B. Munro reported that "gradually the people of the city awoke to the fact that they no longer had city manager government in anything but name."[20]

Although two directors had protested against the turmoil and factional disputes, the directors were included in the recall petitions. The Pasadena Association, which led the recall efforts, debated whether the recall should include the two directors and, according to Munro, the majority of the association members concluded: "the board as a whole was so constituted that it would never function satisfactorily. To apportion the blame among individual members did not seem practicable, nor would it serve any purpose. The charges and counter-charges of each group against the other were so tangled as to defy unraveling. To institute recall proceedings against some of the board, and not against the others, would merely intensify the factional quarrel and draw the Pasadena Association into it."[21]

The mayor was recalled by the voters in Detroit in 1930, in Seattle in 1931, and in Los Angeles in 1938. The occasional recall of a mayor is not surprising, given the fact that the mayor is required to make decisions on controversial issues and often possesses relatively broad discretionary powers that can be abused.

RECENT RECALL ATTEMPTS

A survey of the use of the recall in local governments since 1970 sheds light on the frequency of its use and the charges directed against public officers compared with an earlier period. Charles M. Price surveyed the secretary of state in 26 states to obtain data on the estimated number of local government recalls in the period 1970–79.[22] Table 4.4 contains the results of his survey, revealing that the most frequent use of the recall is in Oregon, where there were 1.17 recalls per 10,000 population, and nonuse of the recall in Hawaii, Maine, Minnesota, North Dakota, and Wyoming. California with 396 recall elections had the largest absolute number of recall elections, followed by Oregon with 280 and Michigan with 193.

Three members of the school board of the municipality of Anchorage, Alaska, were recalled on December 15, 1992, and a fourth member of the seven-member board escaped the recall election by resigning.[23] The sample ballot for two of the school board members reveals that they were charged with making decisions with two other members by means of telephone calls and without the decisions being made at a regular school board meeting (Figure 4.1). Each member maintained that the allegations were false, yet the three members were removed by votes of 73.06 percent to 26.94 percent, 67.28 percent to 32.72 percent, and 67.52 percent to 32.48 percent, respectively.

In Arizona, voters in the city of Tombstone removed two of three councilmembers subject to recall petitions, with charges against one being "failure to represent his constituents in Ward I in a professional manner" and against the second member being "total disregard of city problems — in lieu of personal vendetta. Has not represented best interest of Ward II. Non-cooperation with fellow city officials and public."[24] The following year, Camp Verde town voters recalled a member of the council with petitions stating "this business license ordinance is unfair, unwanted, unneeded, ridiculous, and discriminatory. This ordinance among many being passed without benefit to the community as a whole. Over regulation never works."[25] Pima County voters in 1994 recalled County Assessor Alan Lang, who received only 7.5 percent of the votes cast in the recall election (Figure 4.2).[26]

TABLE 4.4
Local Use in Recall Option States, 1970–79

State	Estimated Number Local Recalls*	Census Population (in thousands)	Number of Recalls per 10,000
Oregon	280	2,385	1.17
Nebraska	32	766	0.42
Alaska	15	416	0.36
Idaho	20	856	0.23
Michigan	193	9,185	0.21
Nevada	12	637	0.19
California	396	21,886	0.18
Washington	62	3,680	0.17
Arizona	25	2,335	0.11
Louisiana	35	3,928	0.09
Colorado	20	2,625	0.08
Montana	5	766	0.06
Massachusetts	15	5,778	0.03
Georgia	16	5,041	0.03
Ohio	22	10,697	0.02
New Jersey	6	7,344	0.01
South Dakota	1	688	0.01
Kansas	? (a few)		
Missouri	?		
Arkansas	?		
Texas	?		
Hawaii	0		
Maine	0		
Minnesota	0		
North Dakota	0		
Wyoming	0		

*One can only conjecture on the number of times local officials were casually threatened with recall, but it does happen occasionally in recall active states. Local election officials in California estimated that approximately 60–70 percent of recalls filed successfully qualify for the ballot. Based on the California data, it can be estimated that approximately one-half of the local officials facing a successfully qualified recall will be removed from office.

Source: Charles M. Price, "Recalls at the Local Level: Dimensions and Implications," *National Civic Review* 72 (April 1983): 203.

FIGURE 4.1
Sample Ballot

MUNICIPAL OFFICIAL BALLOT
SPECIAL ELECTION
DECEMBER 15, 1992

A
A

MUNICIPALITY OF ANCHORAGE

SAMPLE BALLOT

MUNICIPAL OFFICIAL BALLOT A
SPECIAL ELECTION
DECEMBER 15, 1992

I HAVE VOTED

HAVE YOU?

MUNICIPAL OFFICIAL BALLOT A

Question 1:   Dorothy Cox

GROUNDS FOR RECALL AS SET FORTH IN PETITION

Dorothy Cox, Anchorage School Board, committed misconduct in office and failed to perform prescribed duties by drafting, endorsing and imposing confidentially on the Superintendent, during an executive session, an action item consisting of nine new management and control policy directives that (1) were composed and developed during a round of private telephone calls among only four Board members, closed to public scrutiny, without public notice and open meetings, that (2) were never formally adopted in a regular school board meeting.

Dorothy Cox committed misconduct in office and failed to perform prescribed duties by engaging in a round of private telephone calls among only four Board members, closed to public scrutiny, without public notice and open meeting, for the purpose of secretly plotting to later vote to oust the duly elected Board President before the end of his term, without first placing this item on a published agenda, without first hearing public comments, and without deliberating with other Board members in the telephonic scheming.

STATEMENT OF OFFICIAL

Before you vote, it is important for you to know the truth about the recall.

Under state law anyone can say whatever they like when they file a recall petition, whether it is true or false. The claims made in this petition are false.

This election is really about the future of our school district and our children. Dr. O'Rourke's disregard for the School Board, and Darryl Jordan's lack of leadership on the Board, left our district unable to function. As a member of the majority of the publicly elected board, we felt a legal responsibility to try to change the ineffective direction of our district.

Now Darryl Jordan's sister-in-law, Connie Bennett, is personally attacking members of the School Board and is placing our district and our children's future at risk.

We took a risk when we decided enough was enough, but our children's future is important. We felt we needed to take action. We have been attacked for doing what is right.

I urge each of you to vote against this recall.

Let's get back to the business of working for our kids and providing the best education possible for our community.

Shall Dorothy Cox be recalled from
the office of School Board Member?   YES [+]
                                     NO [+]

TURN CARD OVER

VOTE BOTH SIDES

MUNICIPAL OFFICIAL BALLOT A

Question 2:   Walter Featherly

GROUNDS FOR RECALL AS SET FORTH IN PETITION

Walter Featherly, Anchorage School Board, committed misconduct in office and failed to perform prescribed duties by drafting, endorsing and imposing confidentially on the Superintendent, during an executive session, an action item consisting of nine new management and control policy directives that (1) were composed and developed during a round of private telephone calls among only four Board members, closed to public scrutiny, without public notice and open meetings, that (2) were never formally adopted in a regular school board meeting.

Walter Featherly committed misconduct in office and failed to perform prescribed duties by engaging in a round of private telephone calls among only four Board members, closed to public scrutiny, without public notice and open meeting, for the purpose of secretly plotting to later vote to oust the duly elected Board President before the end of his term, without first placing this item on a published agenda, without first hearing public comments, and without deliberating with other Board members in the telephonic scheming.

STATEMENT OF OFFICIAL

This recall petition alleges that I violated the open meetings laws by conspiring with three other board members to draft a letter to Mr. O'Rourke and to replace Darryl Jordan as president of the School Board.

These allegations are false. The letter to Mr. O'Rourke was drafted by me alone. The letter requested Mr. O'Rourke to comply with the policies of the Anchorage School District and with the provisions of his contract. I believe that it was my responsibility, as the Board president, to take this action.

Other board members and I did privately discuss Mr. Jordan's ineffective leadership and the need to replace him as president of the Board. However, the Alaska Supreme Court has specifically ruled that public bodies may meet in private to elect and remove their officers. Thus no violation of the open meetings laws occurred.

Unfortunately, the law permits Mr. Jordan and his supporters to make false accusations against me on this petition. The simple truth is that I have not violated any laws. What I have done is to serve you to the best of my ability. With your support, I will continue to serve you and the best interests of our community's children.

Shall Walter Featherly be recalled from
the office of School Board Member?   YES [+]
                                     NO [+]

Lejune Ferguson
Municipal Clerk
December 15, 1992

VOTE BOTH SIDES

FIGURE 4.2
Special Recall Election

SPECIAL RECALL ELECTION

STATEMENT FROM NATIONAL ORGANIZATION OF WOMEN:

WITH LESS THAN A YEAR SERVED OF HIS FOUR YEAR TERM, COUNTY ASSESSOR ALAN LANG HAS BROUGHT NATIONAL ATTENTION AND EMBARRASSMENT TO OUR COMMUNITY. HE HAS MISMANAGED HIS ELECTED OFFICE, AND HAS SHOWN EITHER ARBITRARINESS OR FAVORITISM IN MASSIVE REASSESSMENTS OF PROPERTY THROUGHOUT THE COUNTY. OF FOUR CHARGES OF SEXUAL HARASSMENT AND RETALIATION THAT HAVE BEEN FILED AGAINST HIM, TWO ARE STILL PENDING AND TWO HAVE BEEN RULED AGAINST HIM, INCLUDING FINDINGS OF ATTEMPTS TO INTIMIDATE WITNESSES AND BUG HEARINGS. HIS OFFICE IS CURRENTLY THE SUBJECT OF NUMEROUS INVESTIGATIONS.

ON OCTOBER 18 HE WAS JAILED ON CHARGES OF DOMESTIC VIOLENCE AND A TRIAL IS STILL PENDING. ALAN LANG HAS CALLED EMPLOYEES INTO HIS OFFICE WHILE DISPLAYING A GUN ON HIS DESK; COUNTY EMPLOYEES FEAR FOR THEIR JOBS AND THEIR PERSONAL SAFETY. A SHERIFF'S DEPUTY HAS BEEN STATIONED IN THE ASSESSOR'S WORK AREA TO PROTECT THE PUBLIC AND EMPLOYEES. MASSIVE FIRINGS AND THREATS OF CONTINUED FIRINGS AND RETALIATION HAVE CRIPPLED HIS OFFICE IN THE FACE OF A RECORD NUMBER OR PROTESTS OVER NEW TAX ASSESSMENT · INCREASES. HE REFUSES TO RESIGN; WE HAVE NO CHOICE BUT TO RECALL HIM.

STATEMENT FROM ALAN LANG:

ALAN LANG, YOUR PIMA COUNTY ASSESSOR, INHERITED A COUNTY ASSESSOR'S OFFICE THAT HAD GROWN UNRESPONSIVE THROUGH DECADES OF NEGLECT. SINCE TAKING OFFICE IN JANUARY OF 1993, HE HAS MADE CERTAIN THAT ALL PROPERTY IN PIMA COUNTY WAS REVALUED. SOME PROPERTIES HAD NOT BEEN REVALUED FOR OVER A DECADE. MANY HAD NOT BEEN SEEN BY AN ASSESSOR FOR 30 YEARS. NEW COMPUTER SYSTEMS AND EQUIPMENT REPLACED TECHNOLOGY DATING TO THE 1960'S AND 1970'S. THE COUNTY ASSESSOR'S OFFICE NOW OPERATES MORE EFFICIENTLY. THE ASSESSOR'S RESPONSIBILITY IS TO LOCATE, IDENTIFY, CLASSIFY AND APPRAISE AT CURRENT MARKET VALUE, LOCALLY ASSESSED PROPERTY. PROPERTY IS NOW BEING VALUED MORE ACCURATELY. APPRAISERS WHO ARE VALUING YOUR PROPERTY ARE NOW INSPECTING PROPERTIES SO THAT SERVICE AND ACCURACY IMPROVES. IN SPITE OF A RECORD NUMBER OF VALUATION APPEALS IN 1994, THE ENTIRE PROCESS WAS COMPLETED ALMOST ONE MONTH EARLY. THE PIMA COUNTY BOARD OF SUPERVISORS HAS RENEGED ON A RECOMMENDED PLAN OF DOWNSIZING WHICH ARTIFICIALLY INFLATES THE BUDGET. ALAN LANG CONTINUES TO PURSUE THE ELIMINATION OF GOVERNMENT WASTE WHILE IMPROVING CUSTOMER SERVICE, DESPITE PROTESTS FROM HIS CRITICS. ALAN LANG KEPT HIS CAMPAIGN PROMISES TO IMPLEMENT TECHNOLOGICAL ADVANCES IN THE ASSESSOR'S OFFICE AND IMPROVE PUBLIC SERVICE TO YOU.

COUNTY ASSESSOR / ASESOR DEL CONDADO

	WAITE, REX	306 →
	ARMENTA, RALPH	307 →
Vote for not more than 1	LANG, ALAN	308 →
Vote por no mas que 1	LYONS, RICK	309 →
	MURRAY, STEVE	310 →
	STRUNK, DELBERT C.	311 →

As noted, the largest number of local government recall elections are held in California. Under an order issued by U.S. District Court Judge Manuel L. Real, the Pasadena School Board, by a three to two vote, implemented in 1970 a school integration plan that generated the first recall campaign in the history of the school district as integration opponents sought to remove the three members who voted for the plan. On October 14, 1970, the district voted narrowly to retain the three members as the result of an exceptionally high turnout of black voters.[27]

University students and radical politicians in 1971 elected three radicals to the Berkeley City Council. In August 1973, a recall election was held while most students were away from the city, and D'Army Bailey, a radical black council member, was recalled by a vote of 18,567 to 11,548.[28] Bailey contended that the issue was not radicals versus others, but race. Recall proponents charged him with being uncompromising and an obstructionist who brought the government to a standstill and magnified racial conflict."[29] Approximately 40 percent of the voters participated in the election.

The recall, attracting national and international attention, was the attempt by the White Panthers, a fringe group, to recall San Francisco Mayor Dianne Feinstein in 1983. The mayor during the previous summer persuaded the board of supervisors, by an 11 to 1 vote, to enact an ordinance making it illegal to have a handgun, with a few exceptions. It would not have been surprising if the anti-gun control groups launched a recall campaign against the mayor. Formed in the 1960s, the White Panther party launched a recall campaign. Thomas W. Stevens, one of their leaders, stated that the gun control ordinance was unconstitutional and added "we're Communists. We're on the Marxist, Leninist, Maoist, Castroist side of most questions."[30] Other groups opposed the mayor because she vetoed a "live-in lover" bill and a rent-control bill, never attended the annual gay parade, and allegedly broke the hotel workers strike by arrests. The groups collected approximately 35,000 signatures.

Feinstein retained her seat in the April 26, 1983, recall election by a vote of 127,043 to 20,269 or 81.2 percent of the votes cast.[31] Absentee ballots were 36 percent of the ballots cast in the election. The mayor raised in excess of $344,000 in campaign funds, and the cost to the city of holding the election was approximately $450,000.

In December 1984, Stockton City Councilman Mark Stebbins was removed from office in a recall campaign led by former Councilman Ralph L. White, who had led the May 1984 recall campaign that Stebbins had survived.[32] White, who lost the 1983 election to Stebbins, was elected to the council in the second recall election. The charge against Stebbins was an unusual one. White, who is black, maintained that Stebbins lied when he said he was black and pointed out that Stebbins has blue eyes, light brown hair, and white skin. The district had a population that was 37 percent black and 46 percent nonwhite Hispanic.

San Diego held its first and only recall election on April 9, 1991, when the recall of city council member Linda Bernhardt was on the ballot. The petitions charged her with voting for a pay raise for herself, placing her roommate on the city payroll as her chief aide, hiring a political lobby-ing firm to raise contributions from developers to retire her campaign debt, accepting contributions from developers after promising not to accept such contributions, moving into the fifth district to campaign for a council seat, and moving out of the district after being elected to the coun-cil. She was recalled by a vote of 15,240 (70.91 percent) to 6,251 (29.09 percent).[33]

Connecticut lacks a constitutional or statutory provision specifically authorizing the employment of the recall. Nevertheless, a number of cities and towns used the state's Home Rule Act to draft charters providing for the recall. In 1985, the Connecticut Supreme Court invalidated these char-ter recall provisions.[34] Five towns — Bristol, Milford, New Haven, Strat-ford, and Westport — earlier had obtained special charters from the gen-eral assembly authorizing the use of the recall.

Milford voters on July 28, 1968, recalled an alderman and a board of education member in a campaign that revolved around Project Concern, which involved the busing of 25 "inner-city" students from New Haven to Milford public schools.[35]

A major dispute erupted in the wealthy suburban town of Westport, Connecticut, as the result of a three to two vote of the Westport Board of Education on December 7, 1970, to allow the busing of 25 black children from the city of Bridgeport to Westport schools under the Project Concern program. The town charter authorizes the employment of the recall if valid signatures equal to 15 percent of the electors are filed with the town clerk.[36] Town Clerk Joan M. Hyde on January 7, 1971, certified to the board of selectmen that 282 petitions containing 3,918 signatures of elec-tors were filed and 3,770 signatures were accepted.[37] Hyde on December 14, 1970, sought an opinion from town attorney John W. Boyd as to whether the recall provisions of the town charter were legal, and she was advised on December 15, 1970, that the provisions were legal "since they were initially proposed by the Charter commission and enacted by the Legislature as a Special Act pertaining to the Town of Westport."

The town had a population of approximately 30,000, including approx-imately 40 black middle-class families. No charge of misconduct was directed against board of education Chairperson Joan Schine, who cast the deciding vote against holding a referendum on the issue of busing the Bridgeport school children to Westport schools.

John C. Gilmore, a broadcaster and leader of the Recall Committee of Westport, stressed that he was opposed to school experimental programs run by amateurs.[38] The committee posted a letter to residents maintaining:

The smokescreen of Project Concern is being used to alter the quality and character of all our schools.

We are against this. You may not be; but we are sure you agree with us that the school board officials should not be allowed to decide the fate and future of this town.[39]

Housing for low-income families was virtually nonexistent in Westport, which, at the time, had a zoning bylaw requiring two to four acre lots for homes. Gilmore explained: "The busing of kids into this town to let them go to school and play with white kids — all that does is ease your conscience. What they should do is open up Westport and establish decent housing for blacks. Let the government use its welfare money to buy up some of these two- and four-acre places and give them to blacks."[40]

Opponents of the recall filed suit to block the recall election, and the Superior Court for Fairfield County on March 31, 1971, enjoined permanently the holding of the recall election on the ground that the town charter recall provision applied only to town officers "who have no constitutional or statutory basis for existence," and members of the Westport Board of Education are charged with duties by the state constitution and state statutes.[41]

A survey of 81 counties by the Association of County Commissioners of Georgia in 1976 revealed that only counties had state legislative authorization for the recall and that the only recall election held to date was in Douglas County in 1975.[42] Subsequently, the state constitution and statutes were amended to allow the use of the recall against all state and local government elected officers.

On May 7, 1980, three of Barrow County's four commissioners were recalled by voters fearing an increase in taxes because the commissioners had approved the underwriting of hospital revenue certificates that were to be retired with revenues generated by the hospital.[43] Dougherty County voters retained Commissioner Gil Barret on January 12, 1982, but citizens unhappy with the proposed location of the Dougherty County landfill failed to secure the required number of signatures to force the recall election of the chairman of the county commission.[44] On March 30, 1982, voters recalled all five members of the Greene County Board of Commissioners and all three members of the Jones County Board of Commissioners.[45] The Greene County commissioners were recalled because they hired a county police chief over the objection of the sheriff; the Jones County commissioners were recalled because of a sharp increase in taxes.

Whereas an attempt to recall four Richmond County commissioners who voted to create a county police department failed in March 1984 because of a lack of the requisite number of valid signatures to call a recall election, voters on November 26, 1985, recalled the entire Banks County Board of Commissioners by a two to one margin.[46] Banks County voters in 1983 had approved a bond issue to construct a new courthouse, but a dispute erupted over the location of the new building in Homer. The chairman wanted the new building to be located behind the existing courthouse, and the other two commissioners favored a site, donated by a local bank, on the outskirts of Homer that required a considerable amount of fill. A deadlock ensued because the chairman refused to approve site preparation payments.

Attempts in 1986 to recall a Bartow County commissioner for voting for a zoning ordinance and recall of a Dawson County commissioner for "excessive taxation" failed for lack of the required number of signatures.[47] Two Seminole County commissioners were subject to a recall attempt launched by voters protesting high taxes, but no recall election was held, because the commissioners resigned their positions following grand jury indictments that were *nolle prosequi* by the district attorney.[48]

Two of the five Pike County commissioners were recalled in 1987 for "poor performance of duties and nonresponsiveness to the electorate," and attempts to recall two Bryan County commissioners failed for lack of a sufficient number of valid signatures.[49]

As noted in Chapter 2, the Georgia Supreme Court in 1988 invalidated the state's recall statute.[50] This action resulted in an immediate sharp decline in the number of recall attempts, because only the voters in the counties with special legislative authorization could employ the recall. The Georgia State Legislature, however, enacted a new recall act in 1989.[51] No statewide recall election was held in the period 1986–96, but 38 local government recall elections were held.[52]

The recall is not authorized specifically by the constitution and statutes of Hawaii, but the state's constitutional and statutory home rule provisions allow the four general purpose local governments in the state to adopt charters providing for the recall.[53] The only recall election in the state was held on October 5, 1985, in Honolulu, where three members of the city council, who had changed their party registration from Democrat to

Republican, were recalled, including one who was recalled by a margin of 49.8 percent to 49.2 percent.[54] The changes in their party registrations gave the Republicans control of the city council and led to the replacement of the chairman, a Democrat, with a Republican. The three members explained that they changed their party affiliations because the change would allow them to work more effectively with the Republican mayor.

In Kansas, all 69 eligible voters cast in person or absentee ballots in the 1984 recall election of Chairman Wayne Worthington of the Valley Township Drainage District, and he was removed by one vote.[55] He was charged with refusing to allow public inspection of records, holding meetings in violation of state law, and refusing to attend meetings or secure funds allocated for the district to control floods.

Recall petitions were filed in August 1991 against two members of the board of education of the Unified School District 259 in Kansas.[56] More than 23,000 signatures were collected, with 17,995 required for a recall election. After the filing of the petitions, one member resigned. The other member was charged with violating the state open meetings act and was recalled by a vote of 37,264 to 30,369.

Voters in District 3 of Hamilton County, Kansas, recalled two county commissioners on February 6, 1996.[57] Each commissioner was charged with misconduct and incompetence in office. Specifically, they were accused of violating the Kansas open meetings law, authorizing construction of a golf course "in a clandestine fashion, the hiring of a 'big city' lawyer to concoct a financing scheme with the sole purpose of avoiding an election on the issue and payment of $80,000 for work already completed on a golf course which a private company was supposedly building (and paying for) under the finance scheme."

On August 30, 1995, voters in Ward 1 and Ward 4 of the city of Osawatomie, Kansas, recalled their respective ward member of the city council, who was charged with violating the state open meetings act by holding closed sessions and approving a three-year contract with the city manager in one of the closed sessions.[58]

On April 2, 1996, Ora Martindale survived an attempt in Kansas to recall him from the District 1 seat on the board of education of Unified School District No. 322 by a vote of 81 (64 percent) to 46 (36 percent).[59] Charges against Martindale were:

That he has repeatedly ignored school district and school board policies, including those regarding classroom visitation and evaluation of personnel, and has publicly misrepresented his actions in this matter.

That he has violated district and board policies on the handling of parent/teacher conflicts by inappropriately intervening in a process designed to settle such disputes at the lowest possible level.

That he has exceeded and abused the authority of his position on the school board for personal gains, and has misused his position as Board of Education President by actively participating in the evaluation of certified teachers.

That by placing his own interests above that of the school district he has acted contrary to the best interests of the students and patrons of the district which constitutes a failure to perform the statutory duties for which he was elected.

Martindale justified his conduct in office in the following statement:

School district policy does not prohibit a parent from visiting a classroom. You, as parents, have a right to know what is happening in your child's classroom.

The correct procedure to handle parent-teacher conflicts is to meet with the teacher, then the principal, then the superintendent. I have documentation to prove that I followed these steps.

A parent's presence in a classroom is not an "evaluation of certified teachers." At no time did I give the board documentation concerning any certified teacher. All parents have the right to state an opinion.

My only interest is the welfare of the students and the rights of parents to know what is happening to their child in the classroom.

All of these charges were discussed before lawyers representing the school board and the teachers' union. All charges against the board and against me personally were dropped by the union.

I will continue to fight for the just treatment of students and the rights of parents as long as I am your school board member. I urge you to vote FOR students and FOR parents by voting NO on this ballot.

There were 75 recall attempts of local government officers in Louisiana between February 15, 1966, and October 21, 1995.[60] Forty officers were recalled. A forty-first recall election was held, but the concerned village police chief resigned his position simultaneously with the election. A total of 29 school board members and six chiefs of police were recalled.

Thirty-five Maine cities and towns have adopted a home rule charter that authorizes voters to employ the recall, with two charters requiring 500 and 3,000 signatures, respectively, and the remaining charters requiring a specified percentage of signatures of registered voters to employ the recall, ranging from 10 percent of the vote cast for governor to 25 percent of the number of registered voters.[61]

On March 26, 1996, a special election was held in the city of Biddeford, Maine, on the question of recalling Mayor James M. Grattelo. The charter stipulates that the results of the election are not valid unless at least 40 percent of the voters registered at the time of the previous municipal election vote in the recall election.[62] The mayor was retained in office, because only 23 percent of the registered voters participated in the recall election.[63]

Maryland lacks a constitutional or statutory recall provision for other than school board members, but several local charters authorize the employment of the recall. In 1990, the mayor of the town of Brunswick, Maryland, was subject to a recall election because petition signers maintained that they had lost confidence in the mayor's ability to perform the duties of the office in general and to manage the town's finances in particular. On October 30, 1990, the mayor was recalled by a vote of 805 to 465.[64]

Although Massachusetts lacks a constitutional or statutory recall provision, the General Court (state legislature) has enacted a number of special acts allowing towns to employ the recall. In Stoughton, for example, any registered town voter is authorized "to file with the town clerk an affidavit containing the name of the officer sought to be recalled and a statement of the grounds for the recall."[65] The recall seldom has been used in the commonwealth, but three of the five Norwood selectmen who voted to discharge the town manager were recalled in 1939, and Saugus voters on August 22, 1961, recalled three of the five selectmen because the three selectmen had licensed a liquor store near a boy scout camp.[66]

Norwood voters on September 5, 1978, recalled three members of the school committee who did not vote to reduce the school budget by $600,000.[67] In June 1978, the committee approved an $11.3 million school budget and rejected the town meeting recommendation for a budget reduction. Under Massachusetts law, school committees have fiscal autonomy, and the town meeting must appropriate whatever sum the committee decides to authorize for expenditure. After prolonged discussions, four members of the committee agreed to reduce the budget by $355,000. The chairman and two other members refused to approve the reduction and were recalled. Subsequently, the four member majority of the committee faced a recall election on October 24, 1978, but were retained in office with a voter turnout of only 17 percent.

On December 9, 1978, all five members of the Easton School Committee were recalled for two major reasons.[68] The first reason was the controversy over the appointment of a new high-school principal. The committee did not appoint the assistant principal, who was favored strongly by the electorate. Second, an error in accounting, undetected for five years, necessitated a special town meeting to appropriate an additional $489,000 in 1978, thereby causing the property tax rate to increase by $12.86 per thousand dollars of assessment. Voter turnout in the recall election was 47 percent.

Voters in the town of Hanson held its only recall election on November 6, 1982, when two selectmen were recalled.[69] One selectman was charged with being "unable and incapable of managing and handling the duties of the office of selectman" and "inability to sustain the confidence of a majority of the voters of the Town of Hanson that he can carry out the duties of the office of selectman." A similar general charge was made against the second selectman, who specifically was accused of refusing "to take any action against a town official who had been indicted by a grand jury for several felonies" and straining "the relationship between the town and Local 1700 of the American Federation of State, County, and Municipal Employee's Union."

On December 13, 1984, four of the five Mansfield selectmen who voted to fire the town manager were recalled, but one recalled selectman was reelected on the same ballot.[70] The three new selectmen pledged that they would reappoint the town manager.

Four of five selectmen were removed from office in the town of Wareham on November 5, 1985, in a recall election with a turnout of 4,154 voters or approximately 34 percent of the registered voters.[71] The recalled officers were accused of interfering with the zoning board of appeals and being unfair to certain residents speaking at meetings of the board of selectmen. The recalled chairman of the board of selectmen attributed the recall petition to a longstanding feud between the originator of the petition and a selectman; each was a former chairman of the zoning board of appeals.[72]

On February 9, 1987, voters in a Hull recall election retained the four members of the seven member town planning board who were subject to recall petitions. The recall attempt was sparked when the board of selectmen and the planning board jointly appointed William Robinson, who had been defeated for reelection to the board in the spring, to fill a vacancy on the planning board.[73] Critics, who desired a moratorium on development, complained that five of the seven members of the planning board were employed in the construction industry. One petition simply stated that the member had performed his responsibilities in an unsatisfactory manner but added "grounds of recall and removal do not carry an implication of misconduct but rather carry an expression that voters desire an opportunity to recall said member prior to his expiration of term."

A two to one vote of the selectmen of Westborough, Massachusetts, not to renew the contract of the town coordinator in 1987 led to voters in a special town meeting petitioning the General Court to enact a special law allowing the use of the recall in the town.[74] The General Court enacted the requested law, but no recall election was held.[75] The town clerk reported in 1996 "there have been times when people have wanted to do it, but upon reading the process, they don't."[76]

Voters in Rockland on August 20, 1989, removed two selectmen accused of discharging the police chief without giving a reason and being rude to citizens who appeared before the board of selectmen.[77] Approximately 40 percent of the 8,693 registered voters participated in the recall election, compared with 28 percent in the March town elections.

In 1970, a recall movement was sparked in Detroit when the board of education implemented a state law by creating seven districts with a school board in each district. Concerned that the decentralized school system might perpetuate the segregated school system, the four member majority of the seven member board voted to change the feeder pattern for several high schools, thereby necessitating that many inner city black students would have to ride buses up to five miles to their schools on the outskirts of the city. The recall drive, supported by the city police union, stemmed in part from the central school board planning the boundaries of the new districts and failing to mention the boundaries during the public hearings held on the plan to decentralize the system.[78] The four members who voted for the changes were recalled.[79]

Voters in Benton Harbor, Michigan, on May 18, 1976, recalled the mayor and three city commissioners who had voted not to renew the contract of the city manager.[80]

Mayor Jesse P. Miller of Highland Park, Michigan, who defeated the incumbent mayor in a 1975 recall election, faced a recall election on February 19, 1977, on charges that he failed to eliminate pornography from the city and did not cooperate with other city officials.[81] The mayor survived the recall election by a vote of 16,525 to 5,784 in an election with a turnout of 31.53 percent of the registered voters.[82]

On May 9, 1978, Birmingham, Michigan, voters recalled three city commissioners who voted to provide housing for poor and senior citizens.[83] Approximately 34 percent of the 14,937 registered voters cast ballots, which was slightly less than the turnout of voters in the April 1978 referendum and recall election, when voters defeated the proposed housing plan and recalled three other city commissioners who had supported the plan.

Mayor Michael Boyle of Omaha, Nebraska, was reelected to a second term in 1985 with 60 percent of the votes cast. Shortly after his second inauguration, a recall campaign, generated in part by his conflicts with the police, was launched but failed to collect the required 19,669 signatures.[84] A second recall attempt was launched by Citizens for Mature Leadership in October 1986 and also focused on the mayor's conflict with police and his dismissal of Police Chief Robert Wadman, who had refused to discipline three police officers involved in the arrest of the mayor's brother-in-law, who was charged with drunk driving.[85]

The recall proponents charged the mayor with the arbitrary dismissal of the police chief, failure to sign a city council resolution commending Mothers Against Drunk Driving, conflicts with a Keep Omaha Beautiful campaign, "angry and profane telephone calls," a "cruel statement" relative to a member of the city council, and general abuse of power. Citizens for Mature Leadership collected more than 35,000 signatures, a number greater than the number of voters who cast ballots for the mayor in the general election.[86] On January 16, 1987, 98,441 voters participated in the recall election, which resulted in the removal of the mayor by a 56 percent to 44 percent margin.[87]

Voters in several other Nebraska local governments in 1987 launched 66 recall campaigns by November. Only 22 attempts were successful, including 13 officers in municipalities under 9,000 population.[88] An attempt to recall the nine member school board of School District 32 in Scotts Bluff County failed, because the voters retained the incumbents.[89]

Mayor Dick Zellaha of Alliance, Nebraska, was recalled on December 15, 1987, by a two to one vote margin.[90] He had been charged by the Committee to Recall Mayor with harassing police officers, misuse of city materials, inability to conduct the city's business in a dignified manner, and conduct unbecoming an elected officer.

In January 1971, two groups — Community Action Council and Citizens Independent League — each circulated petitions in Jersey City, New Jersey, for a recall election of Mayor Thomas J. Whelan, who had been indicted by a federal grand jury in November 1970 on extortion charges.[91] Although the league filed more than 31,000 signatures in January, City Clerk Thomas F. X. Smith determined that 13,098 signatures were invalid, and 28,670 signatures were required for a recall election.[92] However, New Jersey Superior Court Judge Samuel A. Larner, who was supervising the counting of signatures, ruled that the Community Action Council could combine its signatures with the league's signatures to produce more than the required number of signatures.[93] Nevertheless, the recall election was not held, because the mayor was convicted on federal felony charges and vacated his office.[94]

Citizens to Make Mayor-Council Government Work launched a campaign in July 1983 to recall Mayor Michael J. Matthews of Atlantic City, New Jersey, on charges that he was inept, inefficient, and responsible for excessive city spending.[95] Matthews was the first popularly elected mayor after the city changed from the commission form to the mayor-council form of municipal government. He defeated James L. Usry by 359 votes. The latter was unsuccessful in his court challenge of the election results and led two recall attempts. On March 13, 1984, voters recalled Matthews by a 7,162 (63 percent) to 4,144 (37 percent) vote and replaced him with Usry.[96] Matthews was under investigation by a federal grand jury during the recall campaign and was indicted by a grand jury on March 27, 1984.[97]

In the far west, voters in the White Pine County School District in Nevada in 1996 recalled two members of the board of school trustees on charges that funds of the district had been misappropriated and that trustees violated the trust of the citizens of the county and state.[98] The attempt to recall a third member was invalidated because the member had not served the time in office required before a recall election could be held.

On June 19, 1978, a letter of intent to circulate petitions to recall Mayor David Rusk of Albuquerque was filed with the city clerk and listed as the ground for the recall the mayor's announcement that the city would seek to purchase a $200,000 liquor license as part of a downtown revitalization program.[99] Recall proponents failed to secure the required 8,805 petition signatures by the deadline of August 18, 1978.

Mayor Edward Munoz of Gallup, New Mexico, on April 17, 1990, survived a recall attempt by a vote of 2,135 to 1,995. He maintained that the liquor industry was behind the recall move because he proposed erecting billboards at the state border notifying motorists they were about to enter "the drunken-driving capital of the nation."[100]

Mayor Dennis Kucinich of Cleveland, Ohio, in March 1978 fired Police Chief Richard Hongisto on television and thereby sparked a recall campaign that resulted in the collection of the required number of valid signatures to hold a recall election.[101] Kucinich sought a court order to have many signatures discarded on the ground that only persons who had voted in the November 1977 mayor election could sign the petitions, but the trial court and appeals court rejected his request and the Ohio Supreme Court refused to hear the appeal. In the first mayoral recall election in the city's history, the mayor survived by a 276 vote margin — 60,308 to 60,032.[102]

Recall elections have been relatively common in Oregon. Table 4.5 reveals that 67 recall elections involving 168 officials were held between

1974 and 1979, and 69 officials were recalled. School board members most frequently faced recall elections and accounted for 61 percent of the total number of such elections, followed by city councilmen (18 percent) and county commissioners (8 percent).[103] Thirty-nine of the 102 school board members subject to recall elections, 11 of the 31 city council members, and 6 of the 14 county commissioners were removed from office.[104]

TABLE 4.5
Oregon Recall Elections — 1974–79 by County

County	Officials Involved in Recall Elections	Officials Successfully Recalled	Number of Recall Elections
Clackamas	31	11	11
Douglas	24	10	8
Lane	20	6	6
Jackson	13	9	7
Marion	13	7	5
Polk	13	2	7
Linn	9	1	3
Umatilla	7	3	2
Yamhill	6	2	2
Curry	4	3	3
Columbia	4	0	2
Harney	3	3	1
Klamath	3	3	1
Coos	3	3	2
Malheur	3	2	1
Multnomah	3	0	1
Josephine	2	2	2
Washington	2	2	1
Jefferson	2	0	1
Deschutes	2	0	1
Grant	1	0	1
Total	168	69	68

Source: John Houser, *Recall Elections Since 1974* (Salem, Ore.: Legislative Research, 1980), p. 3.

Relative to Oregon officials elected at a general election, the number of votes originally cast was larger than the number cast in 22 of 33 cases, but voter turnout in recall elections was higher than in the original elections held at times other than when general elections are held.[105] Voter turnout in school board member recall elections was higher for 54 of the 59 officials involved than in their original elections.[106]

An attempt to recall Mayor Frank L. Rizzo of Philadelphia was launched on April 17, 1976, when former U.S. Senator Joseph S. Clark was the first person to sign a recall petition, with 145,448 signatures required for a recall election. The recall drive was commenced after the city announced it faced an $80 million budget deficit and would have to raise taxes. The Citizens Committee to Recall Rizzo collected approximately 211,000 signatures, but city election commissioners, by a two to one vote, on August 25, 1976, invalidated close to 70,000 signatures on technical grounds, including omission of a middle initial or improper notarization of petitions.[107] On September 16, 1976, Judge David Savitt of the Philadelphia Court of Common Pleas overturned the actions of the board of elections and noted that the invalidation was based on "strained inferences" of provisions of the city charter and was "a triumph of form over substance" that, in certain instances, involved a process that was "blatantly false and misleading."[108]

Savitt's decision, however, was reversed by a four to two vote, with one abstention, of the members of the Pennsylvania Supreme Court, who invalidated the recall provision of the Philadelphia home rule city charter.[109] The majority decision was based on a section of the commonwealth's 1874 constitution specifying procedures for the removal of public officers.[110] As noted in Chapter 2, former Dean Jefferson B. Fordham of the University of Pennsylvania Law School criticized the court for failing to consider the 1968 constitutional home rule amendment under which Philadelphia adopted the recall.

Of the 70 Pennsylvania home rule charters, 38 authorize the use of the recall, but the validity of such recall provisions has been called into question by a 1995 ruling of the Pennsylvania Supreme Court that included a review of the *Rizzo* decision.[111] The case involved Kingston Citizens for Change, which filed a petition seeking the recall of Mayor Gary R. Reese in 1995 under provisions of the municipality's home rule charter.[112] The court invalidated the charter provision by holding that all elected officers are subject to the exclusive method for their removal set forth in section 7 of article VI of the Commonwealth's constitution.[113]

A decision of the Providence, Rhode Island, Parks Commission to dismiss Parks Superintendent James W. Diamond led to a campaign to recall Mayor Vincent A. Cicanci on grounds of corruption and mismanagement.[114] Earlier in the year, the mayor was indicted on charges of extortion and beating a man he alleged was having an affair with the mayor's wife. Opponents of the mayor needed a total of 13,249 signatures or 15 percent of the registered voters to force a recall election. The city's board of canvassers disqualified the petitions for a lack of the required number of signatures, but the need for a recall was removed when the mayor resigned from office on April 24, 1984, after pleading no contest to charges of assault with a dangerous weapon and assault on a man and received a suspended five-year sentence.[115]

On February 7, 1911, voters recalled Mayor Hiram G. Gill of Seattle, Washington, who was charged with corruption, especially in the police department, and mismanagement of the lighting department.[116]

On April 3, 1970, petitions were circulated against five members of the Tacoma, Washington, city council, accusing them of agreeing to appoint Floyd Les as city manager without consulting other members of the council and awarding a cable television franchise by ignoring advice of experts.[117] The five members were recalled on September 15, 1970, by votes of 25,034 to 13,492, 25,308 to 13,072, 24,952 to 13,467, 25,131 to 13,367, and 25,407 to 12,847.[118] The city council was left without a quorum, and the governor appointed a new member to provide the council with a quorum.

On July 10, 1979, a recall election was held in the city of Puyallup, Washington, to determine whether three members of the city council — charged with holding a meeting in violation of the state open meetings law, interference with department heads, and firing of the city manager — should be removed from office. All three were retained in office by votes of 499 to 311, 527 to 311, and 407 to 238.[119]

In Wisconsin, voters on June 21, 1988, removed the three member Lawrence Town Board, who were charged with inefficiency and neglect of duty.[120] Mayor Thomas Redner of Hudson was removed from office on December 12, 1989, by voters opposed to a parimutuel race track.[121] A recall effort to remove the Sheldon Town Board chairman and two supervisors failed on September 18, 1990; they had been charged with neglect of duty.[122] Similarly, an attempt to remove three Beaver Dam city council members by the Beaver Dam Tax Action Group failed on August 6, 1991.[123] Voters in LaCrosse, however, on July 14, 1992, removed four members of the school board who had implemented the busing of students to achieve economic integration.[124]

On July 28, 1992, Hallie Town Chairman David Meier and board member Ronald Steinmetz were recalled by the Hallie Citizens Committee, which objected to special tax assessments for municipal water services.[125] Opponents of a decision to close an elementary school were successful in recalling three members of the Wittenberg-Birnamwood Board of Education in 1993. Similarly, opponents of a busing plan to integrate Asian-American students into white grade schools succeeded in recalling five school board members who had supported the plan on December 14,

1993.[126] Sheriff Steve Elmer of Green County was recalled from office in November 1993 for firing his chief deputy.[127] On January 25, 1995, three Mineral Point school board members who supported construction of a new school survived an attempt by Responsible Pointers to remove them from office.[128] Although members of the school board are elected at-large, candidates for election in a recall election must seek election to particular seats.

SUMMARY AND CONCLUSIONS

Our review of the use of the recall to remove local elected officers from office reveals that the use is considerably more common than the use of the recall to remove state public officers, reflecting in part the much larger number of local government elected officers. The relatively few attempts to remove statewide elected officers is a product of the difficulty of collecting the requisite number of signatures.

Local government recall elections most commonly are held in California, Michigan, and Oregon — states that have numerous local governments with recall provisions. Charges against public officers contained in recall petitions cover a gamut of subjects and may be specific or broad. The nature of the charges generally has been similar over the years, although charges involving liquor interests were made more commonly during the early years of the recall and charges involving school busing for racial integration purposes did not appear until the 1960s.

Recall petition charges generally relate to malfeasance, misfeasance, and policy differences. The evidence reveals that the recall has not been overused or employed frivolously.

Chapter 5 evaluates the recall as a governmental instrument by examining in detail the arguments of the proponents and opponents.

NOTES

1. H. S. Gilbertson, "Conservative Aspects of the Recall," *National Municipal Review* 1 (April 1912): 207.
2. Ibid., p. 208.
3. Ibid., pp. 208–9.
4. Ibid., p. 209.
5. Ibid., p. 210.
6. F. Stuart Fitzpatrick, "Some Recent Uses of the Recall," *National Municipal Review* 5 (July 1916): 381.
7. Ibid.

8.   Ibid., p. 382.

9.   J. Otis Garber, "The Use of the Recall in American Cities," *National Municipal Review* 15 (May 1926): 260.

10.   Ibid.

11.   Frederick L. Bird and Frances M. Ryan, *The Recall of Public Officers: A Study of the Operation of the Recall in California* (New York: Macmillan, 1930).

12.   Ibid., p. 107.

13.   Ibid., p. 191.

14.   Ibid., p. 201.

15.   Ibid., p. 248.

16.   Ibid., p. 250.

17.   Ibid., pp. 259–70.

18.   Roger H. Wells, "The Initiative, Referendum, and Recall in German Cities," *National Municipal Review* 18 (January 1929): 32.

19.   William B. Munro, "Pasadena Uses the Recall," *National Municipal Review* 21 (March 1932): 166.

20.   Ibid., p. 163.

21.   Ibid., p. 165.

22.   Charles M. Price, "Recalls at the Local Level: Dimensions and Implications," *National Civic Review* 72 (April 1983): 199–206.

23.   Letter to author from Municipality of Anchorage Election Coordinator Rosemary Sliz, dated June 3, 1996.

24.   Letter to author from City of Tombstone Clerk Regina Duran, dated March 12, 1996.

25.   Letter to author from Camp Verde Deputy Town Clerk Susan Marshall, dated March 4, 1996.

26.   Letter to author from Pima County Elections Manager Mitch Etter, dated April 1, 1996.

27.   Steven V. Roberts, "Pasadena Voters Support School Board Members Who Back Integration Plan," *New York Times*, October 15, 1970, p. 28.

28.   "Black Councilman Loses in Berkeley Recall Vote," *New York Times*, August 23, 1973, p. 26.

29.   "New Ouster Move on Coast Ends Term of a Councilman," *New York Times*, December 22, 1984, p. 10.

30.   Wallace Turner, "Fringe Group Forces Ouster Vote on Coast Mayor," *New York Times*, February 9, 1983, p. A24.

31.   Wallace Turner, "San Francisco Mayor Jubilant Over Recall Victory," *New York Times*, April 28, 1983, p. A14.

32.   "New Ouster Move on Coast Ends Term of a Councilman," p. 10.

33.   Letter to author from San Diego City Clerk Charles G. Abdelnour, dated April 9, 1996.

34.   *Simons v. Canty*, 195 Conn. 524 (1985).

35. Letter to author from Milford City Clerk Alan H. Jepson, dated July 16, 1996.

36. *Charter of the Town of Westport, Connecticut*, chap. 30, § 8.

37. Legal documents and correspondence provided to author by Westport Town Clerk Joan M. Hyde, April 2, 1996.

38. Douglas Robinson, "Drive to Recall School Board Head Divides Westport," *New York Times*, December 22, 1970, p. 35.

39. Ibid.

40. Ibid., p. 37.

41. *Sherman et al. v. Kemish et al.*, case no. 142221, Connecticut Superior Court for Fairfield County, March 31, 1971.

42. "Recall Provisions Rare in Georgia," *Georgia County Government Magazine* 28 (August 1976): 44.

43. "Recall Eliminates Three in Barrow County," *Georgia County Government Magazine* 32 (May 1980): 44.

44. "Recall Fails Against Barrett of Dougherty," *Georgia County Government Magazine* 33 (February 1982): 67.

45. "Recall Successful in Jones and Greene," *Georgia County Government Magazine* 33 (April 1982): 13.

46. "Recall Fails in Richmond," *Georgia County Government Magazine* 35 (April 1984): 21; "Banks County Recalls Three Commissioners," *Georgia County Government* 37 (December 1985): 53.

47. "Recall Fails in Bartow County," *Georgia County Government* 37 (June 1986): 76; "Dawson Recall Results Fall Short in County," *Georgia County Government* 38 (July 1986): 40.

48. "Two Seminole Officials Resign Before Recall," *Georgia County Government* 39 (July 1987): 2.

49. "Two Vacancies in Pike County Due to Recall," *Georgia County Government* 38 (April 1987): 33; "Recall Results Mixed in Bryan, Haralson," *Georgia County Government* 39 (January 1988): 11.

50. *Mitchell v. Wilkerson*, 372 S.E.2d 432 (GA. 1988).

51. *Official Code of Georgia Annotated*, §§ 21-4-1–21-4-20.

52. Letter to author from Director H. Jeff Lanier of the Georgia Election Division, dated April 18, 1996.

53. *Constitution of Hawaii*, art. VIII, §§ 1–2; *Hawaii Revised Statutes*, chap. 50.

54. "Officials Who Joined G.O.P. Lose Recall Vote in Honolulu," *New York Times*, October 7, 1985, p. A17; letter to author from City Clerk Genny Wong, dated April 24, 1996; see also *Revised Charter of the City & County of Honolulu*, §§ 12-101–12-103.

55. "Kansas Recall Decided by One-Vote with One Hundred Percent Turnout," *Election Administration Reports* 14 (March 5, 1984): 5.

56. Letter to author from Sedgwick County, Kansas, County Commissioner of Elections Marilyn K. Chapman, dated March 13, 1996.

57. Letter to author from Hamilton County Clerk Beverly Holdren, dated April 12, 1996.

58. Letter to author from Miami County, Kansas, County Clerk Kathy Peckman, dated March 7, 1996.

59. Letter to author from Pottawatomie County Clerk Gwen Harris, dated April 3, 1996.

60. Letter to author from Louisiana Secretary of State Fox McKeithen, dated April 8, 1996.

61. Geoffrey Herman, "Municipal Charters: A Comparative Analysis of 75 Maine Charters," *Maine Townsman*, August 1992, p. 12.

62. *Charter of the City of Biddeford, Maine*, art. 7, § 5.

63. Letter to author from the Biddeford, Maine, City Clerk, dated June 24, 1996.

64. Letter to author from City Administrator Richard B. Weldon, Jr. of Brunswick, Maryland, dated May 13, 1996.

65. *Massachusetts Acts of 1921*, chap. 400, §§ 21–27.

66. "Saugus Selectmen Recalled," *Worcester* (Mass.) *Telegram*, August 24, 1961, p. 6; *Report Relative to Recall of Local Officials* (Boston: Massachusetts Legislative Research Council, 1979), p. 46.

67. *Report Relative to Recall of Local Officials*, pp. 45–46.

68. Ibid., pp. 43–44.

69. Letter to author from Hanson Town Clerk Sandra Harris, dated March 30, 1996.

70. Letter to author from Mansfield Town Clerk Judith F. Scott, dated November 23, 1982; Joan Vennochi, "Mansfield Split After Recall Election," *Boston Globe*, December 15, 1982, p. 29.

71. Ray Richard, "Wareham Unseats 4 of 5 Selectmen," *Boston Globe*, November 6, 1985, pp. 1, 32.

72. "Wareham Selectmen are Challenged," *Boston Globe*, August 30, 1985, p. 64.

73. Letter to author from Hull Town Clerk Janet Bennett, dated March 29, 1996; Susan Bickelhaupt, "Petition Asks Recall of Planners," *Boston Globe*, November 27, 1986, p. 29.

74. *1987 Annual Report* (Westborough, Mass.: Town of Westborough, 1987), pp. 70–74.

75. *Massachusetts Laws of 1987*, chap. 311.

76. Letter to author from Westborough Town Clerk Nancy J. Yendriga, dated April 29, 1996.

77. "Voters Boot Two 'Rude' Selectmen," *Keene* (N.H.) *Sentinel*, August 21, 1989, p. 8.

78. Jerry M. Flint, "Integration Plan Fought in Detroit," *New York Times*, June 13, 1970, p. 51.

79. Jerry M. Flint, "Michigan Blacks Wary on School Change," *New York Times*, October 4, 1970, p. 60.

80. "Mayor and Commissioners Recalled," *International City Managers Newsletter* 57 (June 21, 1976): 3.

81. William K. Stevens, "Detroit Suburb that Recalled Its Mayor Voting Today on Recall of His Successor," *New York Times*, February 19, 1977, p. 11.

82. Letter to author from Highland Park City Clerk Jean Green, dated February 13, 1984.

83. "Michigan Town Recalls 3 in Dispute Over Housing," *New York Times*, May 10, 1978, p. 18.

84. William Robbins, "Opponents of Omaha Mayor Pressing Recall Effort Today," *New York Times*, November 4, 1986, p. A16.

85. Ibid.

86. William Robbins, "Omaha Mayor Battling on Eve of a Recall Vote," *New York Times*, January 13, 1987, p. A16.

87. "Omaha, Neb. Mayoral Recall Produces Large Voter Turnout," *Election Administration Reports* 17 (January 19, 1987): 6–7.

88. "Nebraska Voters Discover Recall Elections for Local Officials," *Election Administration Reports* 17 (November 23, 1987): 5.

89. Ibid.

90. Charlotte F. Ahern, "Voters Change Their Minds, Recall Elected Officials," *City & State* 5 (January 4, 1988): 28.

91. Thomas F. X. Smith, *The Powerticians* (Secaucus, N.J.: Lyle Stuart, 1982), pp. 261–62; "31,000 Ask Recall of Mayor Whelan," *New York Times*, January 12, 1971, pp. 1, 22.

92. Fox Butterfield, "Recall Petitions on Whelan Voided," *New York Times*, January 30, 1971, pp. 1, 31.

93. Ronald Sullivan, "Jersey City Petitions Held Valid for Recall Vote," *New York Times*, March 9, 1971, p. 62.

94. Letter to author from Jersey City, New Jersey, City Clerk Thomas F. X. Smith, dated February 24, 1984.

95. Donald Janson, "Committee Seeks Recall of Atlantic City's Mayor," *New York Times*, July 12, 1983, p. B4.

96. "Atlantic City Mayor Recalled, Replaced, Still Challenging Petition Sufficiency," *Election Administration Reports* 14 (March 19, 1984): 5.

97. Alfonso A. Narvaez, "Ex-Atlantic City Mayor Indicted on Federal Charges of Extortion," *New York Times*, March 28, 1984, pp. 1, B2.

98. Letter to author from White Pine County School District Interim Superintendent Virginia B. Terry, dated July 15, 1996.

99. Letter to author from Albuquerque City Clerk Mille Santillanes, dated April 15, 1996.

100. Jonathan Walters, "Mayor Won't Drop Liquor Issue," *Governing* 3 (July 1990): 60.

101. Iver Peterson, "Mayor's Personality Sparked Cleveland Recall, Foes Say," *New York Times*, June 14, 1978, p. A19.

102. "Cleveland Mayor Survives Recall Vote: Recount Due," *Knickerbocker News*, August 14, 1978, p. 17A.

103. John Houser, *Recall Elections Since 1974* (Salem, Ore.: Legislative Research, 1980), p. 3.

104. Ibid., p. 4.

105. Ibid.

106. Ibid.

107. Christopher Lydon, "Court Set on Rizzo Recall Petition," *New York Times*, August 26, 1976, p. 19.

108. Ben A. Franklin, "Court Backs Petition on Rizzo Recall Vote," *New York Times*, September 17, 1976, p. 1.

109. "Vote to Recall Rizzo is Barred by Court," *New York Times*, October 1, 1976, pp. 1, A13.

110. *Constitution of the Commonwealth of Pennsylvania*, art. 6, § 7. The original section 4 was renumbered by a 1966 constitutional amendment as section 7.

111. *In re Petition to Recall Reese*, 665 Atl.2d 1162 (1976).

112. *Kingston (Pennsylvania) Home Rule Charter*, § 704.

113. *In re Petition to Recall Reese*, 665 Atl.2d 1162 at 1167 (1976).

114. "Recall Effort Against Mayor of Providence Is Under Way," *New York Times*, October 24, 1983, p. A16.

115. "Providence Mayor Receives Felony Sentence in Assault," *New York Times*, April 24, 1984, p. A14.

116. "Recall in Seattle," *Outlook* 97 (February 25, 1911): 375–76.

117. "Tacoma's Mayor Facing a Recall," *New York Times*, April 5, 1970, p. 33.

118. Information provided by Art Seeley of the Pierce County (Washington) Auditor's Office on April 10, 1984.

119. Ibid.

120. Gary Johnson, "Lawrence Voters Kick Town Board Out of Office," *Eau Claire Leader*, June 22, 1988, p. 1.

121. "Hudson Mayor Defeated in Recall," *Eau Claire Leader*, December 12, 1989, p. 1.

122. "Town Recall Effort Fails," *Eau Claire Leader*, September 19, 1990, p. 1.

123. "Recall Votes Fail to Oust Alderman," *Wisconsin State Journal*, August 7, 1991, p. B2.

124. "School Chiefs Ousted in Recall Election," *Wisconsin State Journal*, July 15, 1992, p. 1.

125. "Officials Out," *Wisconsin State Journal*, July 29, 1992, p. 1.

126. "Wausau Busing Foes Triumph," *Wisconsin State Journal*, December 15, 1993, p. 1.

127. "Green Sheriff Fires Top Deputy: Same Move Brought Fatal Recall," *Wisconsin State Journal*, May 12, 1994, p. 1.

128.   Ed Trevelen, "3 Veterans Survive Recall Vote," *Wisconsin State Journal*, January 26, 1995, p. 1.

5

The Recall: An Evaluation

The recall is a modification of conventional representative government and reflects the historical citizen distrust of governments and government officers (as explained in Chapter 1) and the desire of voters to be able to hold elected officers continuously responsible. The early debates over the desirability of the recall, an unconventional device, involved emotional arguments, particularly with respect to the recall of judges and judicial decisions. Experience with the recall has led in general to the evaporation of most emotional arguments, but strong views are held by both proponents and opponents. The recall raises fundamental questions about the nature of representative government and the role of the electorate in the governance process.

The proverbial deference of candidates for elective office to public opinion is well-known. The key question is the extent to which the successful candidates should defer to the sentiments of the electorate on major divisive issues. Is the recall needed as a spur to ensure that elected representatives will be truly representative of their constituents? The device clearly is a perpetual reminder that sovereignty resides in the voters.

This chapter evaluates the recall by examining the arguments of proponents and opponents in light of experience with the recall described in Chapters 3 and 4. These arguments interestingly date to the early part of the twentieth century. Conclusions about the desirability and efficacy of the recall are drawn and are utilized in Chapter 6 to develop model recall provisions for state or local governments that decide to adopt the recall or reform existing recall provisions.

ARGUMENTS IN FAVOR

Five major arguments have been developed and forcibly advanced in support of the recall by its early proponents who were populists, progressives, and municipal reformers seeking to make elected government officers more fully accountable to the electorate. Not surprisingly, several of these arguments also were advanced in support of the initiative and the protest referendum that frequently were promoted jointly with the recall as reform measures, particularly at the local government level.

Strengthen Popular Control

The recall is supported on the same ground as electoral democracy; that is, the recall strengthens popular control of government by allowing voters to remove public officers who are corrupt or incompetent or who fail to reflect accurately the views of the electorate on major issues. In other words, voters should possess the power to replace officers who are "misrepresentatives" instead of "representatives" of the electorate. The recall clearly is founded upon the right to petition for the redress of grievances guaranteed by the U.S. Constitution and most state constitutions.

Andrew Jackson placed great faith in the "common man" and distrusted government officers. In a December 8, 1829, message to the U.S. Senate and House of Representatives, he stressed:

There are perhaps few men who can for any great length of time enjoy office and power, without being more or less under the influence of feelings unfavorable to the faithful discharge of their public duties. . . . They are apt to acquire a habit of looking with indifference upon the public interests, and of tolerating conduct from which an unpracticed man would revolt. Office is considered as a species of property; and Government rather as a means of promoting individual interests than as an instrument created solely for the service of the people. Corruption in some and in others a perversion of correct feelings and principles divert Government from its legitimate ends, and make it an engine for the support of the few at the expense of the many.[1]

Jackson was arguing for rotation in office as means of protection for the citizenry against corruption and promotion of self-interest. The

Jacksonian theory of voter control through a multiplicity of elected officers serving short terms proved to be inadequate and facilitated boss rule, because voters lacked information to discriminate among large numbers of candidates.

Although the recall was only six years old, William Allen White wrote in 1910 that "this tightening grip of the people upon their state government . . . has been intelligent, gradual, well-directed growth of popular power."[2] Delos F. Wilcox, an advocate of popular government, compared the elected officer with an ambassador plenipotentiary and added that "he is a servant with power, but he had his specific instructions or is presumed to be acquainted with his master's will, and if he fails to recognize his responsibility or if he misinterprets his instructions, he may be recalled at any time."[3]

Herbert S. Swan maintained that the impeachment process can be utilized only if malfeasance is involved and that officers guilty of misfeasance or nonfeasance are immune from removal by the process.[4] He also pointed out that a candidate when elected may have held views comporting with the views of the electorate on particular issues but that future events may have changed the views of the electorate and the officer holds to his original positions. Under such circumstances, he argued, voters should be able to exercise popular control by removing the officer. He emphasized that "so long as the voter may not at any time recall his chosen representatives his franchise is only a remnant. The right to elect and the right to recall — each complements the other. A full and complete electoral franchise includes both."[5]

While serving as governor of New Jersey, Woodrow Wilson advocated the recall of administrative officers as a device for restoring to them "what the initiative and referendum restore to legislators — namely, a sense of direct responsibility to the people who chose them."[6] More recently, Charles M. Price made a similar point in different terms: "The recall strikes at incumbent arrogance. Given all of the advantages of name recognition, availability of money and staff, incumbents normally win reelection in the American system. This, in turn, means that some officeholders can become smug or disdainful in their attitude toward the public. Incumbents in recall-vulnerable communities are forced to be more responsive to the public since they cannot assume they have a lock on their offices."[7]

Electoral System Failures

If the electoral system employed by a government produced public officers who performed all duties conscientiously in accordance with the highest ethical standards and were guided in decision making by the concerns of the majority of their constituents, there would be no need for the recall.[8] As noted, the long ballot makes it difficult for the voter to discern the quality of each candidate and his or her views on major issues. The widespread use of the single-member district system with plurality elections often results in candidates gaining office with only a minority of the votes cast if there are three or more candidates. These candidates may or may not represent adequately the views of the majority of the electorate, particularly if the majority split its votes among two candidates and, thereby, allowed a candidate with a minority of the votes to win the election.

Similarly, the at-large plurality city council electoral system can enable one group — racial, economic, social class — with a minority of the votes to dominate the council and to shut out the views of a majority of votes on certain crucial issues. Semiproportional electoral systems — limited voting and cumulative voting — and the single-transferable vote system of proportional representation produce governing bodies more representative than bodies elected by the single-member district system or the at-large system.[9]

Furthermore, one can argue that there is a need for the recall even if the electoral system does not have the problems associated with the single-member district and at-large systems if there is no incumbent seeking reelection. Wilcox made a strong case for the recall in 1912: "What is more elusive than the character and fitness of a candidate in the heat and haste of an electoral campaign. Who can know the secret weaknesses of his nature? Who can see the invisible strings that are attached to him? . . . The need still remains for a practicable means of discharging public officials who no longer enjoy the confidence of the electorate. The recall is such a means."[10]

Albert M. Kales, an early supporter of the recall, in 1914 linked the emergence of the recall to deficiencies in the electoral system in the following terms:

The movement for the recall began just as soon as it was generally perceived that our system of frequent elections to fill a large number of offices did not prevent the extra-legal government from placing in office men loyal to it. The movement for the recall is the frankest admission that this system of elections has been a failure. The real cause for this failure was the fact that too much voting had overloaded the voter and his resulting political ignorance had delivered him into the hands of an organization which in effect cast his ballot for him.[11]

Frederick L. Bird and Frances M. Ryan advanced a similar argument in 1930: "When the electorate realizes more fully that it is frequently preyed upon, through its government, by certain classes of corporations, it will find even more effective use for the recall."[12] Writing in the vein, George E. Mowry explained that California, in common with several other states early in the twentieth century, "had only the shadow of representative government, while the real substance of power resided largely in the Southern Pacific Railroad Company. To a degree perhaps unparalleled in the nation, the Southern Pacific and a web of associated economic interests rule the state."[13]

The recall, in common with the sword of Damocles, reminds public officers that corruption, inefficiency, or failure to represent adequately the views of the majority of voters will not be tolerated. The device clearly has an admonitory effect on a discrete public officer, encouraging him or her to perform official duties in an ethical and responsible manner. Walter E. Weyl, an early proponent of the recall, pointed out in 1912 that the threat of never being reelected for failing to heed public opinion was not efficacious, because legislators "shrewdly interpreted the word 'never' in a Gilbertian sense, as meaning hardly ever."[14]

Primarily a product of the progressive movement, the recall also was influenced by the other major movements of the time — municipal reform, administrative management, scientific management, and short ballot. The municipal reform movement, in particular, sought to apply the corporate form of business organization and its guiding principles to municipalities.[15] Proponents of the recall described it as nothing more than the application of sound business principles to public affairs and emphasized that every business employer possesses the right to discharge an employee whose performance is unsatisfactory for any reason.[16] They also argued that, because an elected officer had the right at any time to resign his or her position, it would be absurd if voters were denied the right to discharge the officer for unsatisfactory performance.

Herbert Croly contended in 1915 that the recall protects the public from the betrayal of their interest by public officers and added: "If the choice had to be made between a relatively inefficient but entirely popular government, and one which was highly efficient but alien to popular sentiment, any convinced democrat would select the first alternative. Above all else a democratic government must be kept closely in touch with public opinion."[17]

In 1961, the Massachusetts Supreme Judicial Court wrote that the recall is "a device to make elected officers responsive to the opinions of the voters on particular issues. The implication of a recall under the statute is not of misconduct, but only that the voters prefer not to have the recalled official continue to act."[18] The recall, of course, can be utilized to remove officers guilty of misconduct.

Reduction of Alienation and Voter Education

Failures of the electoral process have produced many alienated citizens who are convinced that they are being shortchanged by a closed decision-making process.[19] We use the term "alienation" to mean citizen perceptions that government is unrepresentative and unresponsive and that the average person is powerless to influence significantly the policymaking process. Central to the concept of alienation are citizens' feelings of political impotence and distrust of public officials.

In the view of alienated citizens, traditional citizen participation mechanisms, including public hearings and advisory committees, involve little more than a meaningless ritual. A sense of helplessness pervades the minds of many citizens, who have withdrawn from participation in the political system because they are convinced that so-called representative institutions are incapable of reforming themselves.

The availability of the recall, according to its proponents, has the potential for increasing voter interest in public affairs and reducing alienation because the electorate possesses a device for removing public officers in whom they have lost confidence.

Recall proponents maintain that the device has the related advantage of producing discussion and debate on particular issues, thereby leading to the education of the public. Most recall election campaigns result in the issues generating the removal effort being publicized widely. Proponents are willing to admit that these campaigns can misinform as well as inform the public.

Removal of Restrictions

Several state constitutions, commencing in the 1830s, were amended to incorporate prohibitions and restrictions upon the state legislature as fear of a powerful governor gave way to fear of an irresponsible legislature as the result of scandals associated with canal and railroad building.[20] Subsequent legislative abuses led to the "home rule" movement, which sought constitutional protection against interference by the state legislature with the operations of general purpose local governments and the grant of broad discretionary authority to such governments.[21]

Experts agree that many of the constitutional prohibitions and restrictions add to the cost of government and generally have been inefficacious in achieving their stated objectives because state legislators and chief executives have employed ingenuity to evade many of the prohibitions and restrictions. It is argued that the recall increases the willingness of voters to remove prohibitions and restrictions from state constitutions and local government charters that hamper the operation of and increase the cost of government and lead to officers devoting time to finding ingenious ways of evading the restrictions.

Voters, it is contended, do not need to rely upon constitutional and local charter restrictions and prohibitions to protect their interests because they possess the authority to remove any public officer abusing the public trust. In addition, citizen understanding of governmental operations will be promoted by less complicated state constitutions and local charters that are confined to fundamentals. Croly explained in 1915 that "in the absence of the recall a democracy can scarcely be blamed for reducing the length of official terms, and for using one department to check another."[22]

Lengthening of Terms of Office

A fifth argument in favor of the recall is that it encourages the electorate to approve proposed constitutional and local government charter amendments increasing the term of office of elected officers that, in many jurisdictions, is too short and necessitates continuous campaigning for reelection. Wilcox in 1912 maintained:

Short terms of office and a multiplicity of elective officials impose a double burden both on the electorate and on the officials themselves. . . . The less important the office, the heavier is the proportional burden of the campaign. The shorter the term, the less worth while it is to undertake the campaign at all. On the other hand, the people assume impossible burdens when they attempt to discriminate between hundreds of unknown candidates for scores of obscure offices. . . . The long ballot is the result, in part, of the people's jealousy of irresponsible power. They have demanded the right to retain over many public officials the only sort of popular control that, until recently, has been thought possible. But the device has failed, in many cases utterly and ignominiously. The development of irresponsible party organizations with complete control of the nominating machinery has turned the long ballot into an instrument of tyranny, inefficiency, and corruption.[23]

Continuous campaigning for reelection, of course, is undesirable, because the public officers are forced to take time away from their official duties to further their reelection prospects and may become even more indebted to special interests that contribute campaign funds. It must be admitted, however, that continuous campaigning does have the advantage of keeping the officer in close contact with the views of constituents. Nevertheless, there are other effective means of gauging public opinion in the absence of continuous campaigning.

Advocates of the recall are convinced that citizens should agree to longer terms, such as an increase from two to four years, for elected officers, because the former can utilize the recall as a mechanism to maintain continuous responsibility on the part of the latter. In the view of its advocates, the recall is an admonitory device, and its existence alone is sufficient to ensure that officeholders act responsibly.

ARGUMENTS IN OPPOSITION

Twelve major arguments have been advanced in opposition to the recall, ranging from the existence of other means with due process rights guarantees to restraints placed on energetic officials by the recall to its abuses by well-financed interest groups.

Existence of More Desirable Removal Methods

The primary antipodal reason advanced against the recall is the existence of other and more effective means of removing a public officer from office that do not suffer the disadvantages of the recall, such as the removal from office of an official, by a minority of voters, who had been elected by an overwhelming majority with a high rate of voter participation.[24]

The other methods of removing public officers are employment of the impeachment process, except in Oregon, with charges preferred by one house of a bicameral state legislature and the trial by the other house or a special impeachment court;[25] legislative address (a joint resolution of the state legislature or a resolution of one house directing the governor in 28 states to remove a named officer);[26] statutory or constitutional authorization for the governor to remove officers; and constitutional or statutory provisions automatically removing an officer convicted of a felony. In addition, interpellation of officers may be conducted by a legislative body to uncover evidence that may lead to the employment of one of the above removal methods.[27] These methods of removal, however, cannot be employed simply because an officer does not follow the views of his or her constituents.

Proponents of the recall dismiss the impeachment process as an effective method to remove public officers because of the cost involved and the delays inherent in the process.[28] In fact, few officers have been impeached, tried, convicted, and removed from office. The only officer impeached and removed from office in New York state, the state with the largest number of officials, was Governor William Sulzer in 1913, and the evidence reveals that he was removed because he would not follow the orders of Tammany Leader Charles Murphy, who controlled the state legislature.[29]

Former President William H. Taft, a strong opponent of the recall of judicial officers, maintained that the goal of the recall "can all be accomplished by a provision that if the officer has neglected his duty, or is guilty of malfeasance, he may be removed after a hearing by a court or by the chief executive. This could be made as expeditious as a fair hearing would permit and need not drag through all the courts with the officer still holding his office, but the action of the first tribunal, whether judicial or executive, could oust him, and an appeal, if taken, need not suspend the effect of the ouster until a final reversal of the first decision."[30] Although the Taft argument is valid regarding nonfeasance or misfeasance, the argument does not address the question of the removal of a public officer who has violated an election campaign promise or who took an action, including voting, in opposition to the overwhelming views of his or her constituents.

Avoidance of Additional Mistakes

A second opposition argument is that voters should not be allowed to make additional electoral mistakes during the interim between general elections. In 1912, Ellis P. Oberholtzer opined:

The independent makers, administrators, interpreters, and enforcers of the law are to become the puppets of the people, to obey their changing whims or else to surrender their places to those who shall be more willing to follow popular direction. And why is this done? Because, it is said, of the corruption of legislators, governors, and judges, because of the inability of the people to choose from among their number honest and intelligent men to represent them in the halls of government. The people have failed once; they are to be given the opportunity to fail again in a larger sphere in a more menacing way.[31]

Use for Undesirable Purposes

The use of the recall for philosophical, discriminatory, and emotional reasons is undesirable, according to recall opponents. Oregon Secretary of State Norma Paulus in 1979 advanced a third argument against the recall by objecting to its employment "for philosophical reasons instead of traditional reasons of malfeasance or corruption."[32] It is clear that a major reason for the filing of petitions in 1970 to recall the chairperson of the Westport (Connecticut) Board of Education involved racial discrimination, because the petitions appeared immediately after she cast the deciding vote to authorize the enrollment of "slum" children from Bridgeport in an elementary school.[33]

Taft objected to the use of the recall while the emotions of the voters are aroused and referred to it as "part of what has not infrequently been called 'hair trigger' form of government, by which immediately upon the presentation of an issue, it shall be passed upon by the electorate."[34]

Unnecessary Restraint

A fourth objection to the recall is that it restrains unduly innovative and energetic public officers. Because the recall is similar to the "sword of Damocles," fear was expressed early in the twentieth century that the recall will encourage timorousness on the part of elected public officers. Weyl commented on the "new democracy" in 1912 with particular emphasis upon the recall by observing that the initiative and the referendum tend "to transform these legislators from representatives, possessed of personal, individual opinions . . . into mere delegates; into mere mechanical forecasters and repeaters of popular deliverances; into parrot-like, political phonographs. The recall, by keeping the popular thumb upon the recalcitrant lawgiver, acts in the same way."[35]

Weyl also maintained that an energetic statesman may resign from office or lose his or her spirit of innovation and leadership if subjected to being checked and thwarted continuously in efforts to improve the welfare of the citizenry.[36] The following year, Taft made a similar point relative to the recall: "It tends to produce in every public official a nervous condition or irresolution as to whether he should do what he thinks he ought to do in the interest of the public, or should withhold from doing anything, or should do as little as possible, in order to avoid any discussion at all."[37] Taft, a strong opponent of the recall, was convinced that had the recall been available during an earlier period of the national government, George Washington, James Madison, Abraham Lincoln, and Grover

Cleveland would have been recalled.[38] In his considered opinion, the recall is an extension of the initiative and referendum based upon the proposition "that government must follow the course of popular passion and momentary expression of the people without deliberation and without opportunity for full information."[39]

In 1981, the Association of County Commissioners of Georgia formally objected to the recall because "it enfeebles the whole process of representative government" and "in Hall County it became a tool for swift punishment of a whole board who made an unpopular, although economical decision."[40] The association added: "No one 'bats a thousand' every day. Barring evidence of gross incompetence, office holders should not be harassed by constant threats of recall. . . . Recall should be reserved for extreme circumstances."[41]

President Gil Barrett of the association, who had been subject to an unsuccessful attempt to secure the required number of recall petition signatures, pointed out in 1981 that all recall attempts "have centered on some unpopular decision a county commissioner or a whole board made. In some cases, they haven't had to be unpopular with more than a handful of people for a petition to start circulating and threatening the office holder."[42]

Critics of the recall maintained that elected public officers are delegates who are elected to use their best judgment in making decisions to advance the public interest based upon their analysis of detailed facts on issues, facts that normally are not available to citizens. Furthermore, critics register very strong objections to harassing recall petitions that are libelous and slanderous statements made by circulators of petitions. In the view of the recall's opponents, targeted public officers have their reputations blemished even if petition circulators fail to collect the required number of verifiable signatures or voters retain the officers in a recall election.

Recall proponents as early as 1912 sought to turn the argument that the recall makes innovative public officers timid to their advantage. Wilcox wrote: "Is it courage to do wrong that marks the highest conception of official duty? Is it courage to turn on the people and combat their interests? Is it courage to set up individual opinions and ride roughshod over public sentiment? What kind of official courage is good for public service? Are the Americans a servile people, happy only when they are browbeaten by officialdom? . . . Are they children that their ways should be ordered for them by the political elders?"[43]

Wilcox and Croly were convinced that voters admire courageous elected public officers. Croly in 1915 rejected the argument that the recall

automatically converts all elected officers into automatons lacking independent judgment powers.[44] In Croly's view, elected officers have a
responsibility to lead public opinion by converting voters to their views
on divisive issues. "The fact that he would constantly be threatened with
the loss of popular confidence would act upon a man of independence of
conviction as a stimulus to personal initiative. He would possess an extraordinary opportunity of recommending his opinions to the public. He
could make himself independent just in so far as he was capable of maintaining his leadership of public opinion; and only to the extent would he
as a representative official be entitled to independence."[45]

A Deterrent to Potential Candidates

The fifth argument advanced in opposition to the recall is its deterrent
effect upon many highly qualified men and women who will not seek
elective office for fear it will be employed against them as elected officers
if they take a stand on a controversial issue that is unpopular with a group
of voters. Even if the public officer wins a recall election, he or she would
have endured the harassment of a recall campaign and the added costs of
being a public officer in terms of the time and funds that must be devoted
to a defense against the charges.

Jefferson B. Fordham, a former dean of the University of Pennsylvania
Law School, commented in 1976 on the proposal that Utah should adopt
the recall in the following terms: "A compelling policy objection to the
proposal as a whole is that it has a distrustful thrust not conducive to entry
into public service by able individuals of independent spirit and lively
sensibilities. Were the measure adopted it would provide a ready weapon
for attack upon a public officer at public expense for whatever reason.
What is of primary importance is a constitutional scheme and a political
climate that are congenial to public service by individuals of the highest
quality."[46]

Writing in 1912 and in the light of then current political conditions,
Wilcox anticipated this argument by explaining that political conditions
that were not the products, but rather the progenitors, of the recall were
responsible for the reluctance of highly qualified individuals to seek
public office. "It is the unseemly striving, the expense of the competitive
canvass for voters, the secret obligations to the political machine and
the business interests that finance it, the insufferable dullness of legislative stagnation while the official performers mark time waiting for the
political impresario to nod, the innumerable checks devised under our

government to prevent decisive political action — it is these things that deter so many high-class citizens from seeking careers in the public service."[47]

Partisan Use

Recall opponents advance as a sixth negative argument against the recall its potential for employment for partisan purposes. A candidate who lost in the general election may promote a recall election in anticipation of a smaller turnout of voters and the possibility of recalling and replacing the public officer. An editorial in *Georgia County Government Magazine* asked readers to "notice how many recall campaigns are led by candidates defeated in the last election. That should tell you something."[48]

In addition, the recall may be employed to change the political party control of a legislative body. In 1983, two Democratic state senators were recalled by Michigan voters, as described in Chapter 3, and their replacements were Republicans, which gave the Republican Party control of the senate. The former Democratic majority floor leader complained that the affirmative vote to remove the two senators from office was smaller than the opposition vote in the 1982 general election.[49] He asserted that the recall stifles "visionary planning" and represents a "signal to the public that the best way to get something done is to being a recall procedure."[50]

Increased Governmental Costs

The seventh argument against the recall is that taxpayers have to fund the increase in governmental costs associated with calling and holding a special recall election and, in some jurisdictions, a second election to select a replacement for a recalled officer.

Wilcox admitted that governmental costs are increased if a recall election is held but maintained that these costs can be offset by the savings resulting from the lengthening of the term of office, which in 1912 generally was two years, thereby reducing the number of more expensive general elections by 50 percent.[51] He also was convinced that voters are willing to bear the expense of a recall election "for the sake of correcting a grave political mistake."[52]

Undesirable Simultaneous Elections

By holding a simultaneous election for a successor in the event that the public officer is removed from office, according to critics, the recall may result in the election campaign for a successor overshadowing the reasons advanced for the recall, thereby encouraging the electorate to devote inadequate attention and analysis to the question of whether the officer should be recalled.

This objection to the recall is avoided if a second election is held only if the officer is recalled. As noted, however, a second election increases governmental costs and also may have a smaller turnout of the electorate that could result in the election of a candidate in a two person race by a minority of the registered voters.

Frivolous Harassment

A ninth objection to the recall is the possibility of the circulation of frivolous recall petitions solely for the purpose of harassing conscientious public officers and possibly discouraging them from seeking reelection to office.

The White Panthers, a group of approximately 20 radicals in San Francisco, successfully collected the required number of signatures on petitions to force a recall election on April 26, 1983, on the question of whether Mayor Dianne Feinstein should be removed from office. Thomas W. Stevens, a spokesman for the organization, declared "we're on the Marxists, Leninists, Maoists, Castroist side of most questions" and sought the recall of the mayor because she signed a city ordinance banning the possession of pistols.[53] He added the ban would penalize poor persons unable to secure adequate police protection. As explained in Chapter 4, the mayor was forced to raise more than $344,000 in campaign funds to defeat the recall attempt, and the city and county of San Francisco spent approximately $450,000 to distribute an information pamphlet to each voter and to conduct the recall election.

Georgia County Government in 1988 editorialized: "In some counties recall has become a popular game played by people who enjoy being interviewed by the media and having 'power' to disrupt local government for a time. If those people who spend so much time with recall campaigns would get involved in the political process during normal election campaigns, they would have a much better opportunity to bring about positive change in government."[54]

United Concerned Parents of Oxford, Massachusetts, utilized the town charter recall provision in 1983 against three members of the school committee. In response, committee member Deborah L. Moiles wrote a letter to the editor of a newspaper, raising four questions about the petition circulators: "Who are these people who, except for their spokesperson, remain anonymous? Where are the United Concerned Parents of Oxford when budgetary cuts are proposed that affect the majority of Oxford school children? Where are they at PTO meetings when help is needed in the schools to offset the loss of aides due to budget cutbacks, or when it comes time for town meeting and support is needed for the school budget? Just how concerned are they?"[55] Moiles noted that none of the organization members had enough interest to take out nomination papers the previous year and "they have decided not to submit the 2,000 signatures they say that they have on recall petitions but instead to hold them and watch the three members of the committee they sought to recall."[56]

Abuse by Special Interest Groups

In common with the initiative and the referendum, the recall can be utilized by well-organized and well-financed organizations to achieve their special interests. Taft in 1913 alluded to the use of the recall by "malignant enemies" to prevent a public officer from performing his duties.[57] In other words, a group can intimidate an officer by threatening political recrimination in the form of the recall if the officer adopts a policy opposed by the group.

A 1979 editorial in *The Sunday Oregonian* commented: "A diagnosis of southern Oregon's recall epidemic suggests but does not conclude, that a right-wing conspiracy is one course of recall fever. Conservative elements have been driving forces in many of the recall drives."[58]

Inadequate Reason for Recall

The eleventh argument holds that the reason(s) prompting a recall election in fact may not be of such magnitude as to warrant the removal of a public officer. As explained in Chapter 2, the recall can be employed for any reason(s) in state and local governments where it is legally a political question and not a question requiring legal cause for removal.

Theodore C. Sharpe in 1971 maintained that many reasons for employment of the recall "are petty and parochial," including errors of judgment.[59] He also added that the recall has discouraged public officers from "committing glaring political sins."[60]

A clear example of an inadequate reason for using the recall was the removal from office of all members of the Easton (Massachusetts) School Committee because they appointed a person from another state, instead of the assistant principal, as the new high-school principal.[61]

Destroys Judicial Independence

Finally, opponents object to the recall of judges on the ground that they should not be subject to partisan political intrigues and forced to write opinions that will court favorable public reactions. In 1911, the American Bar Association approved a resolution denouncing the recall of judges on the ground it that destroys their independence.[62]

As explained in Chapter 1, immediately following the development of the recall, there was strong opposition to its application to judicial officers. This opposition led Taft to veto the joint congressional resolution admitting the Arizona territory to the union because the proposed state constitution authorized the use of the recall against all public officers, including judges.

Attorney Rome G. Brown argued before members of the Minnesota State Bar Association in 1911 that the recall of judges conflicts with the fundamental principles of governments in the United States and stressed:

The basic purposes and object of the judiciary are that the members of the court pass judgment only after issue is joined, with a hearing upon the facts, and then only upon and consistently with the elementary principles of personal and property rights expressly guaranteed by the fundamental law; and, further, that no member of the judicial tribunal should be influenced in any degree by outside considerations, whether in advance of, or during, or after the hearing; and that, without prejudice, and uninfluenced by any ulterior considerations, as to past, present and future, he should, in his conclusions of law, apply the law to the facts, with due regard to the constitutional guarantees, and without fear or favor or any predetermination as to the result, and that his final adjudication should be an order or decree, logically and consistently following from the facts and the conclusions of law impartially found.[63]

Opponents of the recall of judges also argued that supposed judicial evils have been exaggerated and that any that exist can be remedied by other means, including the impeachment process and removal for cause. Concern also was expressed by opponents that the existence of the recall would make it more difficult to persuade highly experienced lawyers with a judicial temperament from standing for election as judges.

Early proponents of the employment of the recall to remove judges from office were unconvinced by these arguments. To them, the recall was based upon the principle that the electorate must have a mechanism for keeping all executive, legislative, and judicial officers continuously accountable.[64] They were convinced that judges do more than simply interpret law; judges are lawmakers. So long as they function as policy determinators, proponents asserted that judges must be kept responsible to the voters in the same manner as the other policymakers — legislators and executives.

CONCLUSIONS

A weighing of the evidence marshaled by supporters and opponents of the recall clearly favors the former. The infrequent successful use of the recall to remove elected state officers — one governor, eight legislators, and one judge — offers limited evidence of the desirability of the recall. The more frequent use of the device by local government voters permits the evaluator to draw more definitive conclusions.

There can be no denying the fact that popular control of a government is increased if public officers are guilty of sins of commission or omission and aroused citizens decide to remove the officers. Admittedly, election of an officer for a short term, such as one year, is an alternative to the recall, but experience with Jacksonian democracy has revealed the inadequacy of short terms as a device for eliminating corruption in government and holding officers accountable.

The evidence also is substantial that the impeachment process, because it is a judicial one, is a slow process and, furthermore, seldom has been utilized. This process requires charges of malfeasance, misfeasance, or nonfeasance, which may not be the reason(s) for voter dissatisfaction with a public officer. If the officer's position on a major issue does not reflect the will of the electorate, the petition referendum or the recall enables voters to rectify their differences with the officer. It is difficult to disagree with Swan's conclusion in 1912 that the recall complements the regular electoral process.[65]

The evidence is overwhelming that the most common electoral system — the plurality single-member district system — often results in the selection of officers who are not representative of their constituency.[66] The problem tends to be most severe if a three-way race for an office results in the election of a candidate with a minority of the votes cast. The danger of misrepresentation is increased significantly if voter turnout in the election was low.

Threats by voters to cast ballots for another candidate in the forthcoming general election may have little deterrent effect on an elected officer if there always are three or more candidates seeking the office. The recall, on the contrary, makes the officer face the voters on a single issue — removal from office — and there are not other candidates to split the voters.

There may be less need for the recall if incumbent officers are reelected, because their records are known to the voters. In many instances, it is difficult for the electorate to determine the qualifications of candidates if no incumbent is seeking reelection. Under such circumstances, the recall affords the voters the opportunity to correct an election mistake rather than waiting for the scheduled general election to take corrective action.

The recall is an excellent defensive weapon that voters can employ if a public officer violates the public's trust by corrupt or unethical behavior or disregards the opinion of the majority of the electorate on a given issue. With respect to the later point, Chapter 3 describes the 1971 recall of an Idaho senator and a representative for voting a salary increase for state legislators after conferring with constituents, who were opposed to the increase. Chapter 3 also examines the recall of a Republican representative in California who voted for a Democrat to be speaker of the assembly.

One also can make a strong case for the employment of the recall by the electorate if a legislator casts a vote on a major issue directly opposite to the stand he or she took as a candidate. If a recall election is called under such circumstances, the officer has a full opportunity to explain the discrepancy between the campaign promise and the vote and to convince a majority of the electorate that the vote was in their best interests.

Proponents of the recall maintain that the device will reduce the number of alienated citizens who have withdrawn completely from participating in the political process because they will have the ability to remove officers. Evidence is lacking that the availability of the recall is sufficient to convince alienated voters to participate in the political process on a regular basis.

The recall may have influenced constitutional convention delegates, local government charter commission members, and the electorate to remove prohibitions and restrictions in constitutions and charters on legislative bodies. Although a number of prohibitions and restrictions have been removed since the recall became available, it is doubtful that the recall alone was responsible for such removals, because the device tended to be adopted in conjunction with adoption of the initiative and protest referendum, which also increase popular control of government.

There is a positive correlation between the adoption of the recall and the lengthening of the term of office of many elected officers. The availability of the recall, initiative, and protest referendum no doubt helped to convince voters to approve constitutional amendments establishing longer terms of office. Nevertheless, terms of office have been lengthened in states lacking these popular control devices, such as New York.

Turning our attention to the arguments of opponents, they contend that the impeachment process, legislative address, removal of public officers by the governor, and automatic removal of officers convicted of a felony are more desirable removal methods. These methods seldom have been employed and require a considerable period of time for implementation. Whereas automatic vacating of a public office upon a felony conviction of the incumbent is swift, this method cannot be employed to remove an officer for misfeasance, nonfeasance, or an action opposed by a majority of his or her constituents.

Oberholtzer argued in 1912 that the recall is undesirable because it enables voters to make another error in attempting to correct the first error made in the general election.[67] This argument, of course, is an undemocratic one, premised upon the belief that voters are incapable of exercising perspicacious judgment in casting ballots for candidates for public office. On the contrary, we place our faith in the common sense of the voters over a period of time.

There can be no denying the fact that the recall has the potential for use for racial discrimination purposes. Fortunately, the recall seldom has been used for such purposes and has not been so used during the previous two decades.

Taft objected to the recall because he believed that the decisions made would be unsound because the electorate's emotions would have been aroused when they cast ballots.[68] His fears clearly were based upon a misunderstanding of the recall process, which does not permit an immediate vote on removing an officer when an emotional issue arises. In addition to the common prohibition of the use of the recall during the first six months or last six months of an officer's term, petitions must be circulated and verified, which requires a period of several weeks. Furthermore, court challenges of the sufficiency of the number of signatures or charges where required may produce an additional delay in the conduct of the recall election. In general, emotions have sufficient time to cool before a recall election is held.

Does the recall restrain unnecessarily innovative and energetic public officers? Determining the impact of the existence of the recall on the behavior of elected officers is a difficult task, but evidence is lacking that the recall unduly inhibits public officers in the performance of their duties. Individuals who have decided to make representing the public a career are well aware of the importance of keeping in step with public opinion and leading such opinion if they become convinced that a major change in policy would promote the common weal.

Are highly qualified men and women deterred from seeking elective office if the recall is available to the voters? Such individuals clearly are deterred from seeking elective office, but it is doubtful that the recall is the only reason these individuals decided not to seek office.

One must conclude, as the opponents contend, that the recall can be employed for partisan purposes, yet it seldom has been so used. As noted in Chapter 4, successful employment of the recall in Michigan and Wisconsin resulted in a switch in party control of the state senate.

The reader also should bear in mind that constitutional and statutory recall authorization provisions offer protection to public officers against employment of the recall solely for partisan purposes. The provisions typically do not allow the use of the device during the first or last six months of an officer's term of office. Furthermore, a high petition signature threshold makes effective use of the recall for solely partisan purposes a near impossibility. A threshold of 25 to 30 percent of those who cast ballots in the previous general election should be adequate to dissuade the use of the recall for partisan spite. If a public officer, however, has given cause for recall through egregious behavior, the opposition party naturally may take advantage of the public's discontent and circulate petitions for a recall election.

Governmental costs are increased by employment of the recall, but these costs should not deter a state or local government from adopting the recall, because they are a minute fraction of the total expenditures of the government. Democracy costs the taxpayers money, yet no one objects to the cost of regular elections.

There is little merit to the argument that the simultaneous election of a successor in the event that the targeted officer is recalled results in the voters focusing upon the candidates for election rather than on the question of removing the officer. The focus in each recall election has been on the targeted officer. This argument clearly would possess merit if the recall was promoted by the opposition party for the sole purpose of a second opportunity for its candidate to win the office. Under such circumstances, the charges against the officer probably would not involve malfeasance, misfeasance, or nonfeasance but involve differences on one or more policies or the quality of the competing candidates.

The recall can be utilized to harass frivolously a public officer. Fortunately, such use has been exceptional.

In common with political parties, interest groups can use the recall, and evidence reveals that interest group use is more common than party use. Although opponents maintain that there is abuse of the recall by interest groups, one must not lose sight of the facts that most political activities involve interest groups and that such groups possess the right to be involved in any democratic process.

With the exceptions of the states where the recall is limited to legal cause, the device can be employed for any reason. Hence, it is not surprising that a public officer occasionally is removed from office for a reason that an impartial observer would conclude is an inadequate one.

The independence of the judiciary is essential if the ends of justice are to be served. Where authorized, very limited experience does not support the worst fears of the early opponents that the recall would destroy judicial independence and deter experienced lawyers from seeking election as judges. Nevertheless, the exclusion of judges from the recall appears to be a reasonable safeguard to ensure judicial impartiality.

Unfortunately, it is impossible to determine the deterrent effect of the existence of the recall in preventing public officers from committing unethical acts and in prodding them to perform their assigned duties conscientiously and fully. Ethical governance is essential if the public is to have trust in representative government. Voters can employ the recall, if authorized, to remove officers whose actions give the appearance of a conflict of interest (even though the actions do not violate statutory conflict of interest provisions) and also to replace officers guilty of partial or total nonfeasance.

Considering the thousands of local government officers subject to the recall, the device is used rarely and never has been employed in numerous local governments where authorized, as revealed by surveys conducted by the author. Furthermore, the recall clearly has addressed and, in a number of instances, remedied situations in which public officers neglected their duties, spoke ethnic slurs, were indicted for felonies, accepted payoffs from vice interest, and used government employees to work at the officers' homes. In many other instances, local government officers were removed from office because of policy differences with the electorate, including busing of children for school integration purposes.

Although the United States is organized on the national, state, and local planes of government (with the exceptions of many New England towns) as republics or representative governments, voters are the fountainhead of sovereign political power and simply have delegated their authority to public representatives. Consequently, voters possess the authority to reserve to themselves the right to reverse decisions of their representatives and to remove representatives failing to follow majority opinion or betraying the public's trust by their egregious behavior. Although this principle is an obvious one, not all state and local governments have adopted the petition referendum and the recall. Voters in these jurisdictions apparently have been convinced by opponents of the recall that, on balance, it weakens representative government or have discovered insurmountable barriers to adopting the recall.

In sum, the recall has not produced a new era of public official responsibility; yet, the device has not caused extensive disruption of state and local governments, as had been feared by several of the early recall opponents. We agree with the 1930 conclusion of Bird and Ryan that the recall "has been used most effectively, at times, to drive from office unfaithful, incompetent, and arbitrary officials; but it also has been employed, on occasion, without justification or beneficial result."[69]

Chapter 6 draws upon the constitutional and statutory provisions for the recall and experience with the recall (described and analyzed in Chapters 2–5) to develop model constitutional, legislative, and charter provisions authorizing the recall that reflect the sovereignty of the voters and protect elected public officers from frivolous employment of the recall by small disgruntled groups to harass the officers. To reduce the need for citizens to use the recall, suggestions are advanced for authorization of the petition referendum and the indirect initiative and enactment of statutes designed to ensure that the governance process is ethical and open to the extent possible.

NOTES

1.   Henry S. Commager, ed., *The Era of Reform: 1830-1860* (New York: Van Nostrand Rheinhold, 1960), p. 71.

2.   William Allen White, *The Older Order Changeth: A View of American Democracy* (New York: Macmillan, 1910), p. 60.

3.   Delos F. Wilcox, *Government by All the People Or the Initiative, the Referendum and the Recall as Instruments of Democracy* (New York: Macmillan, 1912), p. 171.

4.   Herbert S. Swan, "The Use of the Recall in the United States," in *The Initiative, Referendum, and Recall*, ed. William B. Munro (New York: D. Appleton, 1912), p. 299.

5.   Ibid., p. 306.

6.   Woodrow Wilson, "The Issues of Reform," in *The Initiative, Referendum, and Recall*, ed. William B. Munro (New York: D. Appleton, 1912), p. 88.

7.   Charles M. Price, "Recalls at the Local Level: Dimensions and Implications," *National Civic Review* 72 (April 1983): 206.

8.   Joseph F. Zimmerman, *Curbing Unethical Behavior in Government* (Westport, Conn.: Greenwood Press, 1994).

9.   For details, see Wilma Rule and Joseph F. Zimmerman, eds., *United States Electoral Systems: Their Impact on Women and Minorities* (Westport,

Conn.: Greenwood Press, 1992).

10.   Wilcox, *Government by All the People*, p. 199.

11.   Albert M. Kales, *Unpopular Government in the United States* (Chicago, Ill.: University of Chicago Press, 1914), p. 122.

12.   Frederick L. Bird and Frances M. Ryan, *The Recall of Public Officers: A Study of the Operation of the Recall in California* (New York: Macmillan, 1930), p. 350.

13.   George E. Mowry, *The California Progressives* (Berkeley: University of California Press, 1951), p. 9.

14.   Walter E. Weyl, *The New Democracy: An Essay on Certain Political and Economic Tendencies in the United States* (New York: Macmillan, 1912), pp. 304–5.

15.   Richard S. Childs, *The First 50 Years of the Council Manager Plan of Municipal Government* (New York: National Municipal League, 1965).

16.   For details, see Jonathan Bourne, Jr., "Functions of the Initiative, Referendum, and Recall," *Annals of the American Academy of Political and Social Science* 43 (September 1912): 3–16.

17.   Herbert Croly, *Progressive Democracy* (New York: Macmillan, 1915), p. 325.

18.   *Donahue v. Selectmen of Saugus*, 343 Mass. 93 at 96, 176 N.E.2d 34 at 36 (1961).

19.   Murray B. Levin, *The Alienated Voter* (New York: Holt, Rinehart and Winston, 1960).

20.   Joseph F. Zimmerman, *The Government and Politics of New York State* (New York: New York University Press, 1981), pp. 49–56, 113–16; Frank W. Prescott and Joseph F. Zimmerman, *The Politics of the Veto of Legislation in New York State* (Washington, D.C.: University Press of America, 1980).

21.   Joseph F. Zimmerman, *State-Local Relations: A Partnership Approach*, 2d ed. (Westport, Conn.: Praeger Publishers, 1995), pp. 17–50.

22.   Croly, *Progressive Democracy*, p. 325.

23.   Wilcox, *Government by All the People*, pp. 201–2.

24.   Ibid., p. 236.

25.   The unicameral Nebraska State Legislature possesses the impeachment power, and impeached officers are tried by the supreme court. The New York constitution provides for a Court for the Trial of Impeachments composed of the Senate and the Court of Appeals (*Constitution of New York*, art. 6, § 24). An initiated constitutional amendment approved by Oregon voters in 1910 stipulates "public officers shall not be impeached" (*Constitution of Oregon*, art. 7, § 6).

26.   For a provision providing for address by the senate, see the *Constitution of Pennsylvania*, art. 6, § 4.

27.   Interpellation refers to the requirement that an appointive officer appear before either house of the state legislature "to answer written and oral interrogatories relative to any matter, function, or work of the officer" (*Wisconsin Laws of 1915*, chap. 406; *Wisconsin Statutes*, §§ 13.28–13.30).

28. Charles Kettleborough, "Removal of Public Officers: A Ten-Year Review," *American Political Science Review* 8 (November 1914): 621.

29. Zimmerman, *The Government and Politics of New York State*, pp. 184–85.

30. William H. Taft, *Popular Government: Its Essence, Its Performance, and Its Perils* (New Haven, Conn.: Yale University Press, 1913). A similar position was taken by the Association of County Commissioners of Georgia; see "Supreme Court Strikes Blow for Good Government," *Georgia County Government* 40 (November 1988): 3.

31. Ellis P. Oberholtzer, *The Referendum in America Together with Some Chapters on the Initiative and the Recall* (New York: Charles Scribner's Sons, 1912), p. 455.

32. Benny Willis, "State Officer Says Recalls are Misused," *Eugene Register-Guard*, December 14, 1979, pp. 1B–2B.

33. "Westport Split Over Busing Vote," *New York Times*, December 10, 1970, p. 56.

34. Taft, *Popular Government*, p. 81.

35. Weyl, *The New Democracy*, p. 207.

36. Ibid., p. 307.

37. Taft, *Popular Government*, p. 83.

38. Ibid., p. 84.

39. Ibid., pp. 84–85.

40. "Abuse of Recall Power Substitutes Popularity for Leadership," *Georgia County Government Magazine* 31 (May 1979): 50.

41. Ibid.

42. Gil Barrett, "Recall Act is Being Used to Punish Local Leaders for Differences of Opinion," *Georgia County Government Magazine* 33 (October 1981): 2.

43. Wilcox, *Government by All the People*, p. 178.

44. Croly, *Progressive Democracy*, p. 326.

45. Ibid., p. 327.

46. Jefferson B. Fordham, "The Utah Recall Proposal," *Utah Law Review* 29 (1976): 33.

47. Wilcox, *Government by All the People*, p. 185.

48. "Recall Can be Abused," *Georgia County Government Magazine* 31 (September 1979): 58.

49. Candace Romig, "Two Michigan Legislators Recalled," *State Legislatures* 10 (January 1984): 5.

50. Ibid.

51. Wilcox, *Government by All the People*, p. 244.

52. Ibid.

53. Wallace Turner, "Fringe Group Forces Ouster Vote on Coast Mayor," *New York Times*, February 9, 1983, p. A24.

54. "Supreme Court Strikes Blow for Good Government," *Georgia County Government* 40 (November 1988): 3.

55. Deborah L. Moiles, "Oxford Board Member 'Owns' Her Own Vote," *Evening Gazette*, April 28, 1983, p. 10.

56. Ibid.

57. Taft, *Popular Government*, pp. 82-83.

58. "Recall Fever Infects Oregon," *Sunday Oregonian*, August 12, 1979, p. C2.

59. Theodore C. Sharpe, *Recall* (Grand Forks: Bureau of Governmental Affairs, University of North Dakota, 1971), p. 11.

60. Ibid.

61. *Report Relative to Recall of Local Officials* (Boston: Massachusetts Legislative Research Council, 1979), p. 44.

62. *Reports of the American Bar Association* 36 (1911): 231–32.

63. Rome G. Brown, "Recall of Judges," in Edith M. Phelps, compiler, *Selected Articles on the Recall* (New York: H. W. Wilson, 1915), pp. 131–32.

64. Wilcox, *Government by All the People*, p. 223.

65. Swan, "The Use of the Recall in the United States," p. 299.

66. Rule and Zimmerman, *United States Electoral Systems*.

67. Oberholtzer, *The Referendum in America*, p. 455.

68. Taft, *Popular Government*, p. 81.

69. Bird and Ryan, *The Recall of Public Officers*, p. 342.

6

A Model for Voter Sovereignty

The secular downward trend in voter turnout, in spite of massive efforts to reverse it, including election day registration, is evidence that a fundamental change has occurred in the nature of representative government and that a great need exists for corrective actions. Numerous citizens voluntarily have abdicated their sovereign powers, and their shunning of the polls on election day can be interpreted in many instances as indicating satisfaction with the performance of elected public officers. In other instances, the failure to vote may be deliberate because alienated citizens have given up the electoral process as a mechanism to produce representative government. These eligible nonvoting individuals, however, should not be deprived of the opportunity to remove one or more officers prior to the expiration of their terms if their actions infuriate citizens.

This chapter draws upon Chapters 2–5 to develop model constitutional, statutory, and local government charter provisions to guide jurisdictions considering adoption of the recall or revision of current recall provisions. The model also contains other provisions designed to lessen the need for employment of the recall. In a representative system of government, the recall should be a last resort weapon employed by disgruntled voters only when other avenues for removal of voter dissatisfaction have proved to be of no avail. To reduce the need for the recall, state constitutions should authorize voters to employ the protest referendum to invalidate legislative acts and the indirect initiative as a spur to governing bodies to enact into law bills desired by a majority of the voters. Voter knowledge is power. Hence, recommendations are advanced for open and ethical governance, which will lessen the need for the electorate to utilize the recall and facilitate the obtaining of information to enable them to make a sound decision should a recall election be scheduled.

MODEL PROVISIONS

A self-executing constitutional provision declaring the recall to be a political question, to be interpreted liberally by courts, is the preferable legal foundation for this voter control device. The constitutional provision can be a detailed one or a brief one. The latter is preferable and is illustrated by the provision in the constitution of Louisiana: "The legislature shall provide by general law for the recall by election of any state, district, parochial, ward, or municipal official except judges of the courts of record. The sole issue at a recall election shall be whether the official shall be recalled."[1]

If the constitutional provision is a brief one directing the state legislature to provide for the recall, it is desirable to include the Wisconsin constitutional provision that "no law shall be enacted to hamper, restrict, or impair the right of recall."[2]

The model procedures deal with exemptions and restrictions on use, the application for a recall election, the petition process, verification of voters' signatures, the recall election, filling of any resulting vacancies, and postelection matters. The officer in charge of conducting elections, hereinafter referred to as the "director of elections," should be authorized to promulgate rules and regulations necessary to carry out the constitutional, statutory, and charter recall provisions. Terms, such as "recall committee" and "campaign contribution," in particular, must be defined with care in statutes, rules, and regulations.

All statutory provisions and rules and regulations applicable to general elections should be applicable to recall elections. In addition, it is essential that a statute be enacted that forbids a person to interfere with the circulation of a petition or use a recall petition for purposes of blackmail, extortion, or private intimidation. Furthermore, the statute should make it a misdemeanor for a person to offer to pay a voter money or anything of value to sign a petition or induce a voter to sign or refrain from signing a petition by threat of retaliation against the person's business or discharge from employment or ineligibility for employment.

Exemption and Use Restrictions

As explained in Chapter 3, judges are subject to recall in several states. Attempts to recall a judge are extremely rare and seldom are successful. We agree with Albert M. Kales, who emphasized in 1914: "A judge is one of the most helpless of all elective officers. He can run on no platform; he can have no political program. He can not point dramatically to any achievements on behalf of the people. Whether he is a good judge or not is a matter of expert opinion that only a comparatively few persons are competent to pass upon. His reputation can be easily blasted by the circulation of false statements. He may even be hurt by the performance of his duty in a particular case."[3]

Judges can and do commit wrongs occasionally. Fortunately, such wrongs are not common, and mechanisms exist for addressing them. Judges in all states except Oregon, where there is no impeachment process, are subject to the impeachment process, and in several states, a special judicial panel exists for the disciplining of judges and possesses the power to remove or otherwise discipline offending judges.

Montana is the only state with a statute authorizing the recall of appointed officers. A small number of local government charters permit the recall of administrators. Using the recall election process to remove administrative officers is inappropriate in view of the facts that they were not elected by the voters and that other provisions exist for their suspension and removal if they are guilty of malfeasance, misfeasance, or nonfeasance.

The recall should be prohibited if the only ground for recall is that the officer performed a mandatory duty of the office he or she holds. Furthermore, the recall should not be applicable to an officer who refuses to perform an act because performance would subject the officer to prosecution for official misconduct.

A newly elected public officer should not be subject to the recall during the first six months of his or her term. It is essential that the officer be given a reasonable period of time to prove his or her competence and to establish a policy record before the electorate is called upon to make a judgment relative to removing the officer. If no such prohibition exists, the political party or candidate that lost the preceding general election for the office may launch a recall campaign for the sole purpose of gaining control of the office.

As noted in Chapter 2, a state legislator in several states is eligible to be recalled five days after commencement of the legislative session when he or she assumed office. This policy is an inappropriate one for the reasons given in the paragraph above. If a state legislator or other elected officer is guilty of malfeasance, misfeasance, or nonfeasance during the six-months grace period, there are other mechanisms to resolve the problem, including expulsion of a legislator by his or her house and suspension or removal of an executive branch officer by the governor.

Elected officers should be exempt from the recall during the last six months of the term of office. Elections, with relatively few exceptions, are held in November, with the winners assuming office on January 1. Depending upon the office involved, petitioners typically have up to three months to collect signatures to trigger an election. Hence, the filing of a petition containing the required number of signatures might not occur until October 1, or approximately five weeks prior to the general election, at which time voter turnout would be high.

Proponents of the recall of a public officer who successfully retains office as the result of the recall election should not be allowed to file petitions for a second recall election of the same officer during the same term of office unless the recall sponsors pay the state or concerned local government an amount equal to the expense of conducting the first recall election. This requirement will help to ensure that the recall will not be utilized for a frivolous reason or to harass the officer.

The Application Process

Registered voters desiring to recall an elected public officer should be required to file a notice of intention to circulate a petition to recall a specified officer in person or by registered post with the director of elections signed by a minimum of ten registered voters as individuals or a committee composed of a minimum of ten registered voters of the concerned electoral jurisdiction who sign the notice. The application must contain the residential addresses of the signers and, in the case of a committee, the names and titles of officers, including a mandatory treasurer, in addition to their residential addresses. The name and address of a contact person must be provided in the application.

The notice must be signed before an officer authorized by law to administer oaths or affirmations that the petition and the signatures contained therein are true. If the director determines that one of the sponsors is ineligible to act as a sponsor, a replacement sponsor may be added to the petition.

A refundable filing fee of $100 should be required to discourage the filing of frivolous notices of intention to file a recall petition. This low fee should not discourage a group of determined voters from filing a notice.

The fee should be refundable if the required number of verified signatures is submitted by the deadline for submission of petition sheets.

Each notice of intention must specify the officer whose recall is sought and contain a clear statement of grounds for the recall, not exceeding 200 words. A separate petition must be submitted for each officer whose recall is sought. A copy of the notice must be served by personal delivery or certified post to the officer subject to the petition.

A registered voter who signs a notice of intention to circulate a recall petition should be immune from civil liability for conduct related to the exercise of the right to participate in the recall process.

The notice of intention must be published at the expense of the recall sponsor(s) at least once in a newspaper of general circulation. If there is no newspaper of general circulation within the territory of a local government, the notice must be posted in a minimum of four conspicuous public places, including the seat of the government. Sponsors must submit to the director proof of publication or an affidavit of the posting of the notice.

The targeted officer — within five days of receiving the notice of intention, excluding Saturday, Sunday, holiday — may file a response statement with the director, not exceeding 200 words. If a response statement is filed, the officer also must serve a copy by personal delivery or certified post on the contact person for the sponsors of the recall petition.

The director must keep a record of each notice of intention application and date of its receipt and issue a notice number to the applicant. In addition, the director should be responsible for preparing a ballot synopsis of the reasons advanced by the recall sponsors and the response statement, if any, of the targeted public officer if either or both statements exceed 200 words. The synopsis must be prepared within ten days of the filing of the notice of intention. The director also should be authorized to suggest to the sponsors and targeted officer changes in wording that will assist voters in making their decisions.

The director should be responsible for determining the number of required certified signatures of voters to trigger a recall election and to notify the sponsor(s) and the targeted officer.

No signatures may be collected on a recall petition sheet until the director has approved the form of the petition and printed copies of the official petition sheets. Signature spaces must be numbered consecutively on each sheet commencing with number one, and space provided for the signature and the residential address of the signer.

Each petition must contain a copy of the notice of intention, including the reasons for the recall, and a copy of the targeted officer's response, if any. If the officer did not file a response, the petition must so indicate. In addition, each petition sheet must contain the name and address of the principal recall sponsor or the treasurer of a recall committee.

Recall Petitions

A separate petition must be employed for each public officer whose removal is sought. The separate petition process focuses specific attention on the grounds for the removal of each officer and allows the concerned officer to prepare a written response to appear on each recall petition sheet and on the election ballot, should a recall election be triggered.

It is absolutely essential that the recall statute make it a crime for a person to offer a registered voter money or anything of value as an inducement to sign or not sign a recall petition. Similarly, the statute should stipulate that no person may be paid to circulate recall petitions for signatures of registered voters. The recall is a citizen corrective and, as such, should involve only registered voters as unpaid petition circulators.

Only one circulator should be allowed to collect signatures on a single petition sheet, because no circulator truthfully could sign the required affidavit attesting that all signatures on the sheet were signed in the presence of the circulator, who is legally responsible for keeping all sheets under his or her control.

An intentional violation of circulating, signature attesting, and filing procedures automatically invalidates the petition.

Each petition sheet should warn potential signers that signing the name of another voter (impersonation) is a misdemeanor, with the exception of signing a petition sheet in the presence of a person incapable of signing his or her name because of a physical infirmity. In addition, signing more than one petition or signing a petition while knowingly not a qualified voter is a misdemeanor.

Each signer should be instructed to sign and print his or her name on the sheet legibly and to include his or her full residential address, including street or box number, city, state, and postal code. If there is no street or box number, an adequate description of the location of the address should be included on the sheet.

Each petition circulator must take an oath or affirm before an officer competent to administer oaths or affirmations that each signature is the genuine signature of the person whose name it purports to be. Each circulator must sign each petition sheet, include his or her address and dates between which the signatures were collected, and certify that the circulator witnessed each appended signature written by a registered voter of the electoral jurisdiction of the officer sought to be recalled and that each signature is that of the person whose name it purports to be.

Sponsors of the recall may not notarize a circulator's affidavit. If a sponsor does so, the signatures automatically are disqualified.

A person who signs a recall petition sheet may withdraw his or her signature until 5:00 P.M. on the last date for filing petitions to be verified, unless the petitions were filed earlier, by filing an intention to withdraw signature statement in person or by post with the petition-receiving officer. After a recall petition is submitted for signature verification, no elector who signed a petition sheet may remove his or her signature from the sheet. A person who gives money or receives anything of value for signing a withdrawal statement is guilty of a misdemeanor.

Verified signatures equal to 25 percent of the voters who cast ballots in the jurisdiction for governor in the preceding general election should be required to trigger a recall election of a statewide elected officer or the mayor of a large city. Consideration can be given to basing the triggering percentage of signatures for small local governments on a sliding scale correlated with the number of registered voters. It is easier physically for recall sponsors to collect signatures in a small municipality compared with signature collection in a large city or statewide. Hence, the required percentage of signatures might be as high as 40 percent in small local governments.

To ensure that there is broad geographical support for the recall of a statewide elected officer, the recall constitutional or statutory provision could stipulate that a specified percentage of signatures must be collected in each of one-half or one-third of the counties. The need for such a provision is not great, as evidenced by the rare use of the recall to remove a statewide elected officer.

The deadline for the submission of petition signature sheets to the director for verification should be 120 days after the director's approval of a petition for the recall of a statewide elected officer and 90 days for other officers.

The targeted officer whose recall is sought may challenge in writing the validity of signatures and whether the signers are registered voters of the officer's jurisdiction within 30 days of the filing of petition signatures and must be accorded at least 8 days to check signatures after the director has examined them. If the director rejects the officer's challenge of the validity of one or more petition sheet signatures, the officer may appeal the director's decision to a court of competent jurisdiction.

The director may conduct representative random statistical sampling of petition sheet signatures by means of postcards, telephone calls, or other accepted information-gathering techniques to determine whether the signatures were signed by the persons whose names appear on the sheets. The director must report violations of the petition-signing law to the appropriate public officer for investigation and possible prosecution.

The director must review all petition sheet signatures and make a determination within 30 days of their filing of their sufficiency and notify *in personam* or by certified post, within 3 days of the determination, the sponsor(s) and targeted public officer as to whether the petitions were filed during the eligible time period and contain the required number of certified signatures. Nullification of a signature on a petition sheet does not invalidate automatically other signatures on the sheet.

If the petition lacks the requisite number of verified signatures, the petition may be amended within ten days of the director's determination of the inadequacy. The director must review an amended petition within ten days and determine its adequacy. If the amended petition is found to be inadequate, it shall be returned to the sponsor without prejudice to the filing of a new recall petition.

Should the director find invalid signatures, only the sponsors listed in the notice of intention should be allowed to examine the petitions to determine the reasons why the signatures were rejected.

If the director issues a certificate of sufficiency, the concerned officer has five days to decide to resign the office. If the officer does not resign during this time period, the director shall schedule a special recall election within the subsequent 30 to 45 days, unless a general or primary election is scheduled during this time period, in which event the recall election will be held in conjunction with the regularly scheduled election.

Should the director fail to comply with any of the required procedures, an elector within ten days of the refusal to comply may apply to the appropriate court of equity for the issuance of a writ of mandamus to compel compliance.

The Recall Election

A recall election shall not be held if a vacancy occurs in the targeted office because of resignation, removal by other means, conviction of a felony, death, or inability to perform the duties of the office. Absentee voting should be allowed in a recall election.

Candidates to fill a vacancy resulting from successful employment of the recall may be nominated under the current nomination statute, which should include nomination by petition to ensure that political party bosses do not exclude independent voters. The targeted officer should not be allowed to be a replacement candidate in the event of his or her recall from office.

If no candidate is nominated to replace the targeted officer in the event of a successful recall, the resulting vacancy should be filled by existing methods, which should include appointment by the chief executive officer if an elected administrator is recalled and by co-optation by the governing body if a legislator is recalled. An alternative for filling vacancies on a local governing body that has lost a quorum is authorization for the governor to fill vacancies to produce a quorum.

If the recall of more than one member of a multimember body elected at-large is sought, the nomination petition of each candidate must indicate which member each candidate is seeking to replace.

The recall election preferably should be held in conjunction with a primary or general election, which typically has a higher turnout of voters than a special election. A key question that must be answered is whether the recall election should use a one-question or a two-question ballot. If the recall election simply decides that a public officer will be removed from office, a second election will have to be held to select a successor, and such a special election may have a relatively low turnout of voters. A two-ballot question, involving whether the officer should be removed and selection of a replacement in the event of removal, has the advantage of a larger turnout of voters in most instances.

An alternative is the California provision, which asks voters whether a resulting vacancy should be filled by appointment or by a special election.[4] The advantage of the California approach is that it guarantees that the focus of the recall election will be on the grounds for the removal of the public officer and not on replacement candidates.

Sample recall ballots should be prepared, containing the grounds for recall and the officer's response, and posted conspicuously in places of public gathering, including the building housing the seat of the government. The officer in charge of each polling place should be charged with posting at least four copies of the sample ballot in conspicuous places. Voters should be the sole judges of the reasonableness and sufficiency of the grounds for removing the officer. In common with other elections, recall ballots should be subject to a recount if requested.

A recalled officer should be ineligible for appointment to any other office in the jurisdiction for the remainder of his or her original term of office. Furthermore, an officer subject to a recall election who resigns his or her office also should be ineligible for appointment to any other office for the remainder of his or her original term of office.

If the successor to the recalled officer does not qualify to hold the office within five days subsequent to certification of the results of the election, the office automatically becomes vacant and is filled as provided by law.

The director is to certify that the office is vacant if a majority of the voters favor recall, provided at least 50 percent of those who voted in the previous general election for the office voted in the recall election.

It is essential that the state's corrupt practices act apply to recall elections. The treasurer of the recall committee and the targeted officer must file detailed reports of campaign receipts and expenditures and comply with all requirements of the act. A "contribution" must be defined carefully to include the payment of a gift, forgiveness of a debt or a loan, or provision of nonpersonal services, equipment, supplies, or any other item of value without compensation of money. The term "expenditure" also must be defined carefully to include, among other things, reducing the debt of the incumbent officer or a candidate for the office should it become vacant.

Post Election

If the public officer is recalled, the statute should specify that the elected or appointed successor serves the balance of the recalled officer's term of office. The successor should be subject to the recall except during the immunity periods of the first six and last six months in office.

If the incumbent successfully retains office in a recall election, the state or local government should be directed to pay the personal expenses incurred by the incumbent to retain the office.

The successful employment of the recall can result in the inability of a local government legislative body to take action should a quorum be lacking because of the removal of public officers. The problem, of course, will not occur if state law or local government charter provides for the simultaneous election of replacements for officers recalled or the appointment of sufficient replacements to achieve a quorum. State law and local charters commonly authorize a local government body to co-opt members to fill vacancies on the council. However, co-optation is not possible unless a quorum exists on the council. To deal with this potential problem, the governor should be authorized to fill vacancies to produce a quorum.

THE PROTEST REFERENDUM AND THE INITIATIVE

The protest referendum and the initiative complement the recall as devices voters can employ to ensure that their wishes are followed. The former allows electors by petition to suspend a statute until a referendum is held to determine whether the statute should be repealed. The initiative permits voters to place proposed constitutional amendments and statutes on the referendum ballot. These two devices lessen the need for the recall as a device to remove legislators who enact a statute opposed by a majority of the electorate or fail to enact a bill favored by a majority of the voters. Policy differences between legislators and voters can be resolved by employment of one or both of these devices, thereby removing a reason for employment of the recall.

The Protest Referendum

The referendum is based upon the concept of shared decision making and first was employed in the Massachusetts Bay Colony in 1640.[5] Following the issuance of the Declaration of Independence in 1776, constitutional conventions in Massachusetts and New Hampshire referred draft constitutions to the voters for their action. Although Massachusetts voters rejected the document submitted by the General Court (state legislature), they approved in 1780 a new document drafted and submitted by a constitutional convention.[6] New Hampshire voters rejected a constitution drafted by a convention in 1778 but approved in 1784 a new document submitted by a second convention.[7] The practice of submitting proposed constitutions to the voters spread to Connecticut in 1818 and Maine in 1819 and today is followed by all states except Delaware.

Growing distrust of the state legislature by the electorate in the nineteenth century led to constitutional amendments or new constitutions providing for conditional laws, that is, ones that do not become effective without voter sanction. Most restrictions involve borrowing of funds and taxation and are found today in many constitutions.

The first such restriction was placed in the Rhode Island constitution of 1842, which was drafted by a convention and ratified by the voters. The state legislature was forbidden to incur debts exceeding $50,000 without the consent of the electorate except during a war, insurrection, or invasion.[8] In 1843, the Michigan constitution was amended to prohibit the legislature from incurring any debt without the consent of the voters with the exceptions of raising funds "for defraying the actual expenses of the legislature, the judicial and state officers, for suppressing insurrection, repelling invasion, or defending the state in time of war."[9]

The 1876 Colorado constitutional convention drafted a constitution, ratified by the electorate, containing a maximum property tax limitation that could not be exceeded without the approval of the voters.[10] Similar restrictions have been incorporated in other constitutions relative to state taxation and local taxation.

The referendum entered a new era in 1898, when South Dakota voters amended their constitution to provide for the protest or petition referendum by stipulating that they "expressly reserve to themselves the right . . . to require that any laws which the legislature may have enacted shall be submitted to a vote of the electors of the state before going into effect."[11] The only exceptions to the referendum requirements are laws designed to preserve "the public peace, health, or safety, support of the state government and its existing institutions."[12]

The protest or petition referendum, also known as the "direct referendum" or "citizens' veto," allows voters by petitions to stop the implementation of a new law until a referendum determines whether the law should be repealed. In 1970, the U.S. Court of Appeals for the Ninth Circuit defined a petition referendum as "an exercise by the voters of their traditional right through direct legislation to override the views of their elected representatives as to what serves the public interest."[13]

This type of referendum is similar to the initiative in that action to place a law on the referendum ballot originates with the voters. Successful collection of the requisite number of signatures automatically results in a mandatory referendum.

The protest referendum may be employed in 24 states. In eight states — Alaska, Idaho, Massachusetts, Michigan, Missouri, Montana, South Dakota, and Wyoming — this control device may be used only against an entire law, whereas in the other states, the referendum may be employed against part or all of a law.

The constitutional provision for the protest referendum typically excludes certain topics — appropriations, the judiciary, religion, and special legislation (a law affecting a single local government) — from the referendum. The longest list of excluded topics is contained in the Massachusetts constitution.[14] The Massachusetts General Court on several occasions voted a salary increase for its members, only to see the increase repealed by the outraged electorate employing the protest referendum.

Emergency and appropriations acts are excluded from the citizens' veto in ten states; appropriation and emergency acts are excluded in five additional states and four additional states, respectively.[15] All statutes are subject to the protest referendum in Arkansas, Idaho, Nevada, and North Dakota. Local government charters and state statutes often provide for a petition referendum on a local ordinance or law.[16]

In 14 states, the protest referendum propositions appear only on the general election ballot, where voter turnout will be the highest. In 9 additional states, issues may appear either on a general election ballot or a special election ballot. The governor in California, Maine, North Dakota, and Oklahoma may call a special referendum election to determine whether a law should be repealed. The state legislature in 6 states — Arkansas, Michigan, Missouri, Oklahoma, Oregon, and Washington — may schedule a special referendum election, as can voters in Arkansas and Maine by petition.

To suspend a law and place it on the referendum ballot requires a number of signatures, varying from 2 percent of the votes cast in the last gubernatorial election in Massachusetts to 15 percent of the number who voted in the previous general election and reside in at least two-thirds of the counties in Wyoming.[17] Typically, there is a requirement that a specified minimum number of signatures must be collected in each county or in a specified number of counties, such as a majority in Utah and two-thirds in Wyoming, in order to demonstrate that there is interest in the issue in many sections of the state. The degree of difficulty encountered by dissatisfied voters in utilizing the protest referendum is affected directly by the signature threshold and distribution requirements.

Constitutional provisions require that petitions relative to suspending and repealing a state law must be filed within a specified number of days — typically 90 — subsequent to the adjournment of the state legislature. In Utah, the maximum time allowed is 60 days, whereas Montana allows 6 months. All but four states require a simple majority vote on the question to repeal a law to negate it. In the four states that are exceptions, the number of votes cast on the question must be equal to 30 to 50 percent of the votes cast in the previous general election. The state legislature in only six of the protest referendum states may not amend or repeal the decision of the electorate.

States lacking the protest referendum at the state level authorize the use of this type of referendum at the local level. New Hampshire statutes, for example, authorize the owners of 20 percent either of the land area or lots to petition for a referendum on a change in land use regulations adopted by a town.[18] Residents of Connecticut towns with town meetings are authorized by petition — 200 voters or 10 percent of the registered voters, whichever is less — to force a referendum on any item in the warrant calling a town meeting.[19]

The protest referendum can be employed by conservative or liberal groups or by integrationists or segregationists. Relative to the latter, they employed the device in June 1963 to block the immediate implementation of a public accommodations law in Maryland.[20]

There is no evidence that conservative groups make more use of the protest referendum than liberal groups, but there is evidence that voters take both a conservative and a liberal stance on different propositions on the same referendum ballot. Massachusetts voters in 1982, for example, approved a death penalty proposition (generally considered to be a conservative position) and a bottle deposit proposition and a nuclear freeze proposition (considered to be part of the liberal agenda).

Business groups occasionally use the protest referendum to annul statutes. In 1982, for example, the Massachusetts Soft Drink Association filed petitions for a referendum on the subject of repealing a mandatory bottle deposit law enacted by the General Court.[21]

The protest referendum is a form of citizens' veto designed to correct legislative sins of commission and should be available to voters as a safety valve to be employed to reverse unrepresentative legislative decisions. There is little evidence to date that the protest referendum has weakened representative government by discouraging many able individuals from seeking or continuing in legislative office or by encouraging legislative bodies to shirk their responsibilities by employing often the optional referendum.

Consideration should be given to a new type of petition referendum that, upon the filing of the requisite number of certified signatures, would suspend a law and require the legislative body to consider the repeal or amendment of the law within a specified number of days. Should the legislative body fail to adopt the proposal contained in the petition within the specified period, regardless of whether the legislature is in session on the day the petition is certified, a referendum automatically would be held on the proposal.

The current protest referendum limits voters to a "yes" or "no" choice on the question of repealing the referred law, whereas the proposed new type of petition referendum hopefully would encourage the legislative body to amend or repeal the law in question, thereby obviating the need for a protest referendum, with its attendant expenses.

The Indirect Initiative

The 1898 South Dakota constitutional amendment also authorizes voters to utilize the initiative to propose state constitutional amendments and state laws by means of petitions. San Francisco freeholders in the same year ratified a new city-county charter providing for the initiative and the protest referendum.[22] Public enthusiasm in favor of lawmaking by unassembled voters was strong in the period 1898 to 1918, as 19 states adopted the initiative. All were west of the Mississippi River except Maine, Massachusetts, and Ohio. No state subsequently adopted the initiative until 1959, when Alaska entered the union with a constitutional provision for the initiative. Wyoming adopted the initiative in 1968; Illinois in 1970 adopted a constitution providing for the initiative relative to the legislative article only of the constitution; and Florida adopted the constitutional initiative in 1972.

The constitutions of 23 states currently contain provisions for one or more types of initiatives. Constitutional authorization provisions in some states — Idaho, South Dakota, and Utah are examples — are brief, and implementation is the responsibility of the state legislature. On the other hand, the Colorado and Ohio constitutions contain detailed procedural provisions. In a number of the initiative states, the constitutional provision is self-executing, that is, no implementing legislation is required.

The initiative may be employed in the process of amending the state constitution in 17 states and in 21 states may be employed in the process of enacting ordinary statutes. The veto power of the governor does not extend to voter-approved initiated measures. The participatory device — as authorized by the state constitution, state law, or local charter — may be employed in most states to adopt and amend local government charters and ordinances.

In common with the protest referendum, constitutional provisions authorizing the initiative contain several restrictions. Alaska, California, Massachusetts, Missouri, Nebraska, Nevada, North Dakota, South Dakota, and Wyoming except certain subjects or place restrictions on the exercise of the initiative. Appropriations, emergency measures, the judiciary, and support of the government typically are not subject to the initiative.

The Nevada constitution forbids the use of the initiative to appropriate funds unless the initiated measure provides for the levying of a tax to supply the funds.[23] The Maine constitution stipulates that an initiated measure providing for expenditures exceeding the amount appropriated becomes invalid 45 days after the state legislature convenes.[24]

The California and Missouri constitutions restrict the initiative to a single subject, and the Illinois constitution limits the number of propositions on the referendum ballot of a political subdivision to three.[25] By way of contrast, the Arkansas constitution specifically stipulates "no limitations shall be placed upon the number of constitutional amendments, laws, or other measures which may be proposed and submitted to the people by either initiative or referendum petition."[26]

In contrast to referred propositions, opponents of an initiated proposition can initiate an alternative proposition in the hope that it may be more popular than the proposition they oppose. The anti–bottle deposit groups in particular have employed the initiative to place an alternative measure on the referendum ballot.

The initiative can be direct or indirect. Under the former type, the entire legislative process is circumvented, because propositions are placed directly on the referendum ballot if the required number and distribution of valid signatures of registered voters are collected and certified. The indirect initiative, employed in eight states, involves a more cumbersome process, because a proposition is referred to the legislative body upon the filing of the required number of certified signatures. Failure of the legislative body to approve the proposition within a stipulated number of days, varying from 40 days in Michigan to adjournment of the Maine state legislature, leads to the proposition being placed automatically on the referendum ballot. In three states, additional signatures must be collected to place the proposition on the ballot if the legislature fails to approve it as follows: 0.5 percent and 10 percent of the votes cast for governor in the last general election in Massachusetts and Utah, respectively, and 3 percent of the registered voters in Ohio.

Only the Massachusetts constitution authorizes the indirect initiative for constitutional amendments. To be placed upon the referendum ballot, the initiative proposal must be approved by each of two successive joint sessions of a successively elected General Court or receive the affirmative vote of 25 percent of all members in each of the two successive joint sessions.[27]

The state legislature in five states — Maine, Massachusetts, Michigan, Nevada, and Washington — is authorized to place a substitute proposition on the referendum ballot whenever an initiative proposition appears on the ballot.[28]

The indirect initiative is the preferable type, because it has the benefit of the legislative process, including public hearings and committee review, study, and recommendations. Should the legislative body fail to approve an initiated proposition, voters have been advantaged in their decision-making capacity by the information on the proposition generated by the legislative process.

The indirect initiative is a useful adjunct or complement to the conventional lawmaking process and can be an effective counterbalance to an unrepresentative legislative body. One of the indirect initiative's major advantages is the fact that the device makes the operations of interest groups more visible in comparison with their lobbying activities in a state legislature or a local legislative body. Furthermore, the availability of the initiative increases the citizen's stake in the government.

Support for the indirect initiative does not suggest that it should be employed frequently. It should be a reserve power or last resort weapon, and the relative need for its use depends upon the degree of accountability, representativeness, and responsiveness of legislative bodies.

OPEN AND ETHICAL GOVERNMENT

Aristotle stressed the importance of an educated citizenry in the following terms: "But if the citizens of a state are to judge and to distribute offices according to merit, then they must know each other's characters; where they do not possess this knowledge, both the election to offices and the decisions of lawsuits will go wrong."[29] Similarly, open government is essential for the full and effective functioning of participatory democracy because of the limited resources possessed by citizens in comparison with the resources of elected and appointed public officers. The purposeful withholding or hiding of most information on governmental operations and decisions clearly is unethical and also makes informed citizen participation in the government an impossibility. Similarly, citizens are harmed by other unethical actions of public officers.[30]

Open Government

Information is power, and it is essential that information be available readily to the electorate to assist them in making decisions relative to candidates for election to public offices and employment of the three participatory control devices — the protest referendum, the indirect initiative, and the recall. Open government means that official records and meetings of governmental bodies, with a few necessary exceptions, must be open to the public.

Freedom of Information

To what extent should citizens have access to the official records of a government? There is no simple answer to this question, because all governments have a legitimate need to keep certain records confidential to protect individuals and the general public.

A precise dividing line between confidential and public information does not exist, and it is apparent that citizens cannot play a full role in the governance system if important information is withheld from them. Because confidentiality can be employed as a shield to hide unethical actions and information from the citizenry, a mechanism is needed to resolve disputes regarding the disclosure of official information marked "confidential." The 1977 New York State Legislature addressed this problem by creating the Committee on Public Access to Records, charged with developing guidelines for the release of official information by state and local government agencies and providing advice in the case of disputes.[31]

Ethical problems also are involved in the purposeful delay in providing information in response to requests by citizens, and a conflict can exist between a freedom of information law and a privacy law. For example, the federal Privacy Act of 1974 requires executive agencies to keep personal information confidential, yet the federal Freedom of Information Act requires agencies to make executive branch records available for inspection or copying except "to the extent required to prevent clearly unwarranted invasion of personal privacy."[32]

Open Meetings

In camera decision making has been common and hinders informed citizen participation in the governance process. To throw light ("sunshine") on the decision-making process and to allow citizens to monitor it, many governments in recent years have enacted open meeting laws mandating that decisions be made at public meetings with specified exceptions where the public interest would be injured by an open decision.

These laws help to ensure that high ethical standards will apply to the decision-making process and that *in camera* sessions will be limited to a relatively small number of cases, such as acquisition of property, disciplinary action, salary negotiations, or matters that could prejudice a government's position in a lawsuit.

In adopting an open meeting law, care must be exercised in defining the term "meeting." The Council of State Governments recommends that the term "be defined as the convening of a governing body for which a quorum is required in order to make a decision or to deliberate toward a decision on any matter."[33] In addition, it is essential to define the term "governing body" precisely, require that adequate public notice be given to interested individuals and organizations of the place and time of meetings, and specify the exceptions to the open meeting requirement. Furthermore, complete and accurate records of meetings must be made and maintained, because such records allow citizens unable to attend a meeting to examine the proceedings.

Ethical Government

Freedom of information and open meeting statutes promote ethical government as well as citizen participation in policymaking and implementation. Ethical government also is promoted by conflict of interest statutes, codes of ethics, mandatory information disclosure, internal controls, external oversight, and whistle-blower protection, which reduce the need for employment of the recall.

Conflict of Interest Statutes

Elected public officers swear or affirm that they will faithfully and impartially discharge and perform all the duties of their respective offices to the best of their ability. Unfortunately, not all officers keep their oath or affirmation, and these officers should be removed from office. Because many violations of oaths or affirmations may be subtle ones, it is important that statutes be enacted and supplemented by rules, regulations, and guidelines to assist in the education of officers and the detection of conflicts of interest.

The English common law's rules of trust provide that a government officer has a fiduciary obligation to act solely in the interest of the general public. The common law applies only to public officers involved in a transaction. Statutory conflict of interest provisions usually apply to all officers and employees, whether or not they are involved with a given transaction. These provisions accord recognition to the fact that a citizen appointed or elected to a public office cannot disassociate himself or herself totally from his or her private activities and provide guidance to the officers with respect to forbidden activities. Criminal penalties are authorized to deter venal conflicts of interests.

Constitutional and statutory conflict of interest provisions should be broad and include definition of interest, dual office holding, contracts, gifts, disclosure of confidential information, representing private parties before governmental bodies, outside employment, and postemployment restrictions. Penalties for violations should also be provided. It is essential that the definition of "interest" be broad to include family members but also exclude interests that cannot cause harm to the polity, such as purchasing government bonds or being entitled to receive a service or other benefit offered by the government on the same terms to other citizens. The statute also should allow an officer to retain a private interest, provided it is remote and disclosed.

Codes of Ethics

A large gray area exists between clearly ethical behavior and unethical behavior on the part of a public officer identified by conflict of interest provisions. Codes of ethics have been enacted by legislative bodies to address the ethics of actions falling in the gray area by providing a more detailed frame of reference that facilitates self-regulation of conduct of officers by establishing guidelines with respect to acceptable and unacceptable behavior. The codes acknowledge that they cannot address every conceivable ethical question that may arise in the future and consequently typically provide for a board that is authorized to conduct investigations and to provide advisory opinions in response to inquiries from public officers and employees. In time, the advisory opinions, with names of officers deleted, become a common law of ethics guiding officers and employees in reaching decisions on ethical matters. The board also may conduct a continuing or periodic education program and make recommendations to the legislative body for amendment of conflict of interest statutes and the code of ethics.

Mandatory Information Disclosure

Detection of unethical behavior is facilitated if statutes are enacted mandating that candidates for elective office, campaign committees, lobbyists, and public officers and employees file periodic financial reports. The early disclosure laws — termed "corrupt practices acts" — prohibit bribery, betting on elections, treating, and payment of one voter's poll tax by another individual. In the late nineteenth century, the early acts were supplemented by constitutional and statutory provisions curtailing political patronage and prohibiting assessment of officeholders as a means of raising party campaign funds. More recent statutes regulate the amounts that may be contributed to candidates and the amounts they may spend in primary and general election campaigns. Corporations and labor unions currently are forbidden to contribute to election campaigns in 16 and 8 states, respectively. In addition, Montana forbids regulated corporations to contribute to election campaigns. Candidates, election committees, political parties, and protest referendum, initiative, and recall committees are required to file reports of contributions and expenditures.

In an effort to deter unethical behavior, Congress and all state legislatures regulate interest groups in some manner. Currently, 32 states require lobbyists to register, identify their employers, and reveal the amount of their compensation and expenditures. Unfortunately, lax enforcement of these requirements is common.

A perennial problem is the intertwining of personal interests of an elected officer with the public interest. To deter such intertwining and to detect its existence, public officers are required by constitutions, statutes, initiative and referendum, municipal ordinance, or executive order to make an annual disclosure of their financial interests.

To be effective, the financial disclosure statements must be audited periodically to ensure their accuracy. The nature of the audit, obviously, will be influenced by the specific disclosures made in each statement. Should the number of statements be large, a random audit should suffice as a determinant of the accuracy of the filed statements.

Internal Controls

Constitutional and statutory provisions promoting ethical governance need to be supplemented by internal controls. Making a rigorous screening of applicants a part of the recruitment process, for example, reduces the number of persons with a proclivity to unethical behavior who are hired. Good accounting, central-purchasing, record-keeping, and reporting systems will remove or reduce opportunities for unethical actions. These systems also reveal improprieties and thereby facilitate initiation of corrective actions.

The effectiveness of internal controls is increased if each department or agency has an internal control officer who tests existing controls and develops new or modified controls. Related to internal control officers are inspectors general, who may have government-wide or departmental jurisdiction to investigate alleged unethical behavior.

External Oversight

The historic type of oversight was performed by standing committees of state legislatures, but it has become more common during the past century for a legislative body to create a special committee or commission to investigate allegations of unethical conduct by a public officer(s). These committees and commissions terminate with the filing of their respective reports.

External oversight also is performed in the federal government by the comptroller general and in each state by an auditor or comptroller, whose function originally involved scrutinizing financial transactions and accounts. Commencing in the twentieth century, many comptrollers and auditors initiated program audits that questioned the policy judgment of executive officers.

In addition, external oversight is performed by an independent counsel appointed by the U.S. attorney general. Such counsels or special prosecutors were appointed to investigate the Watergate scandal in the 1970s and, more recently, the Whitewater scandal of the 1990s.

Ombudsmen date to the 1809 appointment of a *Justiteombudsman* (citizen justice officer) in Sweden. Although several governors and mayors of large cities have established an ombudsman office, these offices are not genuine external oversight agencies, because the ombudsmen are appointed by the chief executives to investigate departments and agencies under their control. The state legislatures in Alaska, Hawaii, Iowa, and Nebraska have established a classical type of ombudsman with authority to investigate all complaints filed against executive officers and agencies by citizens. The ombudsman lacks the authority to direct that corrective action be initiated if needed but can use publicity to pressure the concerned officer or agency to adopt the ombudsman's recommendation(s).

Whistle-blower Protection

It is unreasonable to expect public officers and employees to blow the whistle on unethical behavior by an officer if they fear retaliation in the form of discharge from employment, reassignment to another location, lowered performance ratings, or other retaliatory actions. Furthermore, actions must be initiated to change the organizational culture to encourage whistle-blowing.

If whistle-blowing is common and supported by facts, it is apparent that the internal control system has failed and needs to be revised to address the problems identified by the whistle-blowers.

CONCLUDING COMMENTS

Our review of the use of the recall to remove state and local government officers from office reveals that a need remains for this late nineteenth century political corrective, yet this conclusion should not obscure the fact that most elected public officers have performed their official duties in accordance with the highest ethical standards and have been responsive to the citizenry in general.

No system of representation is perfect. Lawmaking by elected representatives may foster the illusion that all proposals receive careful scrutiny prior to their approval, amendment, or rejection. Although giving the appearance of relative simplicity as a political institution, representative government permits the manipulation of citizens, and voters should possess devices to correct such manipulations. If elected officers are guided only by the highest ethical standards and government is open, voters will have no need for employment of corrective devices. The recall supports the development of an ethos guiding the behavior of elected officers based upon the Roman maxim *salus populi suprema lex esto*, that is, "Let the welfare of the people be the supreme law."

In our judgment, four correctives — voting in regularly scheduled elections, the recall, the protest referendum, and the indirect initiative — should be available to the voters on a standby basis as circuit breakers and preferably should be triggered only by gross misrepresentation of the electorate or, specifically in the case of the recall, violation of oath or affirmation of office. The quintessential task for voters is to obtain adequate information to enable them to make rational decisions whether to employ a corrective and, if employed, on the issues placed on the ballot.

With respect to the recall, elected officers can view its nonuse or lack of threats to employ it as a vote of confidence in their stewardship. Such a view is particularly valid if legislators have voted to increase an existing tax or impose a new one and no group threatens to recall the lawmakers who voted for the increase or new tax.

In sum, availability of the recall provides citizens with an incentive to play active watchdog roles in the governance system, because they are armed with a weapon to correct abuses of power by removing the responsible officers, and also encourages public officers to conduct official business in the interest of the citizenry in a responsive manner.

NOTES

1. *Constitution of Louisiana*, art. 10 § 26.
2. *Constitution of Wisconsin*, art. 13, § 12.
3. Albert M. Kales, *Unpopular Government in the United States* (Chicago, Ill.: University of Chicago Press, 1914), p. 125.
4. *California Elections Code*, §§ 27310–7311.
5. Nathaniel B. Shurtleff, ed., *Records of the Governor and Company of the Massachusetts Bay in New England* (Boston, Mass.: From the Press of William White, Printer to the Commonwealth, 1853), vol. 1, p. 293.
6. *Journal of the Convention for Framing a Constitution of Government for the State of Massachusetts Bay from the Commencement of Their First Session September 1, 1779 to the Close of Their Last Session June 16, 1780* (Boston, Mass.: Dutton and Wentworth, Printers to the State, 1832), p. 255.
7. *New Hampshire Constitution of 1784*; this document lacks article or section numbers in part 2.
8. *Rhode Island Constitution of 1842*, art. 4, § 13.
9. *Michigan Constitution of 1835*, amendment 2.
10. *Colorado Constitution of 1876*, art. 10, § 11.
11. *Constitution of South Dakota*, art. 3, § 1 (1898).

12. Ibid.

13. *Southern Alameda Spanish Speaking Organization v. City of Union City*, 424 F.2d 291 at 294 (1970).

14. *Constitution of the Commonwealth of Massachusetts*, articles of amendment, art. 48, the referendum, § 2.

15. In Massachusetts, the General Court may attach an emergency preamble to a law or the governor may file an emergency statement with the secretary of the commonwealth. In either case, a law takes effect forthwith rather than at the end of the 90 days and cannot be suspended by the protest referendum. However, a referendum can be held on the law if the requisite number of signatures of voters is certified.

16. For an example, see *Newport (Rhode Island) Charter*, § 2-14.

17. For details, see *The Book of the States*, published biennially by the Council of State Governments in Lexington, Kentucky.

18. *New Hampshire Revised Statutes*, § 31:64; *Disco v. Board of Selectmen*, 115 N. H. 609 (1975).

19. *Connecticut General Statutes*, § 7-7.

20. Ben A. Franklin, "Petitions Block a Maryland Law to Combat Bias," *New York Times*, June 2, 1963, pp. 1, 70.

21. "Petitions Filed for Referendum to Repeal Bay State Bottle Bill," *Keene Sentinel*, February 17, 1982, p. 15.

22. *Charter of the City and County of San Francisco*, art. 2, chap. 1, §§ 20-22.

23. *Constitution of Nevada*, art. 19, § 6.

24. *Constitution of Maine*, art. 4, part 3, § 19.

25. *Constitution of California*, art. 2 § 8(d); *Constitution of Missouri*, art. 3 § 50; *Constitution of Illinois*, art. 14, § 28-1.

26. *Constitution of Arkansas*, amendment 7.

27. *Constitution of Massachusetts*, articles of amendment, art. 48, V § 5.

28. *Constitution of Maine*, art. 4, part III, § 18; *Constitution of Massachusetts*, articles of amendment, art. 48, the initiative, part III, § 2; *Constitution of Michigan*, art. 2, § 9; *Nevada Revised Statutes*, § 295.025-3; *Constitution of Washington*, art. 2 § 1(a).

29. Benjamin Jowett, translator, *Aristotle's Politics* (New York: Carlton House, n.d.), p. 288.

30. For details, consult Joseph F. Zimmerman, *Curbing Unethical Behavior in Government* (Westport, Conn.: Greenwood Press, 1994).

31. *New York Laws of 1977*, chap. 933; *New York Public Officers Law*, §§ 84–90.

32. *Privacy Act of 1974*, 88 Stat. 1896, 5 U.S.C.§ 552a; *Freedom of Information Act*, 88 Stat. 1896, 5 U.S.C. § 552(a)(2).

33. *Guidelines for State Legislation on Government Ethics and Campaign Financing* (Lexington, Ky.: Council of State Governments, 1974), p. 4.

Bibliography

BOOKS AND MONOGRAPHS

Barber, Benjamin R. *Strong Democracy: Participatory Politics for a New Age.* Berkeley: University of California Press, 1984.

Beard, Charles A., and Birl E. Shultz. *Documents on the State-wide Initiative, Referendum, and Recall.* New York: Macmillan, 1912.

Bird, Frederick L., and Frances M. Ryan. *The Recall of Public Officers: A Study of the Operation of the Recall in California.* New York: Macmillan, 1930.

The Book of the States 1996–97. Lexington, Ky.: Council of State Governments, 1996.

Bruce, Andrew J. *Non-Partisan League.* New York: Macmillan, 1921.

Burdick, Usher L. *History of the Farmers' Political Action in North Dakota.* Baltimore, Md.: Wirth Brothers, 1944.

Charter Removal Provisions. Hartford: Connecticut Public Expenditure Council, 1981.

Childs, Richard S. *The First 50 Years of the Council-Manager Plan of Municipal Government.* New York: National Municipal League, 1965.

Commager, Henry S., ed. *The Era of Reform: 1830–1860.* New York: Van Nostrand Reinhold, 1960.

Croly, Herbert. *Progressive Democracy.* New York: Macmillan, 1915.

Dahl, Robert A. *Dilemmas of Pluralist Democracy: Autonomy vs. Control.* New Haven, Conn.: Yale University Press, 1982.

____. *Polyarchy: Participation and Opposition.* New Haven, Conn.: Yale University Press, 1971.

Ford, Mark L., compiler. *When Voters Change Their Minds: Recall Elections.* Lexington, Ky.: Council of State Governments, 1984.

Ford, Paul L., ed. *The Writings of Thomas Jefferson*, vol. 4. New York: G. P. Putnam's Sons, 1894.

Gaston, Herbert. *The Nonpartisan League.* New York: Harcourt, Brace, and Howe, 1920.

Goldman, Eric F. *Rendezvous with Destiny.* New York: Alfred A. Knopf, 1952.

Guidelines for State Legislation on Government Ethics and Campaign Financing. Lexington, Ky.: Council of State Governments, 1974.

Hicks, John D. *The Populist Revolt: A History of the Farmers' Alliance and the People's Party.* Lincoln: The University of Nebraska Press, 1961.

Hofstadter, Richard. *The Age of Reform: From Bryan to F.D.R.* New York: Alfred A. Knopf, 1955.

Jowett, Benjamin, translator. *Aristotle's Politics.* New York: Carlton House, n.d.

Kales, Albert M. *Unpopular Government in the United States.* Chicago, Ill.: University of Chicago Press, 1914.

Kennedy, John F. *Profiles in Courage.* New York: Harper & Brothers, 1956.

Levin, Murray B. *The Alienated Voter.* New York: Holt, Rinehart and Winston, 1960.

Lowell, A. Lawrence. *Public Opinion and Popular Government.* New York: Longmans, Green, 1926.

Matthews, Harry G., and C. Wade Harrison. *Recall and Reform in Arizona, 1973.* Tucson: University of Arizona, Institute of Government Research, 1973.

Morlan, Robert. *Political Prairie Fire.* Minneapolis: University of Minnesota Press, 1955.

Mowry, George E. *The California Progressives.* Berkeley: University of California Press, 1951.

Munro, William B., ed. *The Initiative, Referendum, and Recall.* New York: D. Appleton, 1912.

Nelson, Bruce. *Land of the Dakotahs.* Minneapolis: University of Minnesota Press, 1946.

Oberholtzer, Ellis P. *The Referendum in America Together with Some Chapters on the Initiative and the Recall.* New York: Charles Scribner's Sons, 1912.

Phelps, Edith M., compiler. *Selected Articles on the Recall*, 2d ed. New York: H. W. Wilson, 1915.

Popularly Elected Officials. Washington, D.C.: U.S. Bureau of the Census, 1996.

Prescott, Frank W., and Joseph F. Zimmerman. *The Politics of the Veto of Legislation in New York State.* Washington, D.C.: University Press of America, 1980.

Report of the Committee to Oppose Judicial Recall. Washington, D.C.: American Bar Association, 1914.

Reports of the American Bar Association. Chicago, Ill.: The Association, 1911.

Rule, Wilma, and Joseph F. Zimmerman, eds. *United States Electoral Systems:*

Their Impact on Women and Minorities. Westport, Conn.: Greenwood Press, 1992.

Smith, Thomas F. X. *The Powerticians.* Secaucus, N.J.: Lyle Stuart, 1982.

Taft, William H. *Popular Government: Its Essence, Its Permanence, and Its Perils.* New Haven, Conn.: Yale University Press, 1913.

Torelle, Ellen, compiler. *The Political Philosophy of Robert M. LaFollette.* Madison, Wisc.: Robert M. LaFollette, 1920.

Weyl, Walter E. *The New Democracy: An Essay on Certain Political and Economic Tendencies in the United States.* New York: Macmillan, 1912.

White, William Allen. *The Old Order Changeth: A View of American Democracy.* New York: Macmillan, 1910.

Wilcox, Delos F. *Government by All the People Or the Initiative, the Referendum and the Recall as Instruments of Democracy.* New York: Macmillan, 1912.

Woliver, Laura R. *From Outrage to Action: The Politics of Grass-Roots Dissent.* Urbana: University of Illinois Press, 1993.

Zimmerman, Joseph F. *State-Local Relations: A Partnership Approach*, 2d ed. Westport, Conn.: Praeger Publishers, 1995.

____. *Curbing Unethical Behavior in Government.* Westport, Conn.: Greenwood Press, 1994.

____. *Participatory Democracy: Populism Revived.* New York: Praeger Publishers, 1986.

____. *The Government and Politics of New York State.* New York: New York University Press, 1981.

____. *The Massachusetts Town Meeting: A Tenacious Institution.* Albany: State University of New York, Graduate School of Public Affairs, 1967.

GOVERNMENT REPORTS AND DOCUMENTS

The Historical Development and Use of the Recall in Oregon. Salem, Ore.: Legislative Research, 1976.

Houser, John. *Recall Elections Since 1974.* Salem, Ore.: Legislative Research, 1980.

Journal of the Convention for Framing a Constitution of Government for the State of Massachusetts Bay from the Commencement of Their First Session September 1, 1779 to the Close of Their Last Session June 16, 1780. Boston, Mass: Dutton and Wentworth, Printers to the State, 1832.

1987 Annual Report. Westborough, Mass.: Town of Westborough, 1987.

Procedure for Recalling State and Local Officials. Sacramento, Calif.: Office of the Secretary of State, 1994.

Recall of Elected Officials in Massachusetts Municipalities. Boston: Massachusetts Executive Office of Communities and Development, 1982.

Recall: At Issue in Utah. Salt Lake City, Utah: Office of Legislative Research, 1976.

Recall Manual '96. Salem: Oregon Elections Division, 1996.

Recall: Report of the Legislative Interim Committee on Intergovernmental Affairs. Salem, Ore.: The Committee, 1976.

The Removal of State Public Officials from Office. Madison: Wisconsin Legislative Reference Bureau, 1980.

Report Relative to Recall of Local Officials. Boston: Massachusetts Legislative Research Council, 1979.

Shurtleff, Nathaniel B., ed. *Records of the Governor and Company of the Massachusetts Bay in New England.* Boston, Mass.: From the Press of William White, Printer to the Commonwealth, 1853.

Statutory Authority Under Home Rule for Recall. Hartford: Connecticut Office of Legislative Research, 1974.

ARTICLES

Abbot, Frank F. "The Referendum and the Recall Among the Ancient Romans." *Swanee Review,* January 1915, pp. 84–94.

"Absentee Ballots Over 36% in San Francisco Recall." *Election Administration Reports* 13 (May 2, 1983): 5, 7.

"Abuse of Recall Power Substitutes Popularity for Leadership." *Georgia County Government Magazine* 31 (May 1979): 50.

Ahern, Charlotte F. "Voters Change Their Minds, Recall Elected Officials." *City & State* 5 (January 4, 1988): 28.

Akre, Brian S. "Recall Effort: Group Says Alaskan Governor Abusing Power." *Times Union,* October 16, 1991, p. B-10.

"Amid Impeachment, Mecham Maintains He'll be Vindicated." *Knickerbocker News,* February 6, 1988, p. 2A.

"Arizona Court Blocks a Special Vote on Governor." *New York Times,* April 14, 1988, p. A32.

"Arizona Governor Won't Quit." *New York Times,* February 1, 1988, p. A28.

"Atlantic City Mayor Recalled, Replaced, Still Challenging Petition Sufficiency." *Election Administration Reports* 14 (March 19, 1984): 5.

Balousek, Mary. "2-Week Reprieve for Petak." *Wisconsin State Journal,* February 21, 1996, p. 1.

"Banks County Recalls Three Commissioners." *Georgia County Government* 37 (December 1985): 53.

Barnett, James D. "Fighting Rate Increases by the Recall." *National Municipal Review* 11 (July 1922): 213–14.

———. "Operation of the Recall in Oregon." *The American Political Science Review* 6 (February, 1912): 41–53.

Barrett, Gil. "Recall Act is Being Used to Punish Local Leaders for Differences of Opinion." *Georgia County Government Magazine* 33 (October 1981): 2.

Bartley, Bruce. "Recall Elections High Mark in State." *Eugene Register-Guard,* December 9, 1979, p. 25A.

"Berkeley to Vote on Black's Recall." *New York Times*, August 19, 1973, p. 39.

Bickelhaupt, Susan. "Petition Asks Recall of Planners." *Boston Globe*, November 27, 1986, p. 29.

"Black Councilman Loses in Berkeley Recall Vote." *New York Times*, August 23, 1973, p. 26

Block, A. G. "A Twisted Tale of Revenge." *California Journal* 27 (January 1996): 34–36, 39–41.

____. "Democrat Bounced from Allen Recall Ballot." *cjWeekly*, November 6, 1995, pp. 5–6.

Bourne, Jonathan, Jr. "Functions of the Initiative, Referendum, and Recall." *Annals of the American Academy of Political and Social Science* 43 (September 1912): 3–16.

Brown, Rome G. "Recall of Judges." In *Selected Articles on the Recall,* compiled by Edith M. Phelps. New York: H. W. Wilson, 1915.

Butterfield, Fox. "Recall Petitions on Whelan Voided." *New York Times,* January 30, 1971, pp. 1, 31.

"California Voters Recall Ex-Speaker of the Assembly." *New York Times*, November 30, 1995, p. A14.

"Campaign to Recall Arizona Governor Prove a Failure." *New York Times,* October 7, 1972, p. 64.

"Cleveland Mayor Survives Recall Vote: Recount Due." *Knickerbocker News*, August 14, 1978, p. 17A.

Cohen, Michael. "Recall in Washington: A Times for Reform." *Washington Law Review* 50 (1974): 29–55.

"Constitutional Law—Recall of Public Officers: Discretionary Acts Cannot be a Sufficient Basis for Recall." *Washington Law Review* 48 (1973): 503–14.

Cox, Gail D. "The Trials of Gov. Evan Mecham." *National Law Journal* 10 (March 28, 1988): 1, 8–9.

"Dawson Recall Results Fall Short in County." *Georgia County Government* 38 (July 1986): 40.

Endicott, William. "A Turn Around Political Track." *Sacramento Bee*, February 3, 1996, p. A3.

Fitzpatrick, F. Stuart. "Some Recent Uses of the Recall." *National Municipal Review* 5 (July 1916): 380–87.

Flint, Jerry M. "Michigan Blacks Wary on School Change." *New York Times*, October 4, 1970, p. 60.

____. "Integration Plan Fought in Detroit." *New York Times*, June 13, 1970, p. 51.

Fordham, Jefferson B. "Judicial Nullification of a Democratic Political Process — The Rizzo Recall Case." *University of Pennsylvania Law Review* 126 (November 1977): 1–18.

____. "The Utah Recall Proposal." *Utah Law Review* 29 (1976): 29–37.

Franklin, Ben A. "Court Backs Petition on Rizzo Recall Vote." *New York Times,* September 17, 1976, p. 1.

____. "Petitions Block a Maryland Law to Combat Bias." *New York Times,* June

2, 1963, pp. 1, 70.

Garber, J. Otis. "The Use of the Recall in American Cities." *National Municipal Review* 15 (May 1926): 259–61.

Gilbertson, H. S. "Conservative Aspects of the Recall." *National Municipal Review* 1 (April 1912): 204–11.

"GOP Leader Quits California Post." *Times Union*, September 15, 1995, p. A-6.

"Green Sheriff Fires Top Deputy: Same Move Brought Fatal Recall." *Wisconsin State Journal*, May 12, 1994, p. 1.

Grumet, Barbara R. "Who is 'Due' Process?" *Public Administration Review* 42 (July-August 1982): 321–26.

Gruson, Lindsey. "Arizona is Facing a Legal Question." *New York Times*, April 6, 1988, p. B7.

____. "Mecham of Arizona is Convicted by His State's Senate and Ousted." *New York Times*, April 5, 1988, pp. 1, A16.

____. "Arizona Senate Begins Impeachment Trial of Mecham." *New York Times*, March 1, 1988, p. A13.

Healan, Hill. "The Recall Act—Good Intent and Faulty Application." *Georgia County Government Magazine* 33 (February 1982): 103.

Herman, Geoffrey. "Municipal Charters: A Comparative Analysis of 75 Maine Charters." *Maine Townsman*, August 1992, pp. 5–15.

"Hudson Mayor Defeated in Recall." *Eau Claire Leader*, December 12, 1989, p. 1.

Janson, Donald. "Committee Seeks Recall of Atlantic City's Mayor." *New York Times*, July 12, 1983, p. B4.

Johnson, Gary. "Lawrence Voters Kick Town Board Out of Office," *Eau Claire Leader*, June 22, 1988, p. 1.

"Judge Beats Recall." *Knickerbocker News*, May 12, 1982, p. 2A.

"Judge Who Suggested Boy in Rape Reacted 'Normally' Draws More Ire." *New York Times*, August 26, 1977, p. A14.

"Kansas Recall Decided by One-Vote with One Hundred Percent Turnout." *Election Administration Reports* 14 (March 5, 1984): 5.

Kettleborough, Charles. "Removal of Public Officers: A Ten-Year Review." *American Political Science Review* 8 (November 1914): 621–29.

Knudson, Thomas J. "Arizona Governor Dismissive of Foes." *New York Times*, July 13, 1987, p. A18.

Lazarovici, Laureen. "Machado Recall Fails." *cjWeekly*, August 28, 1995, p. 12.

____. "Machado Foes Say They Have Enough Signatures." *cjWeekly*, May 29, 1995, p. 6.

____. "Horcher Recalled Emphatically." *cjWeekly*, May 22, 1995, pp. 1, 11–12.

____. "Machado Recall May Be Headed for Ballot." *cjWeekly*, May 8, 1995, p. 5.

Lindsey, Robert. "Deukmejian and Cranston Win as 3 Judges are Ousted." *New York Times*, November 6, 1986, p. A30.

Lydon, Christopher. "Court Set on Rizzo Recall Petition." *New York Times*, August 26, 1976, p. 19.

"Mayor and Commissioners Recalled." *International City Managers Newsletter* 57 (June 21, 1976): 3.

"Michigan Ouster Votes Threaten Democratic Control in Legislature." *New York Times*, December 2, 1983, p. A22.

"Michigan Town Recalls 3 in Dispute Over Housing." *New York Times*, May 10, 1978, p. 18.

"Michigan Voters Recall Backers of Tax Hike." *Public Administration Times* 6 (December 15, 1983): 1.

Moiles, Deborah L. "Oxford Board Member 'Owns' Her Own Vote." *The Evening Gazette*, April 28, 1983, p. 10.

Munro, William B. "Pasadena Uses the Recall." *National Municipal Review* 21 (March 1932): 161–67.

Narvaez, Alfonso A. "Ex-Atlantic City Mayor Indicted on Federal Charges of Extortion." *New York Times*, March 28, 1984, pp. 1, B2.

"Nebraska Voters Discover Recall Elections for Local Officials." *Election Administration Reports* 17 (November 23, 1987): 5–6.

"New Ouster Move on Coast Ends Term of a Councilman." *New York Times*, December 22, 1984, p. 10.

"Officials Out." *Wisconsin State Journal*, July 29, 1992, p. 1.

"Officials Who Joined G.O.P. Lose Recall Vote in Honolulu." *New York Times*, October 7, 1985, p. A17.

"Omaha, Neb. Mayoral Recall Produces Large Voter Turnout." *Election Administration Reports* 17 (January 19, 1987): 6–7.

Peterson, Iver. "Mayor's Personality Sparked Cleveland Recall, Foes Say." *New York Times*, June 14, 1978, p. A19.

"Petitions Filed for Referendum to Repeal Bay State Bottle Bill." *Keene Sentinel*, February 17, 1982, p. 15.

Press, Charles, and Kenneth VerBurg. "Recall Reverses Party Composition of Michigan Senate." *Comparative State Politics Newsletter* 5 (April 1984): 7–8.

Price, Charles M. "Paying the Tab for Recall Elections." *California Government & Politics Annual* (1996-97): 76–78.

____. "Recalls at the Local Level: Dimensions and Implications." *National Civic Review* 72 (April 1983): 199–206.

"Providence Mayor Receives Felony Sentence in Assault." *New York Times*, April 24, 1984, p. A14.

"Recall can be abused." *Georgia County Government Magazine* 31 (September 1979): 58.

"Recall Effort Against Mayor of Providence is Under Way." *New York Times*, October 24, 1983, p. A16.

"Recall Eliminates Three in Barrow County." *Georgia County Government Magazine* 32 (May 1980): 44.

"Recall Fails Against Barrett of Dougherty." *Georgia County Government Magazine* 33 (February 1982): 67.

"Recall Fails in Bartow County." *Georgia County Government* 37 (June 1986): 76.

"Recall Fails in Richmond." *Georgia County Government* 35 (April 1984): 21.

"Recall Fever Infects Oregon." *Sunday Oregonian*, August 12, 1979, p. C2.

"Recall Provisions Rare in Georgia." *Georgia County Government Magazine* 28 (August 1976): 44.

"Recall Results Mixed in Bryan, Haralson." *Georgia County Government* 39 (January 1988): 11.

"Recall in Seattle." *Outlook* 97 (February 25, 1911): 375–76.

"Recall Successful in Jones and Green." *Georgia County Government Magazine* 33 (April 1982): 13.

"Recall Votes Fail to Oust Aldermen." *Wisconsin State Journal*, August 7, 1991, p. B2.

Richard, Ray. "Wareham Unseats 4 of 5 Selectmen." *Boston Globe*, November 6, 1985, pp. 1, 32.

Robbins, William. "Omaha Mayor Battling on Eve of a Recall Vote." *New York Times*, January 13, 1987, p. A16.

——. "Opponents of Omaha Mayor Pressing Recall Effort Today." *New York Times*, November 4, 1986, p. A16.

Roberts, Steven V. "Pasadena Voters Support School Board Members Who Back Integration Plan." *New York Times*, October 15, 1970, p. 28.

Robinson, Douglas. "Drive to Recall School Board Head Divides Westport." *New York Times*, December 22, 1970, pp. 35, 37.

Romig, Candace. "Two Michigan Legislators Recalled." *State Legislatures* 10 (January 1984): 5.

"Saugus Selectmen Recall." *Worcester Telegram*, August 24, 1961, p. 6.

Schaffner, Margaret A. "The Recall." *Yale Review* 17 (August 1909): 206–9.

"School Chiefs Ousted in Recall Election." *Wisconsin State Journal*, July 15, 1992, p. 1.

Scolaro, Joseph A. "Petak, GOP Question Over 6,400 Signatures." *Racine Journal Times*, March 7, 1996, p. 1.

——. "Petak: Dems Involved in Recall." *Racine Journal Times*, February 2, 1996, p. 1.

Sentell, H. Perry. Jr. "Remembering Recall in Local Government Laws." *Georgia Law Review* 10 (1976): 883–915.

Stevens, William K. "Detroit Suburb that Recalled Its Mayor Voting Today on Recall of His Successor." *New York Times*, February 19, 1977, p. 11.

Sullivan, Ronald. "Jersey City Petitions Held Valid for Recall Vote." *New York Times*, March 9, 1971, p. 62.

"Supreme Court Strikes Blow for Good Government." *Georgia County Government* 40 (November 1988): 3.

Sych, Lawrence. "State Recall Elections: What Explains Their Outcomes?" *Comparative State Politics* 17 (October 1996): 7–25.

"Tacoma, in Recall Election, Votes Five Councilmen Out of Office." *New York Times*, September 17, 1970, p. 30.

"Tacoma's Mayor Facing a Recall." *New York Times*, April 5, 1970, p. 33

Taylor, Charles F. "Municipal Initiative, Referendum, and Recall in Practice." *National Municipal Review* 3 (October 1914): 693–701.

"31,000 Ask Recall of Mayor Whelan." *New York Times*, January 12, 1971, p. 1.

Thompson, Carl D. "The Vital Points in Charter Making from a Socialist Point of View." *National Municipal Review* 2 (July 1913): 416–26.

"Town Recall Effort Fails." *Eau Claire Leader*, September 19, 1990, p. 1.

Trevelen, Ed. "3 Veterans Survive Recall Vote." *Wisconsin State Journal*, January 26, 1995, p. 1.

Turner, Wallace. "San Francisco Mayor Jubilant Over Recall Victory." *New York Times*, April 28, 1983, p. A14.

____. "Bid to Oust San Francisco Mayor Polarizes Splinter Groups." *New York Times*, March 26, 1983, p. 6.

____. "Fringe Group Forces Ouster Vote on Coast Mayor." *New York Times*, February 9, 1983, p. A24.

____. "California's Chief Judge Is Facing a Recall Move." *New York Times*, October 15, 1982, p. A13.

"Two Seminole Officials Resign Before Recall." *Georgia County Government* 39 (July 1987): 69.

"Two Vacancies in Pike County Due to Recall." *Georgia County Government* 38 (April 1987): 33.

Vellings, Mary L. "Assembly GOP, Long Subservient, Relishing Chance to Rule." *Sacramento Bee*, January 29, 1996, pp. 1, A6.

Vennochi, Joan. "Mansfield Split After Recall Election." *Boston Globe*, December 15, 1982, pp. 29–30.

"Vote to Recall Rizzo is Barred by Court." *New York Times*, October 1, 1976, pp. 1, A13.

"Voters Boot Two 'Rude' Selectmen." *Keene (N.H.) Sentinel*, August 21, 1989, p. 8.

Walters, Jonathan. "Mayor Won't Drop Liquor Issue." *Governing* 3 (July 1990): 60.

"Wareham Selectmen are Challenged." *Boston Globe*, August 30, 1985, p. 64.

Warner, Sam B. "Criminal Responsibility for Statements in Recall Charges." *National Municipal Review* 15 (February 1926): 118–22.

"Wausau Busing Foes Triumph." *Wisconsin State Journal*, December 15, 1993, p. 1.

Weinraub, Lori K. "Arizona Governor Officially Told to Resign or Face Recall Vote." *Schenectady Gazette*, January 27, 1988, p. 2.

Wells, Roger H. "The Initiative, Referendum, and Recall in German Cities." *National Municipal Review* 18 (January 1929): 29–36.

"Westport Split Over Busing Vote." *New York Times*, December 10, 1970, p. 56.

Willis, Benny. "State Officer Says Recalls are Misued." *Eugene Register-Guard*, December 14, 1979, pp. 1B–2B.

"Winner in War Over Judge's Words." *New York Times*, September 9, 1977, p. B1.

Wold, John T., and John H. Culver. "The Defeat of the California Justices: The Campaign, the Electorate, and the Issue of Judicial Accountability." *Judicature* 70 (April-May 1987): 348–55.

Zimmerman, Joseph F. "Initiative, Referendum, and Recall: Government by Plebiscite?" *Intergovernmental Perspective* 13 (Winter 1987): 32–35.

UNPUBLISHED MATERIALS

City of Tacoma Interdepartmental Communication. From Assistant City Attorney Geoffrey C. Cross to City Manager Marshall McCormick, dated August 25, 1970.

Houser, John. *Recall Elections Since 1974*. Salem, Ore.: Legislative Research, 1980.

Minutes of Special Meeting of the Tacoma City Council, dated September 29, 1970.

Press, Charles, and Lawrence Sych. "Participation in State Recall Elections." A paper presented at the annual meeting of the American Political Science Association, Chicago, Illinois, September 3–6, 1987.

Sharpe, Theodore C. *Recall*. Grand Forks: University of North Dakota, Bureau of Governmental Affairs, 1971.

"Statement of Board of State Canvassers for State Senator, District Twenty-One Recall Election, June 4, 1996." Madison, Wisconsin, June 12, 1996.

Index

ABOUT THE AUTHOR

JOSEPH F. ZIMMERMAN is Professor of Political Science in the Graduate School of Public Affairs, State University of New York at Albany. He is author of numerous studies, including *Interstate Relations: The Neglected Dimension of Federalism* (1996) and *State-Local Relations: A Partnership Approach* (1995), both published by Praeger.